An Ocean Between

100% American-100% Ukrainian

By Stephanie M. Sydoriak

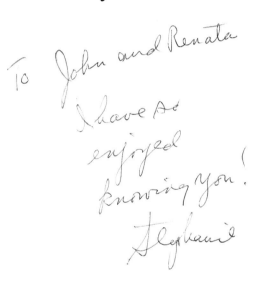

To John and Renata

I have so enjoyed knowing you!

Stephanie

Published by Stephanie M. Sydoriak

ISBN 978-1-105-39851-3

Acknowledgements

Had not my immigrant parents, Elias and Mary Chopek, been my constant and fascinating storytellers, I would not have been able to write this book about their early lives in Ukraine and their later lives across the ocean in America. My sister, Anna, completed their stories in later years by telling me her experiences as an immigrant child in the slums of Boston and her career path as a woman lawyer in that same city.

Many members of my family as well as dear friends generously took time to read my manuscript as it evolved. Their suggestions and insights were an invaluable guidance for me. Among them were my daughters: Katherine Lawrence and Chris Sydoriak; friends: Martha Chomiak-Bohachevsky, Lauren Earles, Diane Fritz, Kate Igmunson, Kristen Litchman, Marie Odezynskij, Jennifer Reglien, Jane Reis and independent editor, Tania Casselle. Other friends and family, too many to list, gave me encouragement and support. To all of them, I am deeply grateful.

1936, Chestnut Hill School Easter Assembly

I stood a little behind my father only half listening to his story-telling voice streaming out over the children's heads. I kept my eyes on the dark, wide floorboards at my feet but my ears and peripheral vision focused on the audience. I heard a shrill voice and threw a quick glance to the back of the hall. Was it the witchy principal? My father had filled me with stories about their daily battles every night. I swallowed down the sour taste of panic.

The children were laughing. Were they laughing at his eastern European accent or was he saying something funny? How could these kids in this fancy Chestnut Hill School want to hear how my father, their janitor, had celebrated Easter Day in his little Ukrainian town, anyway? What could Ukraine possibly mean to them? No one in my school had ever heard of it. Including the teacher.

My makeshift costume began to worry me. Would the pieces hold together when I did my Ukrainian dance? I didn't have a costume of my own, so Mama woke me early this morning to fit the various pieces of my older sister's costume to my small body. Mama had to fold the elastic holding the multicolored ribbons to the back of the wreath of bright, artificial flowers onto a safety pin. Now, I felt the pin pressing into the back of my head.

Mama had rolled up the sleeves of the embroidered blouse and secured them with more hidden pins. She had bunched the bright skirt panels at my waist and tied the string of the embroidered apron tightly round and round. To hide all of that mess, she had wound a long, woven sash around my waist at least three times before securing it at the back with yet two more safety pins. I felt very thick in the middle now. The only piece of the costume that belonged to me was the beaded jacket, a name-day gift last year from Mama's sister in Ukraine. It had been too small when it arrived. I knew I'd have trouble lifting my arms when I danced.

I took a deep breath and tried to listen for my cue, but I was distracted by how my father's short, lean frame followed his arms as they pointed or opened wide. His cool, blue eyes moved quickly from one child to another. I wished I could tell him that a few of the long hairs that he combed over his bald top were coming loose. I told my eyes to stop watching and my ears to listen for the words of my cue.

"Now, you see," he was saying, "we always woke up well before the first light of day on Easter morning. We would make a wide parade, stumbling in the deep, darkness, as we walked three times around the church behind the priest. When a little pink light showed itself in the east, the big doors of the bright, candle-filled church opened wide, and we would enter singing the wonderful, exciting hymn, 'Xhrestos Voskres!' which means in English, 'Christ has risen!'

"After the Holy Service, which was more than two hours long, everyone went home and ate the food that their Mamas had made and that had been blessed by the priest on Saturday. It was a cold dinner, because on Easter Sunday, even the Mamas had to have a day when they didn't do any work at all, not even heating up the food they made on Saturday."

I was wondering if the Mamas of these rich kids ever had to work at all. I swallowed hard when I saw my father's eyes moving in my direction. My heart began to bang around in my chest. This morning, Mama told my father that his record was of a men's dance, the Arkan, so I shouldn't be doing it. He had shrugged his shoulders and said,

"This is the only dancing record I have." Mama retorted angrily. "Yes, and she's only a beginner, so even if you had the right music, she doesn't know a whole dance. What do you expect her to do? This is all a joke. But you never listen to me anyway, so what's the use of arguing?"

What was I going to do?

I heard my father say, "After the food was eaten, everyone came back to the square in front of the church and the dancing began." As he turned to the Victrola behind him and put the needle into the groove of the record, he said,

"Now children, my daughter, Stephanie, will show you a little bit of the kind of dancing we did."

The music of the martial dance pounded the walls of the Assembly Room. I heard in my head, 'Rass, dva, rass ih dva,' the count that our dance teacher used to start us moving. My feet followed the pounding beat, and I stepped out, randomly changing the step every eight counts. I added as many of my favorite little twirls as I could fit in. As I suspected, I had to fight the jacket to lift my arm, and the wreath began to move down toward my face, but I couldn't help smile a little with the excitement of

3

feeling how easily my feet found the steps. The music ran its course, and I was startled by the applause of the children. My father told me to bow. Frightened and deeply embarrassed again, I bowed quickly and ducked behind him.

He smiled broadly during the applause while trying to pull me around to his front. Failing this, he pointed me to the desk on his other side. He had covered it earlier with newspaper and spread out my egg decorating supplies. As I sat, I heard him say,

"During all the weeks before Easter, people decorated many eggs so that when they came to the Easter Dances, they could exchange them with friends and family. Now, watch as Stephanie decorates an egg in the old, Ukrainian way."

If he thought I could make a true, old Ukrainian design, he was mistaken. When he lit the candle, I picked up the white egg in my left hand and the special pen my sister had bought in a stationary store in my right. I remembered her arguing with our father a few nights ago. She shook her head and said,

"We've just been learning to make eggs ourselves these past couple of months. She can hardly make a straight line yet. She'll just make a mess of it." I was a little offended, though I knew it to be true. She was fourteen years older than me and had just passed her bar exam in Boston, so she was always right.

But my father had prevailed, and here I was about to show all these rich kids how to mess up an egg. My hands seemed like someone else's hands. They shook as I held the pen in the flame until it got hot. I pressed the pen into a lump of beeswax and back into the flame. When the wax became fluid in the heat, I began to draw a waxy line on the egg. My trembling hands made the dividing line around the middle of the egg look like a snake. Heating and reheating the pen and occasionally pressing it into the lump of wax, I drew simple outlines of flowers and a scattering of circles and stars above and below my snaky line.

I spaced them widely. I wanted this all to be over. Carefully balancing the egg on a spoon, I dropped it into the jar of yellow dye. When it looked yellow enough, I took it out and patted it dry with a rag Mama had tucked into the bag.

Then came the tedious part, covering the insides of all the petals and the stars with a heavy coat of wax to protect their yellow color from the next dip into orange dye. When I was done waxing over the inside spaces of the rest of the circles to keep the orange color intact, the egg was ready for its final dip into the red dye. Just as the egg came to the top of the dye, it slid out of the spoon and made a slight noise at the bottom of the bottle. I had no idea what I'd do if it had cracked. By this time the children had crowded around my table. I was surprised when I looked up, how intently they were watching. I tried to ignore their closeness while I waited for the red dye to set properly, but I couldn't. I took the egg out too soon and the red was splotchy, not smooth like the yellow and orange. I wanted to disappear.

But, at least it was almost over. I put the side of the egg to the side of the flame until the waxy lines began to melt. Rubbing each melted place with the little bit of clean rag that was left, I remembered not to let it touch the flame. Finally, magically, the original white shell of the egg under my first waxy lines as well as the filled-in colors of yellow and orange were free of the blackened wax. I almost smiled, but my second look at the egg horrified me with its crudeness. The lines intended to be straight were drastically crooked. The flowers and the stars looked like a kindergartener drew them. The red was a disaster. Tears sprung to my eyes. I glared at my smiling father. How could he do this to me?

When at last the dark wood-paneled Assembly Room was emptied of children, I stood behind the green, velvet drapes of the large front window to watch the cars gathering at the front of the building. Mothers in coats and fancy hats, and maids in white and black uniforms, greeted the children and drove off with them, some in chauffeured cars. My father called me to stuff the pen and wax and dance record into a cloth bag. "I think the children liked it," he said. He tightened the dye jars firmly. I wadded handfuls of newspaper around them as he put them into the other bag. "You can carry the light bag. I will carry the dyes. But, wait here for me. I won't be long. I have to be a good janitor and check the building before we leave.

I sat glumly. How could he be so happy? Surely he knew I had been a disastrous failure. I was surprised that he held my hand as we walked down the long, green tunnel of Hammond Street toward the distant bus stop. As I entered the bus ahead of him, I was acutely aware of the passengers' eyes puzzling over my unraveling costume. Anger flooded me again.

Tato sat beside me. "Wasn't that a wonderful event, Stefchu! And could you ever imagine that the highest of the high in Chestnut Hill School are interested in our beloved Ukraine and want to learn from us." He turned and fixed his eyes on mine so I would understand that what he was saying was important, "So many of our poor Ukrainians have crossed the wide ocean in the hopes of making a new, maybe better life here. Their bundles were very small, but in their heads, in their hearts, in their feet and in their hands, the carried the memories of their customs, traditions, arts and dances, even though they had little hope of ever truly experiencing them again. And now, here in America, in our church gatherings, at our picnics and weddings, they have been able to open their mouths and let the songs sing to them again. Their feet have begun to dance the old dances. Their hands embroider and make our beautiful eggs." He sighed deeply, and I knew that his familiar exhortation was coming.

 "So, you and your sister as well as all the Ukrainian children in America must learn how to take all these things we have brought across the ocean into your own heads and hands and feet and cherish them just as I and Mama and all your ancestors have. You must always listen carefully and learn as much as you can so that you, in turn, can teach the world about the glories of Ukraine."

Though always stirred into a fine patriotism with his words, I had found these expectations of me difficult to achieve in my own, less prestigious, classrooms. Because neither I nor my elementary school teachers could find Ukraine on a map of Europe, I sometimes wondered if his vision of Ukraine was just part of a mass hallucination of the people at the church.

An Ocean Between

Section I

1887 – 1900 Stories of Ukrainian Childhoods For an American Daughter

My Storytellers

I didn't realize until my later years how lucky I had been to have parents who were such driven storytellers. I had each to myself, Mama at lunchtime, Tato at supper. Tato wasn't home for lunch, because he usually spent his days looking unsuccessfully for work. It was the time of the Great Depression, and he was lucky to find an occasional painting or plumbing job. My sister, Anna, just graduated from high school, did not come home for either lunch or supper. She worked as a stenographer during the day, ate a quick sandwich when she was done, then went to night classes at Portia Law School.

Mama wasn't home at supper because she left the house every afternoon at five to work the two jobs. She returned at five in the morning for a few hours of sleep that I interrupted when I came home for lunch. So, only Tato and I were in the kitchen at supper to share the food Mama had left on the stove.

Both Mama and Tato told their stories to me in Ukrainian. Tato's delivery was the more dramatic and often required the space in front of the Black Beauty stove to become a tiny stage. His stories ranged from his birth in 1887 in the town of Kozova in Eastern Europe through his impoverished early life and on into his life as an immigrant in America. They inevitably ended in a lecture on Ukrainian history or American politics. His words were often beyond my childish, Ukrainian vocabulary, but I never dared interrupt the drama to ask their meaning.

Mama's stories were told in a quieter tone. She spoke with yearning for the sweetness of the Old Country that contrasted so sharply with the bitterness of her life in America. She spoke rarely of history and politics, so I had no trouble understanding her simpler words, bright with the colors of blooming lilacs and the fragrance of baking bread.

When I came home at noon, a potato, prepared in one of her many variations, sat ready for me at my place. Alongside the dish was always my shiny, plastic 'Lil Orphan Annie cup filled to the top with Ovaltine. Mama sat across the table from me. With a deep sigh, she would turn to stare down into the street for a few minutes.

I would wait, a little ripple of worry tickling my head. Maybe a scolding was coming for something I had already forgotten. But probably not, I would reassure myself. She seemed to deem the time at lunch more important for telling her family stories than for scolding her mysterious American child who, most of the time, preferred the streets and woods and the neighborhood pack of boys to being with her. I knew she despaired of ever teaching me to be a respectful, helpful Ukrainian child like my sister, though she obviously hoped that her stories would have some effect.

Once she began, I became so engrossed with her fabled, golden world, I could almost imagine being her mythical, obedient Ukrainian child over there. Her eyes, usually tense, would soften as she took me through her streets, where the red of the poppy fields was redder than any red I had ever seen, where the sunflowers were more golden and the fields shone with more shades of green than I could ever imagine.

When I heard my school bell ring, I would be reluctant to leave her world behind for my American world of school and streets where the bullies were always telling me, 'Why don't ya go back where ya came from' and where the teachers were always asking me, 'And just where did your parents come from?'

Stephanie M. Sydoriak

Mama's Stories

Mama's stories came to me in as many minutes as it took me to eat my lunch. Each day brought a different segment. Gradually I was able to collect the pieces, and visualize her life in Kozova. But from the beginning, there was no mistaking her intense love of that brief beginning of her one hundred years.

How I wish you could have seen our town, our Kozova. Maybe someday I will be able to go back, and I will take you with me so you can see with your own eyes how beautiful it was. Kozova was bigger than a village, but smaller than a city. Still, everyone knew each other, talked to each other, laughed together, and danced together. We had no noise from automobiles, streetcars and subways like here. We had only the sound of the singing birds, squawking roosters and geese, and the moaning wind. We walked everywhere, and only sometimes rode a horse.

Now, Kozova was an important place. Austro-Hungarian government buildings had been built around our town square. Everything was more or less peaceful under the Emperor, Franz Joseph. People didn't complain too much that we were under his rule. Well, maybe people like your father did. Tato was a patriot like you wouldn't believe. Well, you would, because you have seen what a big Ukrainian patriot he is even over here in America.

People came from all around to the courts of Kozova to settle their land problems or quarrels between neighbors. They came to buy and sell things at the market that was usually set up on the square on Fridays and Saturdays. They came with their horses and wagons even though we had a railroad station, because most of our Ukrainian farmers couldn't afford the train.

But also on the square were the churches and synagogue. Our Ukrainian Greek-Catholic church was the biggest. It had a big, round, golden, onion-shaped dome. The Polish-Latin Catholic church was quite a bit smaller. It had a tall, sharp steeple. Even though both churches were Catholic under the Pope, the Poles didn't go to our church, and we didn't go to theirs. The Jews had a square Synagogue with a round top. People from each of these churches were always making parades around the square.

The Austrian officials and rich Polish landowners lived in big houses with Ukrainian servants behind one side of the square. Behind another side was a small section where the Jews lived, and behind the other side, the not-so-rich Polish. Curling around all of this was the rest of the town where we Ukrainians lived.

Our houses were built close to the street with barns behind for the horses and cows, tight fences for the pigs, and little open houses for the chickens and ducks and geese, which were underfoot all the time. And behind all of that, people had enough land to have an orchard, a kitchen garden and even some flowers and bushes.

The roads were dirt, of course, muddy when it rained or when the snow melted, dusty the rest of the time. The bricks of the house walls were made of clay mixed with straw, then baked in the sun. The roofs were steep and high and covered with layers of straw. People took very good care of their houses. Every spring, a day was set aside for the women to sponge on a fresh coat of whitewash and for the men to put back any straw that might have been torn out by the winter winds.

I don't think you can imagine what those straw roofs looked like! I have never seen any over here in America. The cap on the very top, and the four sharp edges coming down to the corners were made so carefully that no rain and snow could ever come in. Oy, how I wish I could go back for just one day to my little house! Maybe this house in America is bigger and stronger, but still my house was more beautiful.

Detail of corner of straw roof

Past all the houses, past the last street, all you could see were the fields to the edge of the earth. In the fall, those fields of wheat and rye turned to a soft gold. They bent with every breeze, looking like some giant golden sheet being shaken by the strong arms of a woman. When I was crossing the ocean, I cried to see the black waves under my boat moving like the wheat fields that I had left behind.

And of course the smells. A blind man could know each month from its smells: the sweet, plowed earth of spring so different from the tired smell of autumn. You cannot mistake the smell of the violets in spring from the marigolds in the fall. And oh, the smell of really cold snow.

Every morning in the growing season, people walked to their fields, some of which were very far from their houses. How I wish you could hear the people singing before the sun rose. Someone would start, and then everyone within its sound would find either a matching note or a harmonizing one. As they got closer to their fields, their voices got softer and softer until you couldn't hear them from your house anymore. I hated the hard work of the fields, but it felt easier when everyone was singing with the same beat as your work. You would think they had sung enough by the time they were going home, but no, they sang in the last red rays of the sun to take their tired feet home. How I wish you could hear them.

Not only did Mama want me to love her town, she wanted me know how she and her neighbors lived in this place. She especially wanted me to share her amazement at the clever tools everyone used. I listened carefully, as though someday, here in America, I might have some need to use such tools myself. Apparently it was important for me to know about the different shapes of plows. She hissed softly so I would know the sound a sickle makes when it cuts through the stalks of grain. She traced the size of the two parts of a flail in the air, and then used the invisible tool to show how it separated grain or linen fibers from their stalks in the fall.

My eyes grew heavy, listening to the details of storing food over the winter: how to pile the potatoes, carrots and cabbages in storage cellars, how to make a barrelful of sour cabbage and how to arrange the fruits in the special smokehouses to dry them for winter. She faltered when she realized the impossibility of imparting any notion of the wondrous smells of the oils made from their wide variety of seeds and grains.

You would have to smell those oils for yourself. American oils have no smell at all, so how could you know?

And then, of course, I had to know about the baking differences of the flours that came from the different grains she had reaped. Her Mama could only afford to pay the miller for the time he took to make coarse flour, so her Mama's bread was always rough and dark. She told me I was lucky, because, like the rich people in Kozova, I was able to have the luxury of soft, white Wonder bread in America every day.

It hurts my heart to remember the many days we had for celebration, besides the big, holy holidays like Christmas and Easter. Each special day was so different from the others. In January we all went down to the river with a big cross made of ice to remember how St. John baptized Christ. It was always so cold! And so many, many Saints' Days, which we celebrated instead of birthdays. I know you always want to celebrate birthdays with presents and a cake like Americans do, but we didn't give presents. Instead everyone whose name was Stephen or Stephanie, say, celebrated together on St. Stephen's day. After going to an early service, we would sing and dance around anyone with that name. Now that was a really happy birthday celebration.

Some other days, the young boys were allowed to do pranks. Oh, they could think of so many ways to surprise the girls! Then, on the longest and shortest days of the year, children went door-to-door singing special songs and begging for a treat. Other days were for boys and girls of marrying age to play games, tell fortunes and dance together. And even more special days than I can remember just now.

Tato said we had too many days for doing superstitious things. Superstitions were a sign of ignorance, he said. I didn't really believe in those things either, but I did what everyone was doing because we were having fun together. So how bad was it for people to throw some leaves in the water to tell their fortunes, or maybe cast some spells to protect themselves from bad witches and evil spirits?

On most of these special days, there was feasting. You could go to any house and get some food. Do you think people here would ever know how to live that kind of life?

I tried, but couldn't imagine the neighbors dancing and singing on Greenfield Rd. Mama's eyes told me she couldn't imagine it either.

In the summer, we didn't need a reason to dance. When there was a bright enough moon, and it wasn't raining, young people would gather on the street corners and oh, how we would dance! Sometimes Marko, the fiddler and Roman, the piper and Nikolai, the drummer played. But even if they didn't come, we could always sing the dancing songs ourselves and just clap the beat.

You would know those dances. They are the same ones the dancers do at our church concerts, only here they do them on a stage in costumes, while over there, we did them on the street corners in our regular clothes. And you would know many of the songs we sang because the choir sings them now, but over there we knew hundreds more.

But I have to tell you, everyone wanted to dance with me. You see I was a very good dancer. I knew all of the steps. A partner could spin me faster than any of the other girls. But of course, the boys liked best to show off their own dancing. Each would take a turn, dancing alone for a bit, trying to do the fanciest and hardest steps, bending his knees the deepest while kicking up his heels the highest. We would whoop and yell for the best one. Tato for some reason was never a singer or a dancer. But he was always there. I think he came to watch me dance.

In America, you marry any time of the year, but in Kozova, October and November were for weddings. You see, you needed three days to play out the story for a wedding: the bride leaving the mother, getting her hair cut and covered with a scarf, the groom coming to get her, and bringing her to his house. Each part of the long story had its own songs for the bride and groom's mothers and fathers and friends to sing. So, there weren't three days in a row in the summer when everybody had to work every day in the

15

fields. Then, of course, during Advent and Lent, the church wouldn't let you marry. So, in October and November, once the harvest was done, it seemed that almost every day we were singing and dancing and eating around some bride and groom.

In the winter, heavy snows came and made the ground white for many months. Our snow didn't turn dirty and melt in a day like here in Boston. No, our snow stayed white enough to make you blind. Because it stayed so cold, it went skreet, skreet, skreet, under your feet. We did our indoor work then.

I loved the twelve days of Christmas that started on Christmas Eve. Christmas was the very best of the holidays. Everyone followed the same customs over those twelve days. We did them exactly the same way we had done the year before, and the year before, and maybe for hundreds and hundreds of years before that. Every year, my Mama and Tato told us all the reasons for everything we did or ate. All these customs came either from Christ's birth, or from wanting to honor all of our family who came before us or were not yet born. Some of the customs came from even before Christ, when people wanted to honor the sun, the moon, the stars, the earth, the animals and all the growing things. I think I am beginning to forget some of these things we did though.

Mama's face changed then from the joy of the past to the reality of the present.

And here in America? Bah! You and Hanya will never know the joy that I had throughout the years in my beloved Kozova. Here, we don't dance and sing in the streets. We don't spend three days making a wedding. We don't celebrate Christmas over twelve days. We don't go out on Greenfield Road and go house-to-house walking through the snow, singing our carols. All I can do is make the twelve foods at Christmas in honor of the twelve Apostles. But of course, I can't find the right foods in the stores to make all of them, and even if I could find the food, I would never have enough time to make all twelve. Tato has never found where to buy some straw to put under the tablecloth to remind us Christ was born in a manger, or a sheaf of wheat to put in the corner to remind us of our ancestors. Over there we could just walk to the barn.

I mourned with her, wishing I could have seen her in those years: happy, singing and dancing. Though other women her age danced at picnics and church dances, Mama helped with the food, then sat with the ladies singing their old songs. No, the young, dancing Mama lived only in her memories of that fabled time, and I knew I would never see her that way.

Tato's Traveling Father and Wicked Mother

Mama seemed to be an intimate witness of Tato's early childhood, though she hadn't really known him until she moved into his neighborhood at the age of twelve. When she began telling stories about Tato's family, her far away eyes came back to the kitchen and looked straight into mine, making me feel vaguely guilty. Her voice hardened and she painted no idyllic scenes. Instead, she told of the family's scandals and accented the stories with raised eyebrows and a shaking head that sometimes went up and down with a cynical smile, sometimes back and forth sadly.

You know, Tato's grandfather had three wives and many children with each wife. The first two wives died young. His last wife was the mother of Tato's father, Ivan, who himself, was the very last of all his father's various children. Ivan's father wasted all the money he had inherited from a family whiskey business by drinking and gambling, and when he died, all that was left to divide amongst all those children was a few small fields and a lot of debt. Tato's father received almost nothing! Even though it had happened a long time before I was born, I often heard people talk about that old scandal of the Chopek family.

When Ivan came to be of marrying age, he was so poor that he could only consider the poorest girls. He looked a long, long time, and whom did he finally come up with? Imagine! A Polish girl, Anyelka! People shook their heads when they heard about that arrangement. She was quite ugly and was well known for her terrible temper, so her Polish family was desperate to get her married, even if it was to a Ukrainian. Her dowry was a small piece of land far from Ivan's piece of land, so a lot of good working time was spent just walking between the two pieces when they did get married. But, the really funny thing was that Anyelka was quite a bit taller than Ivan, which made people laugh. Of course, I only know what people said.

Now, I'm sure Tato, the big Ukrainian patriot, has never told you that you have a Polish grandmother.

Indeed, he hadn't told me. I didn't know what to think about this new information, but, somehow, I knew I wouldn't be asking him about it. Mama, smiling her cynical smile, went on.

Anyway, Anyelka had never gone to school, so she couldn't read or write, but only a few people her age did. She did speak both Ukrainian and Polish, so Ivan made her talk Ukrainian at home, except when her parents came to visit. And of course, with only such small fields, life only got worse for them when they had their first three children, boom, boom, boom. Your father was the oldest. They named him Iliya, but everyone called him by the usual nickname, Hilko. The family was the poorest of all the families in our part of town. Life for your father as a little boy was much harder than it was for me.

When Tato spoke of his wastrel grandfather in our after dinner time, his head went back and forth as well, though never with Mama's cynical look. Just as Tato never mentioned Mama in his stories, he almost never spoke of his mother, Anyelka. I would have liked to have him tell me that she was not the shrew that Mama made of her, though that would have spoiled Mama's stories. So, whether everything Mama told me about Tato was true or strained through later feelings about him and his family, I'll never know.

Tato most often talked about how his father, Ivan, coped with the family's hopeless poverty. Standing in front of our Black Beauty stove, his arms spread wide, the lines on his forehead pressed together and his blue eyes joined with mine, he told his story in a hard, angry voice.

You know, by rights, my father should have been a rich man. In his grandfather's time, a whole section of the city was called Chopekivka, which means, 'place of the Chopeks,' which is our name, of course. In those days, the Chopek family had piled up a lot of money with a whiskey business or something like that. They owned many, many fields. When my grandfather inherited his share of it, he could have continued to hire people to work the fields, sell what was leftover from the harvest after the needs of his family and live a life of great ease.

Unfortunately, it didn't happen that way. My grandfather turned out to be a weak man. He played in every gambling game in town and enjoyed his whiskey. So, the factory was lost, most of the fields were lost, and his money disappeared. Then, stupidly, he began to borrow money, and by the time he understood what enormous rate of interest the moneylenders were allowed to charge in Austria, it was too late. He left only debts and a few very small fields when he died. Such was the curse he left his family. It was a very sad, but very common story of our Ukrainians in those years under Austro-Hungarian rule.

So what could my father do but go to America? The food he grew in his small fields didn't even last to the next harvest. I know I was always hungry. He couldn't borrow money to buy another field, because he understood all about the enormous interest that would keep your neck under the lender's foot. Of course, he could have tried to find work for some of the rich people in the town, but the wages those days wouldn't put more than another slice of bread on the table once in a while.

One day he talked to a man who had just returned from America with a little extra money. It wasn't very much money, but the man had a habit of drinking, so my father thought maybe that was why he hadn't come home with much. My father had no such problem. He had learned the lessons of his father's life. He would be able to hold tightly to whatever he earned. When he saw a notice hanging in the railroad station that said men were needed to work on a tunnel in Boston, he said goodbye to us. On this first trip, he was gone for almost three years. I missed him very much.

I don't know how to explain to you how hard it is to come to a country where you do not understand what is said to you, and you have no words to explain your needs to others. My father, at least, had an older half-brother in Boston, who could give him room and board and show him how to get to the job on the tunnel. But when he was at work, he could only talk with his hands, and that was never enough.

As to the great amount of money he was expecting to earn, he soon learned that it wasn't going to happen. The wages written on the notice in the railroad station were higher than what he was actually paid. The company was taking more money out of his weekly pay for his steamship ticket than what was agreed upon. He had also expected to pay less to his half-brother for the mattress he slept on and the little bit of food he ate. He was depressed to see how little he had left at the end of every week to put into his little savings bag, even without spending any money on drink.

Oh, these capitalists in America knew how to use poor people! Make them work for almost nothing, while they themselves were getting rich beyond imagining, living in great houses with more rooms in each of them than any thirty people could use, maybe even forty. To the bosses, these workers were nothing but work animals, like a horse or a cow, maybe not even as valuable as a horse or a cow. My father had to work ten or twelve hours a day down in that tunnel. He said the workers were called 'Sandhogs.' He saw many men die needlessly from accidents down there.

Now the tunnel he worked in is the one that goes from Boston, under Boston Harbor, up to East Boston. That subway tunnel was the first underwater tunnel that went under ocean water. The workers were digging deep, deep under the water, from each side at the same time, only gaining four feet in a day. They dug with pick and shovel in a space with a great pressure of air to keep out the water. At the end of the day, if they were taken back up to the top too fast, they would be twisted with pain. Many died in that horrible way. My father was always exhausted, often sick, but if he didn't work, he didn't get any money.

It took him three years to fill his little sack of coins. When he came home, he was able to buy another small field in Kozova. Oh, we were all so glad to have him home with us again.

Mama's preference was for stories about his mother, Anyelka. When she spoke about her, Mama's eyebrows took residence high on her forehead, and occasionally her hand went up to her cheek as though completely shocked.

Oh, that Anyelka! Can you imagine? If she had had her way, Tato would not even have gone to school! Tato, who is so smart, smarter than any of the Ukrainians in Boston, imagine if he hadn't gone to school! But, I guess it was hard for her while Ivan was gone to America.

So, when it came time for Tato to go to school, Anyelka went to our priest and begged him to tell the authorities of her situation so she could keep Tato at home to help her, at least until Ivan came home. She kept asking why Tato had to go to school anyway? Neither she nor Ivan had gone to school, and it hadn't mattered. But, between that time and the time when Tato and me were of school age, officials in Vienna decided that all the children in the Empire had to go to school from the age of six to at least sixth grade.

The punishment, if you didn't send your child to school, was a feather pillow for every week the child missed. I remember well how the police wagon came rattling down the streets looking for the homes of children who had missed school. How the mother would scream when the policeman came into her house and took a pillow from the big pile on the bed!

Now, a woman had to do a lot of work to make a pillow. She had to tend the goose from when it hatched out of its shell. She had to pluck its down many times before she had enough to make a pillow. When I came to America, I took the feather pillows and blanket I had made, even though they made a very big, difficult bundle to carry. It was no small thing to give up a pillow you had made.

But, Anyelka hoped that if the priest could talk to the head of the school, she wouldn't have to give up any pillows. Instead, the priest told her to bring Tato to him. He told Anyelka to go outside, so he could talk to Tato alone. When he was done, he told Anyelka that Tato was smarter than any child he had ever seen and he deserved to go to school. Anyelka got very mad at the priest. Some people even said they heard her yelling at him, but he didn't give in to her.

Tato never told me that story, but he talked often about that same priest who seemed to be his surrogate father at times.

I was lucky that when I was an altar boy, the priest would keep me after the service on Sundays and let me sit in the library that was in his home. My mother didn't seem to mind then. If I stayed too late, I just didn't get any lunch. Not all his books were about religion. He had some shelves of his boyhood books, which his own children had read when they were small. Those books were much better than the ones in the school. He also let me read the books that were for older people, books of history and literature. I especially liked to read about the time of our glorious Kozaks, and of course

Shevchenko's poetry that was so rich with his love for Ukraine. I think it was then that I began to be a Ukrainian patriot.

Oh, yes, the priest was a good man. He was always trying to teach people new and better ways to think about each other. Now, for instance, he became friends with the Rabbi in town. This, by itself, was unusual in those days. So, once a year, in the fall when all the farm work was done, each group made a parade. Our group started first. Our band would be at the head of the parade. Then came the priest carrying a big cross. I was always at his side, very proud to be swinging the kadello, the incense burner. After the priest and me, men carried banners from inside the church, and then any women and children who wanted to join us. We marched up and down some streets then around the square to the Synagogue. The Rabbi and all of his people were waiting there in a big crowd. I think the Rabbi would be holding the Torah. Our band, still playing, would move onto the grass of the square, the priest and I would face the Rabbi, and everyone in our parade would bow. Then the band would start a new piece and we'd march back to our big church gate.

Meanwhile, the people at the synagogue would make their own parade with the Rabbi in front. They went around some the streets, chanting, and finally come to our gate where we all were waiting. Then it was their turn to bow to our priest. I think it was a very good ceremony. Some people complained that we shouldn't be bowing to Jews, but the priest ignored them. 'Only join the parade if you want to,' he would say.

I felt that the priest was like a father to me while my own father was in America, but it was nothing like having my own father back in our own house. I couldn't get enough of his stories about his life in America. I just followed him around every minute that I could. I was even eager to work in the fields so I could be at his side. But even with the little bit of extra land he was able to buy, the extra food we grew barely lasted through to the next year. Within two years, he was ready to leave again. I was even sadder to see him go this time.

Mama's eyebrows would slide back when she was done with Anyelka and began to talk about Tato. Her eyes softened.

I didn't know Tato when I started school. We didn't live in the same neighborhood then. He was two grades ahead of me, but I had heard a lot about this smart boy. There were many stories about his clever tricks on the teachers and the students that ended with Tato getting the stick from the teachers. We also knew he was one of the very poorest of children in the school. He was a handsome boy, but he came to school barefoot even when the snow first fell, and then, only in the deepest cold did he have some cloth wrappings on his legs. Now, my father was always sure that I had warm sturdy boots for the winter, and my mother always wrapped me in a shawl. I can't imagine how Anyelka could treat her children that way.

I asked Tato that night how he could possibly run in the cold snow barefoot!

I went barefoot in the snow only a few times. My mother just had a new baby, and she couldn't tend me for a little while. I ran very fast so it wouldn't hurt too much. The teacher put my legs into warm water when I got to school, and the next time, the principal even wrapped some pieces of cloth around my feet and fastened them with strips of leather. I was a little embarrassed, but it felt good to be treated so kindly.

But, you know, my school years were the happiest years of my life. I wanted to know everything: German, Polish, Ukrainian, arithmetic word problems, history, literature, religion. It didn't matter. I would stay later than the rest of the children and go into the tiny, tiny library the school had. It was about as big as a closet. I would read over and over whatever books were in there. I would make up a story for my mother about why I was late, but she never believed me, so she just gave me more work to do at home, after a few whacks with the strap, of course. I really shouldn't have lied to her. But, I did try to help her as much as I could.

Tato never mentioned in his stories to me that he had a reputation for being smart. That was for Mama to tell in a voice full of pride.

It amazed everybody that, though Tato was so poor, he was still the smartest child in the whole school. Whenever there was a gathering of the students, the teachers chose him to do the reciting. When he was older they let him write his own little speeches. So you see, that is probably why he makes so many speeches so easily here in Boston.

Ivan's Second trip to America

Mama's emphasis was on Anyelka, when she talked about Ivan's second trip.

People were saying that maybe this time, like some other men in the village, Ivan wouldn't come back, especially to such a hot-tempered woman like Anyelka. My Mama was always very sorry for Anyelka, but then she had a very big heart. She was a saint, you know. After Ivan went to America the second time, Tato was a little older and he was a big help to Anyelka in the fields. It was then that the priest told Tato that when he finished the local school, the priest would pay his tuition at the Gymnasia, a high school, which was in Ternopil, a city quite a distance from Kozova. When he finished the Gymnasia, the priest would pay for him to go to the seminary in Lviv, which was still farther away. There he would become a priest.

Oh, Tato wanted to go the Gymnasia, all right. But he didn't really want to be a priest, so I don't know if he would have gone even if Anyelka had let him. Anyway, Anyelka got very mad when Tato told her what the priest said. She said she needed him to be home to help her in the fields while Ivan was gone so she would never give her permission. He had to tell the priest that he couldn't go. But he should have gone. Being a priest wouldn't have been all that bad. He could have married me before he took his vows. The Catholic Church over there has always let married men be priests. And the parishes always gave priests and their families a good home. If he had been a priest, he wouldn't have been taken into the army, and he wouldn't have had to run away to America so he wouldn't have to fight for Austria, and we would not have come to this strange place, this America!

When Tato talked of his father's second trip, he would become agitated and pace in front of our Black Beauty stove. His anger was for the capitalists who took advantage.

It was hard for us without my father, but harder, I know, for him. He went deep into America this time, somewhere to work on a railroad. I don't think that he knew exactly where he was. He found that the work was very dangerous with men dying daily in accidents on the job, and besides, along with the very high heat, there were mosquitoes. And with the mosquitoes came a terrible fever. Men began to die faster and faster as the days went on. My father became frightened for his life and decided to escape with his cousin who had left Kozova with him.

The company that had pulled them over there with promises of good money had not told them of the dangers they would face. Why should they? If they died, the company could always hire more people like my poor father and his cousin to step into their empty shoes. People who didn't know the language of the country they were in. People who didn't know how much they should be paid. If a man died, the company never told the family. The only way they found out was if someone who worked with him wrote a letter to the family.

And not only did the company pay almost no wages, like for the tunnel digging he did in Boston, it had a company store to take back those wages. My father, like the rest of the workers needed to buy some food, maybe a pair of shoes now and then. So, he had to go to the store because it was the only one for miles around. The store didn't take his coins. Instead, at the end of the month, he got a written list of what he had bought that month. Of course he couldn't read it. He would have to find someone who could read English, and yes, he had bought every item, but the cost of those items were so high, he had only half as much money in his pay as he needed to pay it off. He said he almost fainted. The store clerk offered to lend him the money, at a very high rate of interest, of course. These Americans were very, very smart and very, very greedy people. They did not give even one breath of care for the human beings risking their lives working for them.

So, my father and his cousin decided there was too much danger there: first, from all the disease around them; then, from the growing debt. Now by rights, they should have worked longer so they could pay back the company from their wages for the steamship ticket from Germany and the railroad trip from New York, but they felt they had been deceived when they signed up. So he and his cousin crawled out of their tent one night. They checked to see that the guards were asleep. For the next few weeks, they traveled only by night, taking long detours to avoid getting caught. They got sick now and then and almost never had enough to eat.

How they found their way back to New York, I will never know. My father said they walked in the direction of the rising sun. It took them more than half a year. It took them almost another year to save enough money doing odd jobs on the New York docks to buy a steamship ticket to get home. When they finally arrived in Kozova, they had stories to tell, but not a penny in their pockets.

Tato said nothing more about his father's arrival. It was Mama who told me about Anyelka's reaction: *Oy, oy, oy, she was so mad that when they were walking home and he told her that he had no money, she began to hit him around his head. People were watching and laughing at her. She had no shame, that one. She could have waited until she got home, but no, right in the street she hit him.*

In later years, I had the chance to ask my aunt, who had come to America with my father, about some of Mama's stories about their mother, Anyelka. From all the details Mama related about Tato's family during his boyhood, I somehow assumed Mama must have seen everything with her own eyes.

My aunt hesitated a bit, then said, *Don't believe everything your mother says about our childhood. For some reason she hated my mother, but my mother was not all that bad. My mother had plenty of reasons for the things she did. Your mother, she wasn't in our house when we were small. She had no idea how we had to live. She didn't live anywhere near us until her father died when she was twelve.*

Still, Mama's version of Anyelka came to my mind whenever I tried to put myself into my grandmother's house. I could only see myself hiding from her.

Mama's Father and Saintly Mother

Some lunches, Mama couldn't tell any stories. Her face might suddenly crumple and she would invoke her mother, swaying back and forth in her chair.

Oy, Mamochka, mamochka, I will come back to you. I want to see you once again and hold your hand again. Oy, oy, Mamo, Mamo! I will come back!

The saintly mother approaching 100

Her face covered with her hands, she would cross to her bedroom, closing the door behind her. I ate quickly then, and moved to another part of the house. She didn't cry when she talked about her father, perhaps because he had died such a long time ago. But her face held the same love whomever she spoke about.

My father's name was Alexei. He was a short but handsome man, a shoemaker. We were not wretchedly poor like your father's family, at least not until my father died so unexpectedly. I was proud of my father. Though he was very poor as a boy, he managed to learn how to be a shoemaker and set up a business. He had to work for several years as an apprentice to a local shoemaker whenever he could be away from the fields and several years more to begin to have enough customers. When he was of marrying age, he was such a good prospect that his family got him a woman whose dowry was a house and two fields. Remember, this woman was not my mother. That comes later.

He made fancy shoes for the wealthy people of the town, because they liked his careful, beautiful work. He also made the cheaper, heavy, farmer shoes because he was a good man. With so much business, he earned enough money to hire men to work in his fields. He and this woman had three sons. She died giving birth to their third son.

Now, for a widower with two small children and a brand new baby to arrange to marry a young woman was almost impossible. The families didn't want their young daughters to care for small children not their own, so my father had to look at older, unmarried women.

It so happened that my mother was already twenty-eight at that time, which was really past marrying age. She hadn't married because her family was too poor to give a good dowry. If she had been beautiful, maybe some man would have wanted her anyway, but though she had a kind face, it was plain. When no one asked to marry her, she began to take care of her brothers' and sisters' children at her house. She knew that when the children grew up, she would spend the rest of her life taking care of children in some rich Polish or Austrian family.

My father, who lived near her house, had already noticed how sweetly she tended the family children. When he asked her parents if she could be his wife, of course, they said yes, so my own darling Mama started her married life with three small stepsons. The two oldest were naughty from the beginning, but the baby, Dmytro, came to love her as if she was his own mother. In a little while, I was born, then my brother, Petro, and then my sister, Katerina. That made six children for my mother to watch over. But of course, you know, she was a saint. Everyone knew she was a saint. Nothing like your father's mother who was very far from being a saint! Oh, very, very far.

Now, when I was born in 1889, my father was very happy to have a daughter after those three sons. He was always making shoes for me. He even made some that squeaked when I walked, because that was the style then among the rich people. They were the most expensive of all the shoes he made. He gave me pfennigs to spend in town, and told my Mama not to make me work so hard when I came home from school. When I was in sixth grade, he showed me how to make a list of the shoes he had sold that day, each with its price, and then on another page, write everything he spent on leather and thread. He trusted me to add everything up correctly. He took me to market to let me watch how he bargained with the leather sellers and sometimes let me do it myself. The older boys were not interested in doing these things.

When I was just twelve, my father came home one day with his face all red. He was shaking. It was a very hot day, and he had taken a drink from a very deep, very cold well. He should have known better. Sadly, in one week, he was dead, probably with pneumonia. On his last day, barely able to whisper, he told the children to leave the room. Mama told me later that he thanked her for all she had done for him and gave her a bag of gold pieces from under his pillow. She wasn't to tell his older sons.

Now, you see, there were different rules in Kozova than America. My father's first wife came into the marriage with the house and two fields. Because these properties were hers, they couldn't go to a second wife when he died, only to her three sons. The fields my father had bought with his shoemaking money would have to be divided among all of his six children and Mama equally. My father understood that we would have almost nothing to live on when he died, so he gave Mama the gold pieces in secret, so she wouldn't have to share them with the three oldest sons.

Mama and her three children had to move out, and my father's oldest son, who was married by then and living in the house with all of us, took the house for himself and his wife. The second brother stayed in the house also, because he would soon marry and build his own house. The youngest of the three brothers, Dmytro, chose to leave with Mama, even though he could have stayed in the house with his older brothers.

You would think those two older boys would have been grateful for all my mother had done for them, but you know, the oldest son's wife wouldn't even let me pick a pear off the tree by the front door after we moved out! I was very sad, but also very glad to leave.

Mama's uncle built her new house, but she had to pay for the materials, of course. He was helped by Dmytro, who was fourteen and strong by then. Some good neighbors helped also. One of those neighbors was your Tato's father, Ivan. He came with his horse and his oldest son, Hilko, which was your father's nickname. He was fourteen just like Dmytro.

Ivan and the boys spread straw in some mud and then Ivan tied his horse with a long rope onto a stake in the middle. The horse would go round and round mixing the mud and the straw together with his hooves. Ivan and the other neighbors shaped the mixture into bricks and when the bricks were dry, they built the walls.

Lots of people came to help make the high straw roof. Mama planted another pear tree in front of the house. We had a party for everyone when the house was finished. But, then, everything became very hard for us. With the little bit of money Mama had left, she bought a small field, which she and Dmytro plowed and planted. When I finished sixth grade, I became mistress of the house and took care of my little brother and sister. That way, my mother could work in the fields. But life was hard. I don't know if you can understand what is hard, my little American daughter. You have such an easy life here. You don't do anything to help me, like I helped my mother, so how would you know what hard means?

To make money for her, I had to sell our eggs, milk, and the cheese and butter my mother and I made from the milk. Sometimes I took a baby pig to market. I took the geese down the long path to the river every day between the tall sunflowers on each side. When I walked, they looked like a hundred suns shining down on me. On the warmer days of the year, I had to carry the family laundry to wash in the cold water of the river. I would soak the clothes first, then spread them on the rocks and beat them with a stick to get them clean. After rinsing them in the river, I'd wring them. I was lucky to have strong arms. When I spread the clothes on the green grass beside the river, they got whiter than with any bleaches I used here in America. When there were other girls and women there, we sang the whole time.

I had to get up very early to milk the cow. When I finished, taking only one pull off some bread to hold my hunger, I brought the cow from the barn to a pasture where a neighbor boy watched her all day. I would get home from the pasture just when the sky was waking up. While I was gone, Mama would take Katerina in her big black shawl and go to church, and except when there was too much snow, she would visit my father's grave after the service. When Mama finally came home, I would have some sweet smelling kasha grains cooked and ready to eat. When she left the house to go to work the fields, she always hugged me and told me that she knew of no one who had a better daughter.

Once, just as I got to the pasture to take the cow home, a sudden thunderstorm broke right over my head. I squeezed myself tight under the cow, holding gently to her udders. The lightning flashed all around, and the rain pelted the ground. And, you know, that cow didn't even move. Only my feet were wet when the storm was over.

I tended our house garden, stopping only now and then to listen to a nightingale singing somewhere in the bushes. You have never heard such singing from a bird, because America's birds know only simple songs. I can hear the amazing sounds even now in my head.

When my little brother, Petro, came home from school, I gave him work to do and had to scold him when he was slow. I always had the evening meal ready when Mama came home. Yes, I was a big help to her, not like you who just goes to play in the woods with the boys and never comes home when I call. Mama could always trust me to do whatever she needed.

During the winters, when Mama didn't have to work in the fields, she took care of my little brother and sister, so I could go to a wealthy Polish home to take care of their three children. That way, I could earn a little money for Mama.

Oh, believe me, none of the servants in that rich house crossed me where the children were concerned. Even though I was only twelve or thirteen, I wouldn't let them ignore me. If, say, they didn't bring some milk or tea for the children as soon as I asked them, I would go right to the mother and tell her. The children loved me. I made up games for them to play and I'd read stories from their books in Polish. I had learned Polish in school, so it was easy for me. Then when I walked home, the children of my neighborhood would be waiting for me, begging me to tell them those same stories in Ukrainian.

It was good that I knew all the languages of our town. I learned Polish and German in school so on Saturday market day, when I brought our things to sell, if there were Austrians who spoke only German, or maybe someone Polish, I could easily bargain with them. I took our things on another day to the Yiddish market. The Yiddish man, who sold his things beside me, taught me enough Yiddish to bargain. I had already learned some Yiddish because a few Jewish women paid me to go to their houses to light their fires on the Sabbath, and they would tell me words just like the man did.

Another good thing was that I could do sums in my head very quickly because of helping my father. Those men at market said that I drove a hard bargain. They said they would hardly make any profit for themselves when they sold the butter or milk again in the city. The Jewish man beside me, taught me how to do all the hand motions that opened and then sealed every sale. I learned exactly how to smack their palms to show I agreed with the final price! My mother was so proud of me. She said she could never have gotten such a good price.

I often felt a tinge of envy for Mama's obvious love for her mother. My envy turned to guilt when she went on and on about her own loving goodness toward her saintly mother. I caught her hidden message about the distance I kept with her when I was in my American world, though it didn't change anything.

Even when my Mama was a young girl, every one knew she was already a saint. She was the young girl chosen to put the cross on top of the entrance arch to our old church. She worked hard all of her life, and in spite of that, never lost her goodness. If you saw her, you would see her holiness.

My mother was very well known in Kozova because she knew all the healing plants. She'd pick them coming and going to the fields, sometimes going long distances to find special ones in the woods. When she came home, her shawl would be full. She sat late into the night, tying them in bundles and hanging them on the storage room walls to dry. On Sundays, after church and dinner, she might sit and fold the dry leaves or flowers into different sized packets.

People came to her all the time with their fevers. Or maybe they had a sty in their eye, or they had a headache, or their heart was beating too fast, or maybe they had had too many babies, or maybe not any. Whatever the ailment was, she always had a packet to give them with her special instructions as to how to use it. Some of the packets were to be made into a tea to drink, while others were to be put into a bag that you soaked in hot water and then put on your chest or back or head or eye. Some were for gargling, some would go in boiling water and you were to breathe in the vapors, and some… well you don't really want to know.

I did, but I knew she wasn't about to tell me.

And she never asked for money! I thought her saintliness went too far. I told her we needed more money than we had. Other healing women certainly asked for money. There was that Zosha who not only sold medicine plants, but she made brews of spider webs and bat wings. She could tell you your fortune, or cast a spell. If you maybe had malaria, she might tell you how to go out to a certain crossroads when there were clouds hiding the moon. If you turned three times and spit over your shoulder, your illness would be cured. People gave her whatever she asked for, because they believed they would be cured, but my mother would only say, 'No, I think it would be sinful to ask for money when someone is in need.'

My mother fasted every Friday until the evening meal. That night, all the old men for miles around would come into our house without even knocking, to eat the perohe that I had to spend all day making. I sometimes had to mix dough for almost two hundred of those little dumplings. And then I would have to roll the dough and cut it all into small circles. And then the hardest part when I would have to tightly pinch the circles together around the filling of mashed potatoes and farmer's cheese so they wouldn't come apart when I'd boil them. And of course the men would complain if there weren't enough oil-fried onions tossed over the perohe when I served them.

You see, old or sick men, when their wives had died, would be turned out of their houses, especially if the house by then was filled with their sons' wives and children. It was the custom for brides and grooms to live in the house of the groom's parents. Old, sick, widowed women had to be cared for by the daughters-in-law living in the house, or maybe, if they were dying a long death, they were sent to a convent. Old men came from miles around to Kozova, because it had a building with narrow beds for them to sleep in at night. But still, they had to find their own food by begging, or maybe doing small jobs somewhere.

I asked Tato that very night why the Ukrainians were so cruel to the old men.

Yes, it seems cruel, but what could they do? The homes got too crowded with the new generations. The houses were very small and every bite of food had to be grown by someone usually on a field that was too small to feed everyone in the house. People were too poor to build a bigger house. But you see, over there, every person knew it was his holy duty to help the homeless men. If a man came begging at your door, you knew the church expected you as a Christian to give him something, no matter how little.

So in a way, the whole community took care of these old men. Even the town doctors went regularly to the old men's home to look after them when they got sick, and they never expected pay. Who does that here?

It was obvious from her frowning face that Mama thought her mother did more for these men than the church and town expected of their people.

For a while after my father died, we would just give any man coming to our door a little milk, or maybe some cheese, but then my mother told one of them he could come on a Friday night and join us at our table. So, of course, not only that man, but also so many men began to come, they would have to wait their turn outside of our house in a line. And how they complained if they had been waiting and the last of the perohe had been eaten! My brothers tried to give each man maybe only three perohe, so as to keep the line moving, and make the perohe last longer, but then they would have to argue with each man about how they couldn't give him any more and tell him sharply that it was time to leave. Now, I always put aside enough of the perohe for myself, because if I had waited until I was done boiling them up and serving them, I would not have gotten any at all!

And some of the men smelled so bad! And of course, I was mad because I had to make all the perohe during the growing season, because my mother would be just coming home from working all day in the field. But I was really angry with her because she didn't seem to care how much the men were eating. I told her how much flour and eggs I was using to make the dough, and how many potatoes and how much cheese I had to use to fill the dough circles with, and how much of our precious oil I needed to fry the onions that I covered them with. I told her my fingers were tired with all the pinching I had to do. We hardly had enough of those things for ourselves, but she has to feed all the old men of the world!

But, my Mama would just smile and say, in the Old Slavonic words of our Holy Book, 'When you make a feast, call the poor, the hurt, the lame, and the blind, and you shall be blessed.' I couldn't believe how much of the Holy Book she knew from memory, even though she never learned to read and write.

On Saturday nights, she rested in her own way. She and her sister would go to the bathhouse for a steam bath. Once they were sitting there, each one took a pull of whiskey from a little flask. Then they would fill a pipe with tobacco and pass it between them, gossiping happily until they were done smoking it. After they got dressed and just before they started for home, they would take a little snuff from a box, and stuff it into their noses. My mother said it was those Saturday evenings that made her strong enough to go on for another week. And of course, going to church on every day that she could. Yes, she was truly a saint.

Mama would look at me then, her thick lids holding a rim of tears for a moment before they spilled onto her cheeks. Then her eyes would sweep heavenward as she chanted her usual lament.

"Oy, Mammochka, Mammochka moya! Why did I leave you? Why did I come to this strange place? I want to touch your hand and kiss your cheek just once again. Oy Mammochka!"

I tried to imagine myself in her Mama's lap. What would I call her? My Mama's Mama? Would she hold me tightly, maybe kiss my cheek, or would she think I was a bad, disobedient American child? Her picture always disintegrated before I could resolve my questions.

Section II

1901 – 1914

Courtship, Marriage and Separation

An Ocean Between

Mama and Tato

Mama met Tato and his family when she moved into the new house in his neighborhood, after her father died. She was twelve, just finishing sixth grade, which would be her last. Tato was fourteen and out of school. The stories she told me about him before she lived in his neighborhood came from the copious gossip she had heard about the Chopeks: the notorious Anyelka, the mild-mannered, usually gone-to-America, Ivan, and their unusually smart, oldest boy, Ilya, nicknamed Hilko. Mama had also known this Hilko by reputation at their school, especially his outrageous antics that got him into so much trouble there.

On the day after Mama and her family had moved into their new house, Mama stepped out to shake out a cloth and was startled to hear screaming in the road.

It was tall Anyelka, running and yelling after little nine-year old Stefan, Tato's younger brother, with a switch in her hand. He was too fast for her and disappeared behind our house. Anyelka turned to the other children playing in front of her house, screaming at them to go away and leave her in peace. I moved quietly back into my house. Why ask for trouble?

I couldn't help noticing that something was always happening around their little house, which was two doors down from ours. With five children there, plus Ivan and Anyelka, someone was always outside. Besides Tato and Stefan, there was a sister between them, Anna, who was eleven and supposedly in charge of the two screaming babies, which were three-year old Marena and the brand-new infant, Michael. Those two came after Ivan returned from his second trip to America. Anyelka was always yelling at Anna to keep them quiet.

But the father, Ivan, seemed very kind. After I had met him when he helped making the bricks for our house, he always had a smile for me. And now and then, I did see Tato going to his job at the railroad station, whenever he wasn't working in the fields with his mother and father, but he didn't speak to me. Later, when he was around fifteen, I saw that he had gotten a dark jacket and necktie for his new job as stenographer at the courthouse. Obviously, he was becoming somebody important, because Ukrainian boys of his age didn't wear jackets or get jobs in the courthouse.

He told me later, when we knew each other well enough to talk, that he wrote down the testimonies of people in court. He had to write as quickly as the person spoke, so he made up a way to use just a few letters for each word. Later, he would write it all out in his beautiful handwriting that he won a prize for in school. He could write those records in Polish, German or Ukrainian, whatever they wanted. Anyelka told him it would be better if he used his fine back to help her in the fields instead of his fine handwriting in the courthouse, but he never wanted to be a farmer. He just gave Anyelka a part of his pay, so she could hire some one to do his work. Anyelka wasn't happy, but what could she do? He was too big for her to beat any more.

I think it was around that time that he began to notice me. He came to the street corners when we were dancing, and I could tell he was watching me. Though I saw that he was very good looking and different than the rest of the boys, I was having too much fun dancing and singing to pay him any extra attention.

About that time, Ivan, who probably couldn't stand to be so long with Anyelka, saw a notice at the railroad station from a steel factory in East St. Louis, and next thing we knew, he was gone for the third time.

When Tato wasn't watching the dancers at night, I knew he was over at the new Chytalnia, a little library and meeting hall. The organizers liked him, so they asked him to give talks to the farmers. Imagine, old farmers coming to hear a boy teach them about animal diseases and building outhouses. Maybe it was the fancy courthouse clothes that made the farmers think he knew so much.

Tato, speaking of those days, never spoke of Mama. It must have been a happy time, though, because he talked of it in a happy, excited way.

Something wonderful was happening just around the beginning of the 1900's. The Ukrainian intelligentsia, the doctors, scientists, poets, writers, artists, musicians, were beginning to wake up and see that we had a language, culture, customs, music and dance that were very beautiful, all our own, and quite worthy of respect. They saw that the ordinary people didn't realize the value of these things, much less their real lack of knowledge about the much simpler things like up-to-date health practices and how to farm better so they would be able to thrive on their small fields.

So, these educated people formed an organization called 'Prosvit', which means 'Education', but it means a little bit more. It means the fire and spirit that comes with education. They began to go about the countryside to begin a great work among the people. The first thing we saw in Kozova was the opening of a Chytalnia, a reading room. The organization filled it with books, some of which you could check out, like at a library here. You can imagine how excited I was. But, the room they got in one of the public buildings was too big for the books they had, so they enclosed the small library space, and used what was left for talks and meetings. I hung around, helping anyway I could, putting out benches and sorting books, so the man in charge noticed me. He asked me if I would be willing to call some meetings, and then read the speeches they would be sending me. I said, 'Of course!'

So I made announcements after the church service for a talk on such and such a night. I studied the pamphlets the organizers gave me to read, and then, trying not to look like I was reading the pamphlet, I would talk to the farmers how certain diseases came from walking barefoot where some animal or person had dropped a pile. I talked to them about making outdoor toilet buildings, but that subject was very controversial. Many years before, Austria had put a tax on such outhouses, and so the people tore them down and vowed not to build any more unless they weren't taxed. And if it was unhealthy? Too bad. Everyone did their business 'over the fence' as they said. That just meant they went anywhere and everywhere. I tried to convince them that if they weren't going to build an outhouse, they should at least wear shoes, but they just yelled at me that no one could afford to do that. This was true, as I very well knew from my childhood.

But best of all, I liked the talks they gave me to read about Ukrainian history, the Kozaks, and all our heroes. I felt I was going to that Gymnasia the priest wanted to send me to, and getting a higher education. Seeing the farmers' faces looking up at me, I began to feel like a teacher and it felt good. But then, when real poets and professors from Lviv came to give lectures, I saw myself as the young ignorant boy that I was.

Mama said she didn't go to the Chytalnia very much because she had begun to develop a little sewing business. Her face shone with a self-satisfied pride.

Soon after we moved into our new house, I began making clothes for my little sister, Katerina and myself. I used our old clothes as patterns for the linen cloth Mama wove every winter. I dyed the embroidery thread, and then copied old embroidery patterns for the collars and sleeves. After a while, I began to make up my own patterns.

Now, by custom, a woman who was getting married had to embroider twelve shirts for her new husband, before they could have the ceremony. That kept her too busy to get into any trouble, and sometimes, it took her so long to make the shirts, she didn't have time to make her own shirt for her wedding. Those days, women didn't wear white wedding dresses like here in America. They wore an embroidered linen shirt. The underskirt with the embroidery around the bottom showed under a straight skirt woven with dyed wool. On top of all that she put on an embroidered apron and a wool jacket embroidered with big flowers in the front corners. But, you know what they look like from church concerts. Of course, here in America, we buy cloth in a store.

Then, a young woman asked me to make her shirt and skirt, then someone else asked, and soon I had a little business going. Of course, I had to sew everything together by hand, because I had no sewing machine. And planning and doing the embroidery on the collars and sleeves and across the front, was tricky, but I got pretty good at it. And, I wasn't going to do it for nothing, like my mother did with her healing plants. I was very sure about that! So, though I still went to the fields for the busy times of planting and harvesting, I gave her some of my money so she could hire someone to help her in my place. I was so glad not to go the fields. I enjoyed my sewing much, much more.

And also, instead of going to the Chytalnia evenings like Tato did, I sang in our big church choir. I sang alto. I went twice a week, once to rehearse just with the choir, and then on another night, when the choir rehearsed with the band.

Now, as you know, Ukrainian churches never use instruments in our Holy Service. With those basses shaking the church, who needed an organ? But, unlike other churches, we had a band. Somehow, the director convinced the priest that we wouldn't go to hell if a band played in church now and then. They played before and after the Service, and maybe with the choir after the priest was done with his sermon.

The choir director had brought back some instruments to Kozova after he studied music at the University in Lviv, and he taught some men and boys to play them. When a lot more men wanted to learn, he convinced the priest to buy some more instruments. Believe it or not, he even taught Tato how to play the clarinet, and Tato was one of those who couldn't sing two notes in a row.

The man was a good director, but he wasn't always patient. When some woman in the church was shrieking instead of singing, he'd lean over the railing and say, 'We don't need any lady-roosters singing today.' Lots of times, the smell of garlic would be very strong coming up from the people on a hot day. Then he'd lean over and say, 'We are about to faint up here from your garlic. What's the matter with you people?'

But, you could just cry with the music, whether it was just the choir or the band, you could feel God, his saints and his angels in that music. And it wouldn't just make the women cry. Even the men cried. But then, the whole church made you think you were already in heaven. So many candles! So many Icons! They were made with gold and strong colors with Jesus and Mary and Joseph and all the saints and angels on the ceiling, the walls and on the Iconostas. You never saw an Iconostas because we don't have one in Boston. It's a carved and painted wooden screen in front of the altar with closed doors in the front to separate the holy place around the altar from the people. When the priest opened the doors during communion, it meant we were now in heaven a little bit.

After rehearsals and after church, Tato would try to walk home with me, but sometimes, other boys got to me first, so he would just walk a ways behind. When he did walk with me, we usually stopped at the well between our houses to talk.

Sometimes, in the early morning, he would see me pumping the handle that brought up water from the well to fill my buckets, and he would run over to help me carry them back to my house. The pump had a long, beautiful, curving metal handle. Sometimes we would pump it up and down together. Sometimes, we sat on a nearby bench and talked.

One night, as we sat by the well, Tato told me about a letter from his father who was working in East St. Louis. His father was living in a boarding house where one man slept in a bed while another man was working. When the second man came home, the first man got up so the second man could sleep on the bed. Anyway, now he wanted Tato to come and work in the factory with him. The work would be hard, but he could make good money to take back home. He would send Tato a steamship ticket whenever Tato decided. Ivan would probably come home with Tato when Tato had to report for his two-year duty in the Austrian army, sometime before he turned twenty.

So now, Tato was asking me, me, who was only sixteen, what he should do? How could I know what he should do? I was really surprised he was telling me about this. All I could ask was what Anyelka thought about it. I was sure she would be against it, but it was worth asking.

He told me he hadn't told her about it yet, but he was sure she wouldn't like it.

So, I just listened, and while he was talking to me, I could hear that he was deciding to go. I didn't think I'd miss him too much, because I had many boys as my friends, but I could tell that he was going to miss me. And yes, his mother was very mad when he told her about the letter. She even slapped him, but he had learned by then that he could do what he wanted.

A Courtship

Tato's first trip to America was always told as an adventure story, both to me, and later, to the children of the Chestnut Hill School. I had happily watched stories like his down at the movie theater: a poor but handsome hero overcoming a multitude of obstacles to reach his goal. Now, I watched his grand adventure play out on my inner movie screen with Tato as the grand hero. Tato didn't say anything about his mother slapping him. He started the story with his dilemma of whether to go or not.

Now, I knew that I had to go in for military service before I turned twenty, but Austria wasn't letting boys between seventeen and twenty leave the country, because they might not come back for their service. I wanted the excitement of seeing America so badly. I thought I would see if I could sneak out.

Before I left, I packed two bags. I put some clothes in one, and in the other, my pillow, a map of Eastern Europe, a comb, a razor, a needle and thread, and some food. At the last minute I buried the twenty-five dollars that my father had sent me deep into my pillow, keeping out a few dollars that I might need along the way, along with my ship ticket. Nothing was easy. I had to cross into Poland, and then into Germany. At every checkpoint, I was handled and questioned very roughly. They ripped out my coat lining at one border. They pounded my pillow everywhere but didn't find the money I had hidden in it. I quickly learned to lie and bribe, and I was only seventeen.

I spent only the smallest amount possible for food, even though I was always hungry. The last train, fit only for animals, I have to say, took me finally to the seaport, Antwerp, in Belgium. I had been traveling for almost three weeks. There, the news was that the next steamship, the Kroonland, would not leave for two weeks.

So there I was, all my papers safely in my pockets, all of them punched, or stamped, or signed, with two weeks to wait in Antwerp, alone, a boy who had never been out of his little town. I could have joined the other men who sat around and played cards and drank for two weeks. But the city looked so beautiful to me, I decided to go out every morning to find something new to look at, something I had never seen in my little town of Kozova. And indeed, every day I saw something that amazed me.

Finally, the steamship came, and I crossed the wide, rough ocean. Many were seasick. I was too, a little bit. In ten days, we were in New York. Because I didn't know any English, either to speak or to read, I couldn't find out how to get to East Saint Louis. It probably would have been funny to an American to see me waving the tickets my father had sent me and trying to talk with my hands and face instead of my voice. So, it was almost unbelievable to me when I was actually getting off the train in East Saint Louis.

I had written to my father that I was coming, but of course, I could not tell him when I would be arriving in East Saint Louis. When I got off the train in that big station, I was suddenly afraid. How would my father find me? How would he know which day to come? I had been traveling for more than a month. Those were the days before you could go find a telephone to make a call and know that there was a telephone at the other end. Telephones are unbelievable! Someday, I hope we can own one.

Anyway, I found a bench that faced the big entrance to the station, and I sat down. The glass everywhere made everything very hot. I sat there all day long, only going to the restroom when I had to. I had never seen such a restroom. The one in our courtroom back in Kozova just had a hole in the floor. Here were white thrones.

By then, I had used all the money my father had sent to me, so I couldn't buy any food. I had no real hope, but I thought that if I sat in one place, maybe someday soon, my father would find me. When my thirst became too great, I went to where I had seen people drinking from some streams of water coming up in a pipe by a wall. What a wonder to see! I got in line and took a long, long drink. When I lifted my head, the man drinking at the fountain next to me lifted his head too. We looked at each other, and it was my father! Can you imagine? It was my father! Oh what a joy it was to see him! He told me that he had been coming every day to the station after work for many weeks.

He took me by streetcar and ferry across that wide, wide Mississippi River to Madison, Illinois, where he worked for the American Car Foundry. So many more, new sights for my young eyes! Billboards were one of the things I had never seen in Kozova. My father brought me to the Ukrainian lady's house where he was a boarder. Ukrainians were living all around, and nearby, a Ukrainian church.

I rested for a day, and then I joined the three thousand or so men who worked at the foundry. It was hot and hard work, either working with the hot metal, or trying to keep up with the production belt that always seemed to go faster than you could work. But, at least they weren't cheating people with a company store and charging for the bed you slept in. I learned just enough English to be able to do my job, and within a half a year or so, I had been promoted to yard foreman. Me, a seventeen-year-old boy! I was out of the hot factory and was not doing such hard labor any more. It was a valuable lesson to me that no learning goes to waste. But, all too soon, it was time for me to go home. I had to report for Austrian Army duty.

Or was it to see Mama again? He never said. Mama said she was sure it was to see her again, though she didn't tell me how she knew.

Tato's father, Ivan, and Tato, taken in East St. Louis

The Secret

Besides enjoying adventure stories at the Saturday afternoon movies, I had quickly become an addict of the love stories. At home, I tried to imagine my mother and father playing out the story of their courtship on the movie screen. Watching them day-by-day, however, I never saw them in the 'happily ever after' part. I never saw them holding hands or exchanging even a slight peck, much less a Saturday matinee, ecstatic kiss. I heard only Hilko and Marena between them, no special loving words, no slightest hint of flaming desire behind the screen of detail Mama always painted when she talked of their teen years.

As for me, I didn't miss him all that much when he went to East St. Louis. As I said, I had boys interested in me. I was still young. I was always doing something with my friends. And of course, I was always helping my mother.

Those days, as I told you, I took over the sewing of our clothes from my mother. While I was sewing, I would be remembering the silk dresses the Polish lady wore. That was the Polish lady where I took care of the children. I would see her playing her piano sometimes in those soft and beautiful dresses. Sometimes, when I was in the children's bedroom, I would take the dresses out of their closet to see how the cloth had been cut to make the dresses fit their bodies so nicely. I began to think of maybe doing some fancier sewing than just shirts and aprons.

So, one day, I went to the dressmaker in town and asked her how I could learn to be a dressmaker like her. She told me her fingers had begun to slow, and she had a dark spot in the middle of her vision, so she would have to give up her business before long. She said to me, 'There are just about enough rich people in town for me to make a living. Maybe you can sew for them when I have to stop. But you have to be an apprentice first, and that costs quite a bit. When you gather enough money, you should go to Berezhane. I can give you the name of a little shop that takes students there.'

I had been able to put away extra coins from my sewing and embroidery, because I had been increasing my fees slowly. I didn't tell my mother about my savings, because she would have wanted to give it away to the poor. On the day I left for Berezhane, I heard, in my heart, my father praising me for trying to improve myself, just as he had. My mother was sad to see me go. She tried to make me stay with her, but I told her this is what I wanted to do, and I'd come home when I could.

Berezhane was a regular city, maybe ten American miles away. I was lucky that my cousin, Olya, let me stay at her house. I found a job in a hospital kitchen on Saturdays to pay her for my food and room. At the shop, I learned all about how to cut cloth to a pattern, and how to use a sewing machine. I learned all kinds of fitting tricks and fancy stitches. I was so excited. I couldn't believe the softness of the cloth I was cutting into. I felt I was part of a bigger world than just Kozova. I was on my way to being somebody, not just a farm working, peasant girl.

I stayed in that shop less than a year. I felt that I had learned enough to start my own business in Kozova, and besides, I had no more money. So, I quit the apprentice shop and went to work for another seamstress in Berezhane. This time I was paid. I learned to work faster, so I could earn my pay faster. It was a very proud moment for me when I was able to buy a sewing machine. I had already written to places in Vienna to get pattern catalogues for the latest fashions from Paris, so, at long last, I went home to a very happy Mama. I was ready to start my own business, just like my father.

I took over the room on the other side of Mama's house. By that time, my young brother, Petro, and our half-brother, Dmitro, had moved out to the barn. They left a few clothes in my room, because the barn did smell a lot. But I wasn't sorry for them. You could get used to the smell. It was actually warmer in there than the house in the winter. You could see the steam from the manure coming out the cracks of the barn. In the summer, if they kept the manure shoveled out, the barn was cool enough. They had a soft pile of hay to sleep on, and a table to play cards on. Of course, what they really wanted was to come and go as they pleased without answering to Mama.

My sister, Katerina, and Mama stayed in the room on one side of the house. I put up my sewing machine and a cutting table on the other side. I worked and slept there on the bench along the wall, but ate with Mama and Katerina. The seamstress did stop sewing, so I went around to all her rich Polish and Austrian customers and showed them my catalogues and the dresses I had made as an apprentice. When they decided to have me make them a dress, they would come to my room to be measured. I had a sample book of the cloth I could order from Berezhane for them to look at. Before long, I had plenty of customers."

While she would be telling this story, she usually had that proud smile on her face, but sometimes the smile disappeared. She would give a quick shake of her head and tears would spill down her face.

"And here in America, what am I? Nothing."

I would have to leave her to her tears then, and either go back to school, or up into a tree to read a library book.

She didn't cry when she spoke of Tato and his father's return from St. Louis, which was marred by the sudden departure of their brothers, a month before, to America. Her brother, Petro, and Tato's brother, Stefan,

45

both close to the same age, had decided to avoid Army duty altogether, and had successfully lied and bribed their way past every border like Tato had done and were now safely in Boston. Apparently, they didn't intend to return.

Otherwise, Mama and Tato's reunion had apparently been pleasant, and he began again to walk her home from rehearsals again. When he was called up to do his two years of Army duty for Austria, he asked her for a picture to take with him. She plucked two pictures from a shoebox one day to show me. One was of her, the other of him.

 I was amazed at how differently they both looked then. Tato, slim and handsome in his uniform could very well have starred in a romantic movie. His gaze was calm and thoughtful behind a thin, slightly curled-up mustache. A long, sheathed dagger hung at his waist. A decorative loop and tassel hung from one shoulder. Yes, I thought, he really could have been a movie hero.

Mama, however, looked nothing like the women that men fell in love with in the movies at the Oriental Theater. Her stocky, almost plump figure was covered from her neck to the floor with a skirt and blouse of a heavy dark material. No hair was visible except for two small, curly tendrils at either side of her forehead. She probably had pulled her hair back into a braid. Her broad, smooth face looked stern in the unsmiling way of old, sepia-toned photographs. Mama pointed to the various parts of her clothing.

I made the blouse and skirt myself. See my clever work putting that different colored tape down the middle and the sides of the front of the blouse. And see how I made the zigzag pattern with the same tape at my wrists. And notice the flare of the blouse at the waist. I paid a lot for the cloth to make the skirt so full.

The coral beads came from my father, not too long before he died. See how many strands there are. I wish I had brought them to America.

The pictures exchanged when Tato left to do his army service

Tato made no mention of the pictures, or how he felt about seeing Mama again when he returned from St. Louis. Instead, he talked about his two-year service that began almost as soon as he arrived.

It was a long two years for me in the Army. But, I was young and everything was interesting to me. I made many good friends, and though it was hard learning how to be soldiers, we still had some time to enjoy ourselves. At first, I pretended to be like many of the recruits from the little villages. Usually, they had been to school only a few years and could barely read or write. I didn't want to volunteer for anything. I just did what I was told. I had no love of Austria, as you well know, and I did not want to do more for them than I had to.

Then one day, I was ordered into the commandant's office. He had received a report on my schooling in Kozova showing all the good grades over those eight years, and he found out that I had been a stenographer at the courthouse. He was angry, because he had asked for volunteers who knew how to write German or Polish, and I hadn't stepped forward. He gave me a lot of rough talk for a while, and even some small punishment, but then he told me I was to be assigned to his office. From then on, I took dictation from him and had to write letters in a special form. I certainly liked doing that instead of cleaning the kitchen and toilets. If it had been a Ukrainian army instead of Austrian, I think I might have stayed on when the second call-up came.

I wished that Tato had talked about his attraction to Mama. Did he really follow her on the streets? I had to take Mama's version, though I felt something was missing.

He never came over to my house when he had a few days at home. He may have been too embarrassed. He had to make it seem like he saw me by chance on the street, which was especially hard in the winter. In the summer, now that I was busy with my business, I didn't go out on the streets to dance as much as I used to. I don't know how he did it, but he always seemed to be walking by just when I was coming out of rehearsals, and he would ask me to walk home with him. Other times, he'd just be walking by when I was coming out of my house to deliver a dress, so we would walk there together.

I think he noticed that other boys were waiting to walk me home after choir rehearsals, and he got worried when my half-brother, Dmytro, told him some friends and brothers of certain boys had come by to ask if my Mama would let them marry me. That's how it was done, you see. The boy wasn't supposed to ask the girl first. If a boy decided he liked a girl, he had to get his brothers or friends to go to the girl's parents to ask them if a marriage would be possible. The delegation would tell the parents about the boy's situation: how much land he had, or if he had some business, or how many cows, how many horses. Then the men would ask the parents what the girl's dowry was. I told my mother very plainly that she was to tell me who came by with such proposals. She was to ask me if I wanted to marry the boy, before she agreed to anything. She did as I said. Since I did not like any of those who came to the house, she had to tell them all, 'No.' Who I married was going to be my choice, custom or no custom.

Finally, Tato's two Army years were over, and he was again a stenographer in the courthouse. I thought he was very handsome, maybe not as handsome as when he was in uniform, but still, very handsome. He was twenty-one when he came out of the Army. Now, men didn't marry until they were at least twenty-three. Women could marry whenever their parents decided, even if they were only fifteen or so. I think he was really worried that I would not wait for him for two more years. So, one night, sitting by the well, he told me he wanted to marry me, if I could wait for him. We talked a long time, and then I told him that I would wait.

Tato knew very well that it was forbidden for the man to ask the woman directly, though I'm sure that he wasn't the first man in Kozova to do it. For all he knew his mother and father could have already chosen someone. That sometimes happened. Both Tato and I were very much against those old traditions, so we didn't feel at all guilty that he and I talked first. After we agreed, I told my mother that I was going to marry Hilko Chopek when he turned twenty-three, so she could tell anybody who came wanting to make a marriage with me that she didn't agree to a match. I told her not to tell anyone that Tato and me had agreed to marry. I think she only told her sister. Fortunately, she had relied on me for so long for so much, she did not want to press her will against mine.

Tato didn't tell his parents anything. Why give Anyelka a chance to scream? The wait for him to turn twenty-three seemed very long, but neither of us wavered. We knew what we wanted.

The Wedding

When at long last Tato achieved the magic marrying age of twenty-three, the first problem of course, was how Anyelka would react. Mama and Anyelka had hardly said more than an occasional 'Hello' since Mama moved into the neighborhood ten years before. Anyelka's 'Hello' usually came with a sharp look, so Mama saw only trouble ahead.

Tato did a very bad thing by asking me first and not telling his parents until much later. Ivan said 'Yes' right away, because he liked me, but Anyelka said 'Absolutely not! He should marry someone with more fields in her dowry. He is handsome. He is working at the courthouse. He could marry a rich girl.'

Hah! So now she was glad he was in the courthouse instead of in her fields! Well, of course, I would have to say that I really had no dowry. What could my poor, widowed mother give me by way of fields or money? Tato was quick to tell Anyelka that I had regular money coming to me from my sewing business, and so I didn't need to bring a big field into the marriage. Anyelka told him that almost anything could stop that money coming in: a baby, an illness, maybe making some bad dresses.

Oy, yoy, yoy! Can you believe that she had the nerve to say that about my sewing, when I had had nothing but praise from everyone I worked for!

Well, Anyelka began to tell Tato of several girls that she would agree to. I think she suspected that Tato and I had already decided to marry. I wasn't there, but I know there was a pretty big argument. Finally, Tato had to tell them that I had already agreed to marry him, and that he would marry me no matter what.

So, Ivan said that though Tato was wrong to ask me first, what was done was done, and Tato had his permission to marry me. Then, Anyelka began screaming and Tato went out the door. I don't know who managed to turn Anyelka around, whether it was Tato or Ivan, but in a few days, Tato sent his brother, Michael, and two of his best friends to my house.

Anyelka said they could not make any arrangements directly with my Mama. She insisted that Tato's delegation should only talk to other men of my family. This was just troublemaking now, because my mother, being a widow, could make the arrangements. I think Anyelka was hoping that my stepbrothers would say no. Anyway, I went to each of my stepbrothers, and I told them that I was going to marry Tato no matter what. They argued with me for a while, but since they didn't have to put any money into my dowry, they had no say on what I wanted to do, so they agreed to act as my sponsors.

Well, one day, Tato's group came to our house. Mama and I, with my sister's help, cooked a lot of food, and I put out a bottle of whiskey and some small glasses for them. Mama, Katerina and I left the room before they arrived, but we listened at the storeroom door. After they had all eaten and drunk some of the whiskey, the rest was quick. I was to marry Hilko Chopek in November of this year, 1911.

What they didn't know was that I had already started embroidering the twelve shirts for Tato, and I was planning my dress. I told Mama it would not be a traditional Ukrainian costume, but one made with a modern pattern from Paris, France. My mother wrinkled her face a little, but then she said it would be all right. You know, she never crossed me in any way. But she did say that tongues might get busy. I told her not to tell anyone who might tell Anyelka.

I went all the way to Berezhane to buy a length of light gray, silk moiré. The rich women didn't wear white like here in America for weddings. My silk cloth glowed like the moon on water. Then I bought a pattern from Paris for a folded over, straight skirt. I made three fancy buttonholes with large pearly buttons on the left side, and ten narrow, long pleats on the right side. The blouse was very fancy with two long machine embroidered inserts. The jacket had sleeves that puffed a little at the shoulders, and then were tight on my lower arms. I put a row of tiny pearl buttons from the wrist to the elbow of the sleeves, and I did some fancy things around the collar. I took my wedding outfit with me to America. See, I took a picture there without the jacket. I don't know why I didn't take my wedding picture. I wore the outfit for special times. It wore out and finally I had to throw it away.

To honor my father, I went back to Berezhane to buy a pair of very fancy shoes with straps and many little fancy-shaped cutouts in the leather. They had a little heel. I bought gray gloves, and after looking in many hat stores, I found a gray felt hat, straight and tall, rounded at the top, with a narrow brim turned down at one side where there was a bunch of pretty gray and white feathers.

Now you would have to know that I was really the first of my social class to wear such clothes for her wedding

The wedding outfit without the jacket or the hat. Picture taken in America.

I was a little afraid, but at the same time, I was determined to be different and modern. I wanted to be somebody, after all. My bridesmaids wore their nicest long black skirts, and I made them each a nice modern blouse, not an embroidered one. I used soft material that I bought in Berezhane. I told Tato to wear the suit he had bought in St. Louis, and to wear a white shirt instead of an embroidered one. He agreed. It didn't matter to him.

But, how Anyelka tried to spoil the wedding for me. You cannot imagine how hard it was when I had to go to Anyelka's house with my twelve embroidered shirts. When I came in, Tato was sitting at the empty table beside his mother, and his brother and sisters were on the benches along the walls. Relatives were standing wherever they could to see whether my shirts would pass Anyelka's inspection, but mostly, I think, to see how much of a fuss she would make.

Anyelka should have stood when I came in and then embraced me to welcome me into the family. Every groom's mother does that. But, no, she just sat there. She didn't offer me a seat, so I stood like a schoolgirl in front of the schoolmaster. You should have seen her! She turned those shirts over and over, poking here and there with her fingernail like a bird looking for a worm. Then she began to count some stitches, trying to find a mistake. She looked at the backside of the embroidery to see if all was neat there as well, and again scratched with her fingernail to see if there were any loose ends. She complained that the front embroidered panel on one of the shirts was a little small, and that another was a little too big, and then that the collar of another had a little curl. She pulled at the buttons on the cuffs, but I had put them on very, very tightly, so she could find nothing wrong. Finally, she tossed them on the table to show me she didn't think very much of them. Tato, on the other side of the table, sat with a stone face. I have no idea what he was thinking. Anyelka just stared at me, so I bowed a little and turned and left their house. Oh, I cried all the way home.

I finally figured out why she was so cold to me that day. Tato could have at least waited until after the shirt inspection, but no, he told her the day before that he and I would not be living in her house after we married.

Now, in Kozova, the bride and the groom always moved in with the groom's mother and father. It was expected that the daughter-in-law would be a servant to the mother-in-law and must do whatever she asked. I had heard horrible stories of how a new bride was treated, how hard she had to work. Knowing, deep in my heart, that no mother-in-law could be meaner than Anyelka, I knew that I could never live in her house.

But, even if I had agreed to move into Anyelka's house, how could we even fit into it? She and Ivan were living with six children in a two-room house. Eight people! Luckily, Stefan had left for America by then, or there would have been nine, and the last two of them just babies!

Oh, those last two babies! As if people didn't have enough already to say about Anyelka! When Ivan got home from St. Louis, Michael, the last of the first five children, was already seven years old when along comes Zoshka! Everyone chattered about how Anyelka was much too old to be having babies. Imagine! Tato was already twenty-one and in the army when Zoshka was born! And then, even worse, a year later another one comes along, poor little Franka. So, of course, Anyelka wanted me to live in her house. It was to take care of those two babies for her!

But, long before, I had told Tato that I would consent to the marriage only if he would move into my house. He could easily fit into my half of the house, even with the sewing machine in one corner. I did not have to argue at all. He was quite eager to leave his house, where he had to sleep on one of the benches along the wall of the main room. His sisters, Marena and Anna slept on the benches along the other side. Anyelka and Ivan had a bed in the other room with the two babies. Fortunately, Michael and Stefan slept in the barn. Michael stayed there alone after Stefan left for America with my brother, Petro. Tato could have slept in the barn with Michael, but he didn't want to smell like a cow when he went to work. I suppose Anyelka expected that Tato and I would sleep head to toe on one of their benches.

Instead of all that, Tato and I decided to put our money together and have my uncle make us a nice bed for the wedding. He made some carving on the headboard. It filled one whole end of my room, but it was so nice to be sleeping in a real bed.

So, that's why Anyelka was really, really mad at me that day. And it never got any better. She told everyone that I was putting on airs. I was worried if she would make some kind of trouble during the wedding. She didn't make big trouble, but she wanted everybody to know how she felt. For instance, the morning of the church wedding the families gather at the bride's house for the blessing of the parents. That's when the parents say that they approve the marriage, and that from now on, the two families would be joined just as the bride and groom.

When it came time for Anyelka to say the customary words, she waited a long time. She looked at me first, then at Tato, then back to me. She sighed a couple of times, then finally, finally, said she approved of the marriage, but it was obvious she was lying. I wasn't wearing my hat then. If I had been, I wouldn't be surprised if she would have said she disapproved, and then what?

Anyway, right after that, I put on my hat, and Tato and I went to stand at the door of the church with our wedding party. All the parents went to sit down at the front of the church. We told the priest, as every bride and groom does at the entrance to the church, that we were marrying as equal partners. The priest put the rings on our fingers, and then we walked in together, down to the altar.

Anyelka was sitting in the front, of course, with all the relatives. When I passed her in my silk dress and fancy hat, my face was in my handkerchief. I was crying, of course, because all brides cry going down the aisle, but still I looked over at her from behind my handkerchief. I saw that her face had become very red. She was staring at the hat as though she was putting an evil spell on it.

Now, you must believe that it was a little harder for me to cry than the usual bride. Because the usual bride would be going to live with her husband's mother and father after the wedding, of course, she would be crying. But I was not leaving my mother, and I wasn't going to live with Anyelka, so why should I cry? Of course, I did cover my face with my handkerchief and shook my shoulders, because it was expected.

The usual bride would have been wearing a crown of flowers, with the ribbons going down her back, but I wore my beautiful hat. I gave it to my bridesmaid to hold during the ceremony when the priest put the green wreaths on our heads. The crowns showed that we were to be the King and Queen of our new kingdom together, you see. I would think that would not happen so easily when you were living in your mother-in-law's house. Then our hands were wrapped together with the long embroidered strip of cloth. When all that was done, I put the hat back on. All in all, it was a beautiful ceremony. The singing between the priest and the choir never stopped. The choir sang their most beautiful hymns for us because I had sung in the choir so long. The deep basses almost shook the windows loose. The director waved at me when we came back down the aisle. The whole service took almost two hours to complete.

We walked to our street with the small band of musicians we hired. There were a couple of fiddles, a flute, and a drum, and they played in and out of our houses and up and down the street for the rest of the day. And of course there was the group of women who came to every wedding. They knew all of the words to all of the songs that have to be sung during the days of the wedding.

Tato went to his house with the band and all the men for some drinks, and I went to my house with the women singers, my bridesmaids, and the women relatives. The women sang all the old songs explaining why my hair was to be cut and hidden. Then my bridesmaids were supposed to sing the wailing songs of sorrow that I was losing my beautiful hair. I was supposed to cry as my mother was supposedly cutting my hair. I was to continue crying when a woman relative wound and tied a kerchief around my head to show that I was now a married woman. The songs would be telling me that I could no longer show my hair from that day to my death to anyone but Tato.

Well, I just refused to do that silly business. I was a dressmaker, after all, a dressmaker of modern dresses. How could I go around with a kerchief always wound around my head? How could I? So, when the women all came to our house, I stood and held hands with my mother and instead of having my hair cut, we just listened to the women singing their sad songs about the weeping bride leaving her mother, and the hair cutting and all the rest. Anyelka sulked. Her lips twitched, but she kept them tightly closed. Whenever it was her turn to sing as the mother of the groom, she almost spit out the words. It took a long time to get through the entire silly business.

At long last, Tato came over with his groomsmen. He stopped at the pile of sticks in my doorway that my bridesmaids had dumped there. According to custom, he was supposed to pick up the sticks and carefully stack them by the stove to show that he would be a good husband. The women were singing naughty and funny songs by then, and everybody was smiling at him. He just moved the pile aside with the toe of his foot and came in and took his place by my side. Anyelka's face was now as red as beet blood, but even she had enough sense not to start yelling like she wanted to.

The rest of the wedding went more or less as it should, with all those many ceremonies, the greetings by our parents with the embroidered towel on a tray with the decorated bread and salt and whiskey on it. When we were eating at the table at Tato's house, some of the guests came to us speaking beautiful verses of blessings and wishes. When they finished, they would drop a few coins into a special bowl. Of course, all the ceremonies over the three days had their own special songs.

Sometimes, the songs were only sung by women, sometimes only by the men. Sometimes only the parents sang. But, everyone knew their parts and all went perfectly. Anyelka looked glum all day, but she didn't do anything unpleasant. Still, the way she looked bothered me.

Many of the houses on our street were open with food at their tables, so all the guests could find a place to sit and eat. When Tato and I were done eating, we went from house to house to greet everyone. The band followed us wherever we went, and then played on the street so people out there could sing and dance. The second day, there were a lot of jokes and pranks, and the third day was for separate feasts with the relatives and the wedding party. But always, of course, people were singing and dancing. When at last it was over, Tato and I began our married life in my house.

But of course, Anyelka had to make some trouble between us to make up for not making trouble at the wedding. As the custom was, we came to her on the day after the wedding was over. We sat at the table as people do when they visit. She brought out some food for Tato, but not for me. Can you imagine that! And the worst thing of all, Tato just sat and ate it quickly. But at least, to his credit, as soon as he was done, he got up and said 'goodbye' and we walked out the door. Yes, he heard from me what an insult he had given me by eating that food, and he heard it many times, even though he insisted that he had avoided a worse scene with his mother by eating some of it. But you see. That was Anyelka! That was the woman I would never, never, let rule over me.

A Baby and the End of an Idyll

Though Mama spoke of being happy in the first months of their marriage, she never looked happy when she was telling me about it. I became confused and unsettled when she had tears in her eyes while talking about how happy she had been.

Everything was so good through those long, early-winter nights. He liked the food that I made for him. He was happy at his courthouse. He was excited at all that was going on at his beloved Chytalnia. He felt important to be given bigger lectures to read. I was making more money, which probably made Anyelka mad. We were happy. I didn't know that it wouldn't last into the next year.

In January, we heard that Stefan was going to marry a woman named Yustena, in Boston. He was around twenty then. Anyelka came every night to complain to Tato that Stefan was not marrying in Kozova, and that Tato should tell him he should wait until he was twenty-three. But worst of all was he was marrying a woman she had never seen! Oh, you should have heard her complain!

And just about then, I figured out that I was going to have a baby. I bought some beautiful white cloth and started to plan the baptism dress. It was a good way to spend my evenings, because of course, most nights Tato was gone, just like here in Boston. It was always more important for him to do these things for the honor and glory of Ukraine, than to stay home with me. Maybe if the Chytalnia wasn't there, he would have stayed home more, I don't know, but probably he would have thought of something. But, to be truthful, at first I didn't mind so much.

Anyway, more and more things were coming to the Chytalnia, speakers, plays, exhibitions, so he was busy getting out the notices for it all. He introduced everything, just like he does now at the church. Why did he have to do all that and not someone else? But what are you going to do with a man like that?

Sometimes I went with him. An opera, Natalka Poltava, came to Berezhane, and Tato borrowed his father's horse and wagon, and we went. That was the most wonderful performance I had ever heard or seen in my life. But I got tired pretty quickly of the talkers who came to Kozova, so mostly I just stayed at home."

Tato never mentioned his marriage and Anna's coming. He spoke instead of the new spirit that had come to Kozova.

When I got back from my first service in the Austrian Army, the Chytalnia had become different. Our priest and a few others had become very active with the organization, Prosvit, which had been growing all over western Ukraine. We now had educated speakers on a regular basis. Some read from their own writings, others talked about some of our great writers of literature, especially poets, others talked about how we could someday have independence. Ukrainian acting companies, as well as big Ukrainian choirs and dancers toured around as well. All of this aroused deep feelings of patriotism in all of us. I especially came to love Ivan Franko's writings and poems about his great pride in our Ukrainian culture. How could I not be part of all this?

Mama's remembered, instead, the excitement surrounding her new baby.

I was happy all that time before Hanya was born in September of 1912. So many people were happy for me too. The birthing woman came, and I didn't have a hard time when Anna was born, not at all like when you were born in that terrible hospital in Jamaica Plain. We baptized her with the name, Anna, but called her Hanya, like everyone called little Annas. The church was full for the baptism. Everyone praised the dress I had made for her. Afterwards, we had a long celebration in the houses and in the streets.

She was a beautiful little baby and always a good little baby too. She let me sleep, not like you. My uncle made us a carved wooden crib that rocked, and many friends gave us this and that, and at last, I was complete. I was a proper Ukrainian woman, with a business, a husband, a home, and a child. I knew already what I had to do as this woman. It was as though everything that happened to me in my life had been teaching me for just this time. I knew that I was now a truly important person in my community. I was truly somebody.

But oh, if I had known what was coming to us in such a short time. I would never have let him waste our time together with all that foolishness at the Chytalnia. The happiness we had after our wedding was a winter, a spring, a summer, and just the beginning of a fall, and no more. Not once since then did I have that kind of happiness. And probably I will never have it again.

I tried to deal with the usual stab of guilt that I had not made her as happy as Hanya had. I consoled myself with the realization that nothing in America had made her happy. She sighed and wiped her eyes carefully before she could go on.

Only a month had passed from Hanya's birth, when a man in a uniform came up to our house on a bicycle and gave Tato a letter covered over with official stampings. Tato was to report back to the Army in Lviv in a week's time.

Of course, the questions flew around the room like chattering bats. Why? How could they do this? We have a child. Didn't the government have enough nineteen-year olds going into the service every year? Why are they calling up those who have already done their two-year duty? And of course we had no answers.

Tato talked to people in the courthouse and at the railroad station. Some of them said Austria was expecting war, like some other European countries. I thought it was just men thinking they know things they can't possibly know. But, there it was. The week was gone in a snap of the fingers, and Tato was on the train to Lviv, and I was alone with Hanya, as I would be until I saw him again in America a year and a half later.

He did come home now and then on leave. Just a quick hello, a few meals and then goodbye again, so for me, he was as good as gone. Once he came home with a bigger crib for that last baby sister, Franka, who was just a little bit more than a year older than Hanya. Just imagine! And Anyelka took the crib from her twenty-four year old son with no shame. Each time he came home he was surer than ever that there was going to be a war. Sitting in peaceful Kozova, I couldn't believe him.

Tato was grim when he talked about his second army duty.

When I went back into the army late in 1912, almost two years before the Archduke was murdered, it was clear that trouble was coming. The Serbians and Bulgarians and the Turks were making little wars, and from everything my outfit was doing, it was very clear to us that Austria-Hungary was getting ready for war. We kept trying to figure out exactly which country we would be fighting.

Anyway, when I came back to my outfit on that first day of the call-up, I was told that I wasn't going to be a stenographer for the commandant. No, it would be maneuvers every day. Different kinds of ground: soft, rocky, and hilly. Once, our troop went into the Carpathians for a bivouac for a week. The mountains were more beautiful than I had expected, but we were dodging live bullets then, and I was often too afraid to look. We dug trenches somewhere every day. We shot all kinds of guns, at all kinds of targets, from all kinds of positions. Sometimes, I felt a very big fear. If this wasn't preparation for real war, I don't know what else it could have been for.

And all the time, I am tortured by the thought, 'You are a Ukrainian patriot and you are going to lay down your life for the country that had stolen and occupied Ukraine for the last hundred and fifty years?' But surely the spirit of my beloved Ukraine was still alive, even after all that time! Oh, I was in great turmoil within myself. Yes, I was afraid. I certainly did not want to die. I was a new husband and father. To die for Austria would be to have wasted my life.

So, a plan began to come to me. It was the spring of 1913 by then. On leave, I took some of the money I had hidden at home and some official papers. Back in Lviv, I bribed an Austrian official for some papers so I could get over the Polish border. Then I went to a Polish official and bribed him for papers to get me into Germany, and then to America. I didn't really trust that either of them gave me the right papers, because I remembered the awful questioning I got everywhere when I was going to America the first time. I knew I was taking a big risk, but what could I do?

And how was I going to tell Mama that I was leaving her and Hanya and going to America? How could I tell her that deserting the Army meant that I could never come back to our beloved Kozova as long as Austria was in power? I knew she would hate living in America without her family and friends and where she wouldn't know the language or the customs. How could I ask her to follow me? I was in such a terrible state. I couldn't eat. I couldn't sleep.

Finally the terrible day came when I had everything together. My best Army friend, who worked in the office where soldiers were assigned for leaves, slipped my papers under his official stamp, and I was on the train to Kozova the next day. I had been back only a month before, so when Mama saw me come in the door, she knew something was wrong. With my heart beating hard in my chest, I told her my plan, and she wailed and cried and told me to please not do it. Please, not to leave her and Hanya. I could hardly keep from crying myself. I told her that I would find work in America and save the money for a steamship ticket for them, and that soon we would be together again. She cried that Hanya was only just past her half year, and how could she travel with such a small infant? She didn't want to go to America; she wanted to stay in Kozova. She didn't believe me when I told her that a war was really coming, and maybe even coming to Kozova, for all I knew. I told her she had to believe me. I very well might die in the fighting, and then she would be alone forever. She looked for a minute as though she believed me.

Mama echoed his description of her reaction to his catastrophic news.

I cried and I begged but there was no way to make him stay. His face was a stone. I put Hanya in his arms and told him to stay for her. He looked at her and said he was going to America - for her. Looking back at me, he said that once I had come to America to join him, she would be able to have a life of freedom there. I told him she was already free here. Anyelka screamed at him, and all he could say after that was that he could not fight a war for Austria.

He was supposed to be back to his Army post in two days. He knew that when they saw that he hadn't come back, they would come after him immediately. But, he would be far away by then. 'If they come here and ask you about me, just tell them I said I was going back to my Army post,' he told me. He packed his things and divided his money between us. He said he'd send a steamship ticket. He took the train that very night.

The amazing thing was that he did not go alone. His sister, Marena, only fourteen years old then, went with him, along with the other Marena, their cousin, who was about the same age. That other Marena came from one of the children of Tato's grandfather's three wives. Anyway, she was a Marena Chopek like Tato's sister. Of course, it was my name now also. Just think, if I had gone at that time, there would have been three Marena Chopeks traveling together! To tell you the truth, I don't know how those two young girls got ready so fast, but then they only needed a few clothes. But how did they get money for a steamship ticket? Had Stefan sent them money earlier? Did Tato give them some? I know Anyelka didn't have any money to give them. Tato's sister, Marena, never told me if they suddenly decided to go when they heard Tato was going, or if they were already planning to run away on their own. I can't imagine what Tato was thinking to take them with him. But maybe he thought he wouldn't look so much like a soldier escaping if he was traveling with two young relatives.

I don't know why the cousin-Marena, was so eager to leave, but the sister-Marena had been a problem to Anyelka, for a long time. Maybe that was because she was too much like Anyelka, stubborn and with a temper. Anyelka made her care for those last, two little babies, and I'm sure Marena was tired of working so hard for Anyelka.

So that was that. I wondered if someone in the town had put a curse upon me. I wondered if God had become angry with me for something I had done, or maybe not done. I talked to the priest and he said I should go as soon as Tato sent the ticket. But how could I ever leave my mother, my family, and my home, my beloved Kozova? I ask you, how could I?

I was afraid to ask her if she stayed of her side of the ocean and Tato stayed on his, would I have been born? I wasn't sure the neighborhood boys were telling me the truth about where babies came from.

Across the Wide, Wild Ocean

And so the separation began. When she told me of this time, her eyes inevitably narrowed with the pain of his betrayal that she felt when he made this decision alone. I wondered if she had ever forgiven him. By the bitterness in her voice when she talked of this time, I assumed she hadn't.

He left me in May of 1913. One minute he was there, holding me, and next minute, he was on the train and gone. I cried and I cried. Every day I cried, even though I knew it was no use to cry. Nothing was going to change. When Hanya's first birthday came, Tato sent the steamship tickets, and I threw them into my big chest. I didn't even want to look at them. Letter after letter, he begged me to come, even though winter was a bad time to be traveling. When I thought of getting on a big boat and crossing the ocean, which I had never even seen, but which Tato and his father, Ivan, had told me about, I was so frightened that I felt faint and had to sit down. And so the winter passed. Hanya was beginning to say a few words. She was beginning to walk, and Tato wasn't there to see it.

The winter was dying. Some of the days were trying to be warm. I couldn't bear to think it was the last Kozova winter I would ever see. Then one day, in the middle of March of 1914, the priest came to my house. He asked me what I was going to do. I told him that Hanya was so small that I was afraid of crossing the ocean with her. I didn't want to leave my Mama, my family, all my friends in Kozova, but I had told him all that before. He just looked at me and said, 'You know, Marena, there are painted women in America, bad women just waiting for lonesome men without their wives. Hilko will be badly tempted there without you. Tempted more than you, as a woman, can imagine. If he falls into sin, it will be upon your soul that the sin will rest.'

So what could I do? Should I condemn myself to burn in Hell? I think the Devil and my soul went round and round for a few days before I could bring myself to tell my half-brother, Dmytro, to get my papers ready. I found the steamship ticket in my chest. But all the time there was a stubborn thought.

So, maybe there was going to be a war, but when it was over, I would come back. Surely, he could come back too, even though he said he couldn't. So, I didn't put the twelve shirts that I had embroidered into the suitcase, well, eleven, because he had taken his favorite, and I didn't put the coral beads that my father had given me before he died. Instead I took only what would fit in my little suitcase after I tucked in plenty of sausages and dried fruit, bread, other things that would keep for a long time. I cried, but I kept telling myself that I would come back, and everything would be safely waiting for me.

Then I put our perena, the feather blanket I had made for our wedding on the bed. On top, I put our three big pillows. I had plucked all the feathers for those things by myself, and I couldn't part with them. I took some rope and tied the pillows and blanket round and round as tightly as I could to make a smaller bundle. Then I put the bundle on the sheet that my mother had woven from linen thread on her loom. I pulled up the edges around the bundle and tied a big knot so that I could hold it all at my shoulder. It was heavier than feathers should be.

During all of this time, my mother pleaded with me not to go. She said that if I go, I should leave Hanya with her. She would take very good care of her. When I came back, Hanya would be here waiting for me, safe and sound. On the day I was to leave, I was so afraid she might snatch Hanya from the floor, I picked her up and held her tight to my bosom. I told my sister, Katerina, to take my suitcase and my bundle. All my friends and my relatives were outside the door, crying. They followed me in long parade to the railroad station. Anyelka wasn't there! Imagine, no goodbye for her own grandchild! When my mother began to stroke Hanya's head and arms, I held Hanya tighter and jumped up onto the train after Katerina had stuffed my things into the door. I was sure Mama was going to try to take her from me. A whistle blew, the train jerked forward, and I couldn't see anyone anymore. I felt like I had died and the train was my coffin.

Sometimes, her story stopped here for tears I knew would not be stopping for a while. I would go to school, or out to play. Other times, she could continue the story, sighing deeply, shaking away her tears, and narrowing her eyes, determined to show me that she had been a woman who coped with her fears and survived.

The train trip was very long. I had to change trains several times. Me, who never had been on a train before. I had to walk very slowly, the bundle over one shoulder, held by one hand, and the other hand carrying the suitcase. I told Hanya to hold tight to my skirt. She was only a year and a half, so I was afraid she would let go, but she always listened to me and was a very good girl. I got to Hamburg with a day to wait for the steamship. But then I heard a man yelling through a big horn in German that we couldn't get on the boat for two weeks, because of scarlet fever. We had to stay within a certain area, so a doctor could check the children every day. If Hanya, or any child got scarlet fever, she would have to go to a hospital, and we wouldn't be allowed on the ship.

They gave us little mattresses to sleep on, in a big covered place. I put my mattress on the very edge of the group. The next day, I saw a little chapel nearby. I took Hanya there every day of the two weeks, and almost no one ever came into the place. Time passed very slowly. Hanya didn't get the scarlet fever, and then it was over.

It's good I didn't know it was such an old boat or I would have worried even more. Tato said he had paid for a newer, better boat. Oh, I was so afraid to climb up those long planks. How could such a big boat be floating? Why didn't it sink when all those people got on? And how could I live in such fear every day until we got to Boston?

I was given the top bed, which if you can imagine, was the third one of the stack. Me, with such a small child! The ladder was very long. I don't know what I would have done if it had been you, always moving the way you did as a baby, always trying to run away from me. Hanya, at least was a very quiet and obedient child. My suitcase fit into a locker along the wall, but I had to put my big bundle at the head of my mattress. I had to sleep sitting up against it, because there wasn't room to stretch out. I slept with her in the bend of my arm, and she hardly stirred. I always held her tightly in my arms and never once let her step foot on the floors of the boat.

I don't know how many sets of three beds were in each of the big rooms in the bottom of the boat, but they were as close together as they could make them. Daylight came from a high row of round windows. At night, oil lamps swinging from the ceiling gave almost no light. Long lines of people waited for the bathrooms. Fortunately they gave us some deep pans with lids. Hanya was afraid at first to go in ours, but I made a joke of it, and she learned. Once or twice, I hid somewhere to go in the pan myself because there was such a long line.

When the boat began to rock a little bit, I could hardly breathe I was so afraid. It was good I didn't know how much worse it was going to get. A few people were already moaning in their beds and throwing up in their pans. I didn't feel sick, so I went up to the top and stood by the railing, watching other boats and some islands go by.

I began to feel a little less afraid. It was sunny, but there was a strong cold wind, and oh, so much water. Still it was better to be there than up on that high, swaying bed.

When we got to the open ocean, the boat rocked much more, and I saw big white clouds straight ahead. Still, I did not get sick. The Jewish lady in the next stack of beds was very, very sick. So was her husband. She was white as her sheet, throwing up into the pan all the time, and she had four children with her. I took care of the children for a few days. At first I took them with me up the stairs to the fresh air. I got food for them.

But then the water began to splash over the rails, and come down the stairs into our room. It splashed up and down the walls and into the bottom beds, and I was glad for the first time that I was so high. Someone said that bad spirits live there in the middle of the ocean, maybe the devil himself. Who but the devil could stir up the water that made the boat shake up and down and side-to-side all at the same time? Such groaning and grinding you never heard! I thought the boat was going to come apart.

I put the older three children into their bed, under their mother's bed and told them to be strong and not bother their sick mother. I took the youngest one into my bed with Hanya and me. Believe me, it was good that I was young and strong, or I never could have climbed up that long ladder with two children while the boat was shaking so hard. A Rabbi began to chant his Hebrew prayers. I heard prayers in German, in Ukrainian, Polish and some I didn't know. Someone began to sing Our Father. I thought we were all going to die together in that big, angry ocean.

The shaking went on, sometimes more, sometimes less, for four days. I could hardly breathe with the stink of the throwing up and the rest that people did in their beds. People couldn't get to the bathrooms, you see. At least my bed was clean, because I did go to the bathroom, but it was really hard with that ladder. I would put Hanya into the arms of a lady in the middle bed when I had to empty Hanya's pot. I had to pull my skirts up high, and hold onto one bed after another, because the water was up to my knees. I couldn't use the toilets on our level. I had to go up to a higher floor.

We were supposed to be on the water for maybe fourteen, fifteen days, but we were on the water for twenty-two days. When they began to run out of food, we got less and less every day. This was hard because I had finished all the food I had. I had been eating it only after the lights went out, because I didn't want anyone to know I had food with me. After all, everyone was hungry, but I was feeding Hanya with my own milk, and all I could think of was that I should not dry up with all of this. Now I was worried.

We were all counting the days to the time when we were supposed to land in Boston. When finally we were tied up to a dock, we were very angry to find out we were in Canada, not Boston! We were in a place called Halifax. They told us we could go on shore, but that in a few hours a new boat would take us to Boston. Everyone wondered how close we had all come to drowning in that ancient boat in that terrible ocean.

I found a man selling apples. I bought a dozen, and sat down and ate one after another. The Rabbi was walking by, and he said, 'Lady, you gonna be sick.' I wasn't sick at all. I remember to this day how sweet and good those apples were, even though it was springtime, and they were a little mushy. I ate ten, then gave the Rabbi one, and fed Hanya pieces of the twelfth.

Then as if we hadn't had enough disappointment, we got to the Commonwealth Pier in Boston on Easter Sunday. No one could pass our papers, because it was a holiday. We stood there, yelling and crying with anger. The relatives and friends waiting on the dock were yelling too. I looked at every face, but I didn't see Tato. Then I heard 'Marena! Marena!' and I saw a small boat and there was Tato, sitting in the front of the boat, looking up to see if he could find me! I shouted 'Hilko! Hilko!' I waved my big handkerchief and screamed even louder. He didn't hear me until his boat was just below the railing where I was standing.

He told me later that he had rented the boat and a man to row it, because he had to see if I was all right after such a long journey. When they were circling the boat, he thought he would never find me. We had to shout to each other, because there was a lot of noise, but he understood that we had a big storm and that Hanya and me were all right. He shouted that he would be back tomorrow and would be waiting for me. Then he waved and the boat went away. To see him, and then to have him go away, just like the last time I had seen him, made me cry and cry, and Hanya said, 'Mama ne plach', 'Mama don't cry'. Oh, she said that so many times to me in the years that followed!

Later on, Tato found out that my ship was the last one to cross the ocean to America with immigrants from the Old Country before the war began. If I had waited even a few weeks longer, I might never have come here. I cannot imagine what would have happened then.

An Ocean Between

Section III

1914-1929 Boston, America

An Ocean Between

Stephanie M. Sydoriak

Slum Life

I was always relieved when Mama was on firm ground again, though her face never showed any relief, any happiness to be off the ocean.

So I was in America! I was so glad to be off the boat, but so frightened, even more frightened than when I was on the water. But, before I could get off the boat, I had to figure out how to hold everything. I tied the rope of the pillow bundle around my left wrist, so my left hand was free to hold the handle of the suitcase. I had to hold Hanya on my right arm. And oh how tightly she wrapped her arms around my neck! Both my arms and my tied wrist were aching before we even started down that shaky gangplank to the dock! I could hardly breathe with people pushing so hard. On the dock, a man with only a suitcase reached for Hanya. 'Let me help you,' he said. My arms were burning, but I held her tightly and said 'No.' He smiled and said he promised to stay close. I gave her to him, but stayed right at his back. Hanya cried loudly, but he made funny faces at her and she quieted.

I couldn't walk a straight line to the immigration building. The floor was moving up and down. The man gave Hanya to me when we had to go into the doctor's rooms. I thanked him with my tears. Then a new fear that we would be sent back. The lady in front of me was coughing, and I heard her wail in Polish that her husband was waiting for her. She couldn't go back to Poland! Then for a few minutes, I started to hope they would send us back. But no! How could I get back on that ocean?

Hanya screamed with the needles. I kept saying, 'No, no!' but they had her on a table and wouldn't let me near her. Finally came the papers and questions from a man in uniform who, thank goodness, spoke German. He stamped everything and pointed to a door. Now, again, another new fear; what would I do if Tato couldn't find me?

People were crowded on the street ahead of me looking for their relatives. I stood there, my knees shaking until I almost fell down. When I saw him pushing through the crowd, I just screamed his name over and over. When he tried to take Hanya from me, she screamed. I don't know what he expected. She was a tiny baby when he left, so how could she know he was her father? He looked so sad when he gave her back to me and took the bundle and suitcase instead. He couldn't hold my hand, so I held onto his elbow. When we crossed a street, I was sure that one of the carts or cars or horses racing by would throw us down. All I could say to him, through my tears, when we got to the other side was, 'So this is Boston, America.'

Hanya a few days after arrival

*My head was banging with the tightness of the people and the noise in the streetcar.
How could people live in noise like this? When we started walking again, I saw paper
and old food and cans and piles of horse kaka everywhere. And so many
people! Women were yelling from their windows. Men were yelling for you to buy
something off their carts. Dark skins. Some were black as ink. Tato said some of them
were probably Armenians or Greeks or Syrians or Africans. Then I saw a different
kind of people. Their skins were not so dark, but they had eyes that slanted up. Tato
said they were Chinese. When I heard them talking in a funny high and low way, I
began to shake again, and I had to press closer to Tato. Tato shook his head to show
he was displeased with me.*

*Finally, Tato pointed to a stoop with four cats on it. As we climbed up to the third
floor, more cats were hissing or meowing the whole way. Hanya was trembling in my
arms. My legs and arms almost gave up on the last few steps. There were no windows,
only a little window in the roof, at the very top of the stairs on the fourth floor. Tato
opened one door and asked me if I needed to use the bathroom. Oy, it was dark and
dirty and how it smelled! I said no, I would never go in there! He said he had bought
some pots to use in our rooms, so I could just carry what we did to the bathroom.*

*Three families lived behind three of those doors, he said, and we would be living behind
the fourth at the back of the hall. I was happy to hear some Polish yelling behind one of
the doors. Our door opened onto the kitchen. Tato showed me what he bought from a*

second hand store: a table and four chairs, a few pots and pans and things to eat; some food in a box outside the bedroom window, and a bed and a bureau in the bedroom. He was proud to show me the crib he bought. I told him it was almost too small for Hanya now. All I did before I got into the bed was feed Hanya from my breast and put her in the crib. I didn't undress or eat what Tato had on the table for me. I couldn't tell if the bed was hard or soft. I fell into it as though I had died again.

Next morning, Tato woke me, because he had to go to work. He tried to show me how to light the stove, but my head was full of a quiet noise, and I couldn't understand him. He showed me how to get water, and then Hanya and I were alone. Tato hadn't told me when I would see my brother, Petro, or his brother, Stefan, and Stefan's wife, Yustena, or their sister, Marena. I wanted to see my brother again so badly. I could hardly remember what he looked like.

Hungry now, I found a piece of bread and salami in the food box, and sitting at the table, I opened the kitchen window. It was good I didn't lean out, because a big splash of garbage came down from above. I could hear it land on the ground far below. Looking as carefully as I could without putting my head out, I saw that the window was on a narrow alley, and you wouldn't believe the smell from all the garbage. Right across from my window was a window to someone else's flat. I could see three dark women around a table. I closed the dirty window and pulled the torn curtains together.

I went back to the bedroom and looked out of that window to the back of the building. Clotheslines full of flapping clothes went back and forth between the buildings. I found out later, we were lucky to be on the back of the building. People with the street in front had to carry their laundry up to clotheslines on the roof.

When I turned, I saw a big cockroach, and when I looked again, I could see them everywhere. I took off my shoe and began to hit them. The ones I didn't kill just ran away, but at least for a little while they were gone. I decided to take my pan to the bathroom. Of course, I was holding Hanya, because she didn't want to be left alone even for a minute. I decided to first carry the oil lamp and put it down for light in the bathroom, then go back to the room to get the pot. When I lifted the oil lamp to see my way in, I screamed loud enough to make poor Hanya scream too. Two big rats were in the corner, their eyes shining at me.

As I was sitting at the kitchen table, my heart still talking to me, I heard a knock on the door and a voice said, 'This is Yustena.' I let her in. She was holding a baby, about the same size as my Hanya. She told me her baby was a Hanya too. She was nice looking, but she seemed very shy. I asked her about my brother, Petro, who had come with Stefan to America four years ago. She told me he was living with her and Stefan just a few doors down the street. Everyone had come here last night, but I was asleep, and they didn't want to wake me.

I cried to her about the cockroaches and the rats, but she just said I would have to get used to them because they were everywhere. She told me that on Saturday, the whole family had an appointment with a photographer, because in less than two weeks, she and my brother, Petro, and her baby Hanya would be going back over the ocean to Kozova. I didn't know if I heard her right. She and Petro were leaving? Why?

'Well,' she said, 'Petro thought he should do his army duty and then marry. He has been thinking about some girl the whole time he has been here.' So I began to think. Tato came here because he thought the war was coming very soon. What if he was right? Why should Petro go back just to fight in a war? And why didn't I even know which girl he wanted to marry so much? And why was Yustena going back with a baby just now with maybe a war coming? I asked her that last question, and she said she was only going for a short visit. Then she asked me, how did Hilko know that a war was coming, anyway?

I felt I was caught in a tangle of ropes. The quiet noise in my head got bigger, and we sat for a while without talking. Then I told her I had never wanted to come to America, but after crossing the ocean, I would be too afraid to do it again. She said she had crossed too, but there hadn't been any storm, so she wasn't afraid to go back. Her parents wanted to see her baby, Hanya, and Anyelka had been complaining in every letter that she had never even seen a picture of Yustena and her baby. Yustena said she had sent Anyelka their wedding picture, and later, one of the baby, but the pictures must have gotten lost in the mail. Or Anyelka threw them away, I thought.

I told her 'Good luck with Anyelka!' Oh yes, I told her everything she needed to know about Anyelka, because, of course, Stefan hadn't told her anything at all about his mother. Yustena was surprised and worried about what I was telling her. 'I think I won't stay there very long. I will tell her I have to go see my mother before I leave. I should be back in about two months.'

When everyone came to see me that night, they were all talking at the same time. So much to ask, so much to tell. I was trying to find out why my brother, Petro, wanted so badly to go back. Tato was telling Yustena again that the war might start, and she shouldn't be going back, and then he was telling Petro that he shouldn't go back either, especially not to the Army. Stefan was also telling them both not to go back. Marena, who was a skinny girl when she left, was a woman now. She was still skinny though, under the silky American dress she wore, and she was still sharp-tongued Anyelka's daughter, arguing with everybody. Yustena was saying over and over that she would be coming back soon. Oh, I felt so dizzy with everyone talking so loud and at the same time. I just wanted to talk to my brother, but that night, it was impossible. I was glad when they all finally went home.

Petro came early the next day. He had stopped his job so he could be with me until he took the boat with Yustena next week, so we could talk all we wanted. I told him how sad Mama was to lose Hanya, and me especially because he, Petro, was gone. Our stepbrother, Dmytro, would probably be going into the Austrian Army too, and then she would have only Katerina. He told me about the girl he wanted to marry. She wasn't anyone special, and I told him so, but he said he loved her, and he just got a letter telling him the marriage had been arranged. I told him all about the terrible ocean, and how hard it had been to take care of Hanya by myself. I told him Yustena was lucky to have him with her to help her with her baby. Then again, I asked him why he would go back to the army when a war was coming. He didn't really answer me. He just said that he never felt comfortable here. Everything was so hard to do, especially trying to learn English. After four years, he still couldn't speak it. We sat and cried together.

That Saturday, we all went to the photographer place and he took a very nice picture. Tato's cousin, Marena, came to be in the picture. I had a chance to talk a little bit with her. She told me she was in eighth grade in a public school. They put her in a special class to learn English when she came here with Tato, because she was only fifteen. This year she was in a regular class. She said it didn't bother her that everyone was younger than her. She could talk English very well now. She told me Tato's sister, Marena, decided not to go to public school when she got to Boston. She went to night school with Tato, instead, and she could talk English too.

*Standing: Marena (Tato's sister), Petro (Mama's brother) Marena (Tato's cousin)
Seated: Yustena (Stefan's wife) Hanya (their daughter) Stefan (Tato's brother) Mama
with Hanya, Tato*

My brother Petro came for the picture, and Stefan and Yustena and their Hanya. We didn't know that was to be the last picture to be taken of that poor little baby. Then, a few days later, we all went with Yustena and her baby and my beloved brother, Petro, to the boat and they were gone!

So, that's how America began for me. With Petro and Yustena gone, I had to go out myself to buy food, but how could I remember the streets? Could I find a storekeeper that would understand me? Lucky for me, a lady who lived across the street tapped on my door and said she was Ukrainian. It was Ksenya who became my best friend. Oh, I just cried and cried to her. I told her I was never afraid in Kozova, and ever since I got on the train and the boat and got to America, I am afraid of everything, most especially the rats and the cockroaches. Ksenya just held me and let me cry. She said, 'don't worry; I will take you to learn the streets and the stores. You will even get used to those rats and cockroaches, believe me.' But she was wrong about that.

A Greek owned the first store she showed me. She said he didn't understand Ukrainian, but I could point to things. Only trouble was he might cheat me a little since I didn't know how much things should cost in American money. But I would learn. She showed me a store with a Chinese man in it. I was afraid of him. She told me I wouldn't need anything in there because I wouldn't recognize anything he was selling. Finally, we came to the store of a Polish Jew. Inside, a lady wrapped up in a big head scarf was talking loud in some funny language. The man threw out his hands like, 'I don't know what you are saying, lady'. So, she bends her elbows and starts flapping them hard, going 'Kvok, kvok' like a chicken. She squats down and throws her hands down below her and says, 'Flyooooop!' Ksenya and I just laugh and laugh. The man goes in the back room and gets out some eggs and she smiles and counts how many she wants. I was surprised how good I was feeling from laughing.

I had to go lots of times with Ksenya before I learned the streets, because I couldn't read the signs, but soon I was recognizing the different shops and the numbers on the buildings, and one day, I went out by myself. I didn't go far, but I was proud of myself. I could see that I could learn new things, but there was so much to learn. I learned to scrub our laundry in the kitchen sink on a washboard using soap powder, instead of on the rocks by the river. I watched how women hung their clothes with wooden pins on the clothesline between the buildings. I learned how to use the gas stove, which was nothing like my wood stove in Kozova. At least I knew how to mend our clothes without a sewing machine. I was so glad when Hanya finally let me put her on the floor and even began to walk beside me on the streets around our flat. But I learned that now I had to watch Hanya more closely, because so many things could hurt her here.

One Saturday, Ksenya took me to a woman's bathhouse many streets away. It was dark and steamy and full of women. I had to put my hands over my ears with the noise banging off the hard walls. She showed me where to put my clothes and how to turn a handle that made water pour out of a pipe over my head. It felt very good to wash myself, especially my hair, but I knew I could never do all this alone. She told me I could always come with her.

She started to take me to the Public Gardens where women from the church would gather now and then. This was a long walk for me, especially since Hanya got tired and I would have to carry her, but when we got there, oh, the blessing of the sun on my face. And to breathe real air, see some trees and bushes and even flowers and sit on the green, cool grass. But, soon, as we women sat talking, we would all start to cry for our mothers and fathers, and for our sweet homes in the Old Country. When Tato came home from work, he would ask Hanya, 'Did Mama cry today? And Hanya always answered in her baby voice, 'Mama plakala.' Mama cried.

A good thing, of course, was that the family was always with us. Stefan was lonesome for Yustena, so he often came to us for supper with sister-Marena, and sometimes cousin-Marena. It was more work for me, but it was good to talk with them. Sunday afternoons, we might go on the subway and streetcar to Chelsea to see Tato's old half-uncle and his family. So, I was busy enough.

Tato's earlier arrival in Boston as an AWOL soldier with the two Marenas was full of difficulties, though not quite the same as Mama's. Where she often cried as she told of those first years, Tato spoke with pride at how he overcame the obstacles of living with little money and no language in a city of a strange country.

I got maybe six or seven dollars when I exchanged my Austrian marks the day I arrived. I was afraid to buy anything, because I was sure I would be cheated, and I needed every penny I had. I studied prices in all kinds of stores. I was lucky to have my brother, Stefan, help me with the streetcars, stores, and streets. Though I had seen these things in East St. Louis, I hardly went out of the solid, little Ukrainian community, except for work. How an immigrant managed in such a big city like Boston with no family or friends, I can't imagine, because even with Stefan, it was hard. Stefan quickly found a job for me where Ukrainians worked, so I didn't need to know English for a little while. Soon, though, I told Stefan to help Marena and me enroll in his night school. Night school was very, very hard, but I knew I had to do it.

The best thing was going to the church with the Marenas, Stefan and Yustena and finding other Ukrainian people. Almost all of the people were from the western, Austrian part of Ukraine like we were. You see, Russia hadn't been letting Ukrainians out of the eastern side for a long time, but the Austrians only tried to keep the young men who would be going into the army. I was told that there were many more Ukrainians in Boston, but they were scattered and didn't go to any church. I think, for some of our Ukrainians, American freedom was maybe a little too much freedom, so away they flew. I soon found plenty to keep me busy at the church, but of course, once I had a little bit of English on my tongue, I began to go further into Boston to see what this city was like.

Sister-Marena got a job in a restaurant. She did very well at her work and at learning English at night school with me. Then not so long after that, Mama and Hanya came, and it was good to all be together again, though Petro, Yustena and Stefan's baby, Hanya, left almost as soon as she arrived. How I wish they had listened to me about the war, though.

Mama had her own opinion about young sister-Marena.

Oh yes, it was good to be together, but Marena was never much help to me. She was either working or running around with her friends. I couldn't believe that she was already talking some English and could go all over the city by herself. She was smart that one, but you didn't argue with her. Tato said I should go to night school with them, so I could begin to learn English too. I screamed at him, 'No, I don't want to go! I am going back to Kozova as soon as I can, so I don't need to learn English.' He just shook his head and said nothing.

But once in a while, when Marena didn't have something better to do, she took me to the big American stores on Washington Street. Those buildings were higher even than the flats we were living in. I thought I'd never be able to climb so many stairs, but Marena took me to some doors right next to the stairs. When they opened, she made me go inside, though I was afraid to be in such a small box. A man closed the door, and then the box started going up. When I felt the big pull on me, I almost fainted, but nothing terrible happened. The man opened the door again, and when we stepped out, we were on a different floor. I saw more dresses, skirts, blouses and coats than I had ever seen in my entire life. And nothing looked like what we wore in Kozova, not even my Paris designs.

I saw some thick towels that I almost bought, but the thin ones were cheaper, and you could dry yourself with them just as well. I bought one. Marena could talk English to the ladies selling things. All I could say those days was maybe, 'hello' and 'goodbye', and 'yes' and 'no'. But, I didn't really need to go to those big stores. Tato often took me to second-hand stores where everything was much cheaper.

But for all the things that were so different, there was one place that was a little bit like Kozova. On the very first Sunday that I was in Boston, our whole family went together to a big Italian church that was letting the Ukrainians use one of their chapels. When I walked in, I thought was this really a church? You know I told you how big and how beautiful our church was with all the gold and bright colors and candles and the big choir and even the band. Here, the walls were white as death itself. The windows were colored and there were two or three statues, but that was all. But it was good to see our people were crowded tightly on the seats and along the walls.

But then, a small priest, Father Pavliak, came out and he, and the people and the little choir and the deacon, began taking their turns singing just exactly like we sang in our church in Kozova. Not so rich and loud as in our very big church, but the same, every word, every melody. Oh, how hard I sang, sometimes through tears, but with such happiness!

After the Holy Service we went down to a room that the Italian priest was letting us use in the basement. Ladies had brought food, everything smelling nicely of potato and garlic and cabbage and onions. Oh it tasted so good. The men took whiskey in the back and brought a glass of beer to the tables, and everybody was talking in Ukrainian. In Ukrainian! It was like being wrapped in my warm perena on a cold winter's night!

But, I saw right away that Tato was the same as in Kozova. There he was standing on a box and telling them about some meeting for the church council. After that, he said to be sure to bring a little more money every Sunday for the second collection, because the church council was looking for a church to buy. I thought he was done, but then he announced a meeting to plan an evening in honor of the life of the poet, Ivan Franko. He would need someone to read some of the poems, especially the ones about freedom for Ukraine, and maybe someone could talk about Franko's life? He was willing to do it if no one else would. Hah! Why would anyone else do it, if he says he would do it? I was thinking I would give him a big argument when we got home, but I was too tired, and maybe a little too happy.

So, little by little I got to know the women at church, even though none of them came from Kozova. Now and then, I had my turn to bring some food. I helped sew costumes for a play Tato was putting together. It wasn't anything like my beautiful life in Kozova with my church, my family, my friends from childhood, but it was better than the nothing I had expected.

War

In June of 1914, Tato came home with the news that Archduke Ferdinand had been murdered in Sarajevo, and that the countries in Europe were pointing guns at each other. The question was not if a war was coming, but when. Mama began to worry about the safety of her family, and of course, about how Stefan was reacting.

Stefan was going crazy He began looking at boat sailings, and wrote one letter after another to Yustena, but letters took a long time to cross the ocean. I kept telling him that maybe everything would blow over, but he just shook his head. In July, Austria declared war. Stefan was crying and shaking all over, saying, 'Yustena, why did you go? Why did I let you go?' Over and over. By August, when every country had joined in the fighting over there, Stefan's eyes had no shine. He hardly spoke.

We tried to help Stefan with all his worrying, but nothing made him feel better. And of course, all the time I thought about how my family might be suffering. Tato read in the papers that the Russians came into Poland to our part of Ukraine and that the Austrians drove them out. The battles could have been right in Kozova for all I knew. No letters were coming from Kozova. I felt so guilty that I had left them to suffer alone.

Tato feared for his family in Kozova, as for all of Ukraine as the war developed. The complicated alliances and battle lines along with the enormous loss of life in central Europe were headlined daily in the Boston papers. Tato, his simple, inadequate dictionary in hand, struggled to translate the newspapers he was reading. Anger and frustration colored his voice when he talked of those war years.

I didn't know what to think when America joined France and England in 1917 against the Germans and Austrians. Poland and Russia were also fighting against the Germans and Austrians, so Austria was sure to be defeated. And, of course, nothing good would come to Ukraine when Austria fell. I always wanted to know more about where the battles were in western Ukraine, but there was no mention of that in the American papers. I began to get the Ukrainian paper, Svoboda, which was printed in New Jersey.

They didn't have much news about the war front either, but there was other news that was very disturbing. Both Russia and Poland were reacting to the strong 'Ukrainianism' that had been growing so strongly since I was a boy. They began to close all those Chytalnias, which I had so loved. They were killing off the intellectuals, the writers who had been fomenting this great love of Ukraine. The ones Russia didn't kill were sent to Siberia to die in horrible prisons. The cruel scythes of Poland and Russia were cutting down all those intellectuals who had been the beautiful flowers of the new growth of Ukrainian patriotism.

By reading the Svoboda, I began to see that there were many deep, dividing, and philosophical struggles between various Ukrainian-American organizations, both political and religious. I studied it all very carefully with a great curiosity.

Occasionally, I got a speaker from New York to explain all this for our parish. I knew people wouldn't come just for a speaker, so I had the parish dancers and singers first and last, with the speaker in the middle, so people wouldn't go home before they heard him. Trouble was, we sometimes couldn't collect enough to pay for his travel.

Mama never shared his need to lead the community.

Oh, yes, Tato was hardly ever home those days, and for that matter, he is still hardly ever home. But, at the beginning of the war, the committee bought a Protestant church on Arlington Street. He worked with the men to clean it up and do the repairs. It was good to have a bigger church of our very own. It had a big basement with a kitchen at one end and a stage at the other. Tato was ready with a play they had been rehearsing at the Italian church, and that was the first thing that we did there. Even people who never went to church came to see it.

Though I was mad at him for all the time he spent away from home, I have to say that play was very good. He played the part of a hunched-over old man who owned a store. There was a young girl and young man who were in love, and they kept coming to the store to meet where their parents wouldn't see them. Well, you can imagine there were all kinds of complications. I don't remember them exactly anymore. Tato, as this very old man, was always stumbling and bumping into things. Knocking things off the shelves accidentally in a very funny way. He got all caught up in lies he was telling the parents about the young people. Anyway, people just laughed at him from beginning to end. He was really a good actor. Tato even put Hanya in the play. She sat on his lap. She was supposed to be his granddaughter, but she didn't recognize him with the big bushy beard, and so she struggled to get off his lap. Everyone laughed at that too which made her cry as she ran across the stage.

Then of course, Tato and Father Pavliak were always going around collecting money. They collected for the church in Boston, for speakers who came to talk to us about the war in Ukraine, for organizations in New York who sent money to help the people in the war in Ukraine. But it was just like trying to collect flowers in winter.

I began to think I should be maybe sewing. Tato was always gone. I had plenty of time, but I didn't know how to start a business like the one I had in Kozova. Then, I heard one of the ladies at the church, Marta, talking about doing embroidery for a Russian lady who had a dress store near Copley Square, a real fancy part of Boston. I asked

Marta to bring me to the shop. I put my wedding skirt and blouse in a paper bag and we went. I was glad that now, at least I had something to show to this lady.

When I saw the Russian lady! Oy, yoy, yoy! She was in black silk, all the way down to the floor, pearls around her neck. Her hair was up on top of her head with a big black comb sticking out. And her face! No real skin anywhere. Everything was thick powder, a little red on her cheeks. Black lines under the eyes and on the eyebrows. Her lips had some red grease on them. I know what we would have called her in Kozova!

But, even with the sight of her trying to hold my eyes, I looked at all the silk and satin clothes hanging on long racks. Mirrors hung on the walls, and there were flowers by the entrance. How did this Russian lady start such a business? I could never look like her, if that was what you needed. Well, she probably learned English quickly, and I knew I couldn't do that. She had to be pretty smart to do all this. I felt small like one of those cockroaches in my kitchen.

No, I thought, you are a good seamstress. Show her! I took my wedding clothes out of the bag. She looked at the blouse and skirt very carefully: the seams, the buttonholes, and the way the sleeves were set in. It was a little bit like Anyelka looking over the twelve shirts I had made for Tato. But then, the Russian lady nodded her head like a 'yes.' I could see that she liked my work. She said something in Russian that I didn't understand. I talked about the skirt in Ukrainian and she couldn't understand me. Nu, what are you going to do? We were in a little back room by then, and I pointed to her sewing machine, shaking my head and pointing to myself, so she could know I didn't have one. She pointed to some embroidery on a dress, and I nodded 'yes' I could do that.

Then we talked with our hands and heads and fingers for the price that I would work for. I tried to make her go a little higher, even though I didn't really know what American money was worth yet. She wouldn't go higher.

But, at least now I had some way of making a few coins while Hanya was small. The embroidery the Russian lady wanted for her silky dresses were high-class designs of very fine flowers and leaves on twisted stems, not at all like the cross-stitch that I had always made. I learned quickly. It was dark in our rooms even in the daytime, so I always had to light the oil lamp, and the cost of the oil took away from what I earned. But, the time went quicker for me.

In 1918, there came the terrible influenza. Tato told me it was all over the world, not just in Boston. So many people died. I tried to keep us all at home, like I kept Hanya at the chapel when the scarlet fever kept us in Hamburg, but of course Tato would never do what I said. But, somehow, no one got sick. It was such a scary time. I worried more and more about everyone in Kozova.

Then, sister-Marena tells us she is getting married to Hilko Woloschuk. Now, Hilko was a lot older than she was, but I would have to say, he was good looking. His hair was black and shiny combed back with lots of pomade. He could afford stylish suits and ties, because he had been working in a wool factory for a long time. Somehow, he and Tato never really became friends. They always seem to be arguing about something.

Marena had three bridesmaids who wore beautiful white dresses and big white bouquets, in the American style. The men who walked with the bridesmaids ahead of the bride had flowers and ribbons on their lapels. I can't imagine how much Marena's dress must have cost. It went to the ground, white, with lots of folds and lace. I truly don't know if I could have made such a dress. And I had thought I had looked so fancy! Her bouquet was even bigger than the bridesmaids' with lots of ribbons tied with little flowers. We wove her wreath from little green, leafy sprigs, just as we would have in Kozova, but then she made a big puff of her veil and attached it to the wreath, which changed it altogether.

Anna: child at left of Bride and Groom:, center, Marena and Hilko Woloschuk Mama and Tato: couple seated at right. Stefan: standing second from left. Cousin Marena: standing, third from right.

I wondered what Anyelka would have thought of all that. Imagine, her daughter having such a fancy American wedding. Stefan looked so sad that day without Yustena and Hanya. I was surprised that their wedding was so big. All the church people came. But it was sad not to have the beautiful customs of Kozova. I know my wedding wasn't exactly according to custom with my fancy dress and hat, and me refusing to cut my hair, but at least all the songs were sung. And we did celebrate for three days with all the rest of the singing and dancing and eating. No, even with all the fancy clothes and flowers, Marena's one-day wedding party in the church basement just wasn't as good as mine.

A few months later in the fall of 1918, the war was over and still no news about our families. We wanted to find out how they passed the war. Was there fighting there in Kozova? Had they had enough to eat? Had the influenza come to the village? Had anyone died? Where was Streyna and where was Streychu's Hanya? Were they safe? When would they come home? But no letters came to our mailboxes. We could only wait and wait and wait.

Letters from Home

Tato rejoiced when the horrific war was over, but when post-war events began to be reported in his Ukrainian paper, the Svoboda, he went from hope to despair.

At the end of the war, the paper was writing that there was a Ukrainian independence beginning. A real Ukrainian government, leaders, soldiers. I was so excited. But all too soon, I was reading that Ukraine had been killed in its cradle and cut in half. Poland fought to get the western part where our families live. The new Bolsheviks who made the Russian revolution kept the eastern half. The war was over for America and Europe, but not for my beloved Ukraine. Once the Polish officials took over their half, they treated any Ukrainians who fought for their independence with great cruelty, and of course, Communist Russia was still a savage Russia. I could only weep.

When finally, the first letter came from Mama's sister, Katerina, all Mama's fears had been realized and worse. Her eyes would grow large with amazement in the telling.

Katerina wrote that many battles had passed through Kozova. The walls of our house had bullets in them. Our family often had to flee and hide in the distant forests while soldiers went through in one direction, then back in another. No one had enough food, because the soldiers, sometimes Polish, sometimes Austrian, sometimes German, sometimes Russian, took what our people were growing or storing. Katerina's health was very bad, though Mama seemed all right. Epidemics, not only influenza, took many babies and weakened those that didn't die. Maybe Tato was right to make me come to America, but oh, how I wanted to be there with my family.

Tato's voice grew hoarse when he told me about the letter from his Army friend. That same Army friend who had put the seal on the paper that let him go on that final leave and escape to America.

I couldn't believe what he wrote! He said he thanked God that he had lost an arm during some war games just after I had left for America. He worked in a hospital after that and he said that the Ukrainian casualties were always the highest, because the Austrians put the Ukrainian units in the most hopeless battles. Our unit had one last battle in the Italian mountains, and not one man survived. If he and I had been there in Italy, we both would have been dead. I wouldn't be here sitting in front of you today telling you about this. For that matter, you wouldn't be here either!

Many letters came after that to the parishioners. Unfortunately, people over there would be punished if they wrote anything unfavorable, so they began to write in a sort of code. The letters were sometimes hard to understand. One letter might say, 'our bulls seem to have some kind of a disease. They run about wildly and try to kill anyone who comes near.' But Bulls probably meant the Polish Police. Another letter might say 'We don't have as many insects as we used to.' Insects might mean food. Someone else might use birds to mean food. It took a while to figure these things out.

One Sunday, a letter came from a cousin of one of the parishioners who had somehow found a way out of Poland and had come to Canada. That letter had no code words, just the plain words from someone who was free to speak. He said that soldiers could demand anything of the people, food, water and even the women, and anyone saying anything unfavorable about the government was put in jail. Now, I ask you, why do men need so much power over others. When I was living in Kozova, all the different nationalities were living in peace. Austria collected high taxes, but they were not cruel. And what is worst of all, all of these people go to one church or another, but when they are in power, they do not act as though they had ever been in a church. I do not understand. I do not understand.

Mama began to feel dread instead of joy when she saw the distinctive blue envelopes from Kozova in the mailbox.

Over and over, only bad news. The worst was a letter from Tato's brother, Michael, who told us that their father, Ivan, died in the typhoid epidemic, just at the end of the war. We had a service for him at the church, though it wasn't the same as if we could have been in Kozova with everyone.

No letter ever came from Yustena, though. Stefan couldn't believe that she still didn't write to him. One day, he got a letter from a friend who said that he had seen Yustena and she looked well, so Stefan began to cry with happiness, but then he began to wonder why his friend said nothing about the baby, Hanya.

Stefan, at least sure that Yustena was alive, kept sending one letter after another telling her that it was time for her and baby Hanya to return. Did she need money? He would try every way he could to get her back to America. She still did not reply.

In the meanwhile, the year after sister-Marena and Hilko got married, little Sophia was born to them. We called her Zoshka. In a year or so little Volodomyr came. We called him Vladko. Marena was very busy then. She had to stop working for a while.

It was many years before Mama finally deemed me old enough to hear the real ending of Yustena's long and sad story. Up to then, she had simply said that Yustena came home eventually. I assumed baby, Hanya, had been left behind for some good reason. I did not question Katerina's identity when she arrived. The day Mama told me the real story she often hesitated, her voice swinging between sorrow and anger.

You see, there was more to the story than I have told you. One day while Stefan was still waiting to hear from Yustena, an unsigned letter arrived while Tato and Stefan were having a beer in Stefan's flat. Stefan began to shake as he read it. Then he began to sob and scream.

'How could she let me hear it like this! Why didn't she write to me herself?' He crushed the paper into a ball, threw it to the floor and folded his arms over his head. Tato took the ball and smoothed it out. He looked first for the signature, but there was none. He read it to himself. It said,

'I am writing to you, Stefan, because Yustena could not bring herself to write to you about what happened. Your daughter, Hanya, got the influenza during the war and died. Because of Yustena's attraction to one of the Altar boys...' Tato thought Altar Boys probably meant Polish soldiers. '... A child, Katerina, had been born not long after Hanya's death. At first, when the war was over, Yustena decided to go back to America with the new child and tell you that it was Hanya. She would explain to you that she was so small for her age because she had been sick during the war. Now she is too afraid.'

Tato tried to put his arms around Stefan to hold him, but Stefan pushed him away. Tato tried to calm him down by telling him that maybe it wasn't true. Why wasn't there a signature, after all? Then he told Stefan to be brave and realize that war was a terrible thing and that we couldn't know how we would have acted ourselves. Knowing Tato, I'm sure he talked on and on, but nothing helped. Stefan would cry for his baby, then scream that Yustena was a whore. Tato wrote to their brother, Michael, for the truth.

When Michael replied, he said that story was wrong.

'What really happened,' he wrote, 'was that Yustena had been cruelly raped.' But Stefan just shook his head and said; 'He is only trying to make it easier for me.'

You cannot imagine how we were all going this way and that. Was it her fault? Tato was saying it could not be her fault. It was the cruelty of the occupying Polish soldiers and must be protested. Sister-Marena was furious. How could she think to tell Stefan the new child was Hanya?

Of course, we tried to keep Stefan busy. But that never helped. Tato kept trying to convince Stefan that he should remember what he promised in church when he married. He should forgive her and support her, whether it was her fault or not. Anyway, after a very long time passed, Stefan told Tato he would ask her to come back.

We were all happy when she agreed to return, but also afraid. More time passed before the Polish authorities gave her the papers, but finally Tato and I and Stefan were meeting her boat. She came down alone. No baby! We were all shocked. Stefan took her baggage but said nothing to her. We all greeted her and put our arms around her, but she just hung her head. I didn't dare ask about the baby. All I could think was that no one could ever have separated me from my Hanya for any reason when I was leaving Kozova.

I think Tato and I did most of the talking on the way back to Stefan's flat. I made tea and put out the little pastries I had brought. Stefan sat in his chair. Yustena sat in hers, sometimes wiping her eyes. Finally, we had to leave, and still they did not say anything. Tato said, when we got down to the street, that maybe Stefan had told her he would only take her back, but not the child. But why hadn't he told Tato?

But, in time, Stefan seemed to accept her. He was always a kind man, like I said, but this had been such a terrible thing. When we went to their flat, Yustena talked a little bit about the war going through Kozova, but almost nothing about how it was to live with Anyelka, even though I asked. She never once spoke about Hanya, who died, or the new baby, who was left behind. They didn't come to see us as often as they did before.

Tato's four siblings and Anyelka in Kozova with little Katerina

Years later, a picture came in a letter from Michael. Tato's brother, Michael, and his sister, Anna, stood in the back, and his youngest sisters, Zoshka and Franka who looked to be about eleven and twelve years old, stood in front of Michael. Sitting in a chair was Anyelka, wrapped in a black kerchief, so you could barely see her face, and next to her, the beautiful little seven-year old who Michael had told us in past letters, was named Katerina. Little Katerina looked so sad. But then, how could she not look sad with her mother gone, and no father? And, don't forget, she was under Anyelka's thumb.

That night, we took the picture to Stefan and Yustena. Yustena got busy with food and didn't really look at the picture, though I kept trying to show her. I told her I thought that Anyelka's face looked twisted under the kerchief. Yustena looked at Tato and didn't say anything for a long time. Finally, she said that during the war, when Ivan was still alive, the whiskey factory had been hit by cannon fire and whiskey began to pour down the gutters. Anyelka got a bucket and was trying to find a place where she could scoop it up, so she could sell it for some food. While she was kneeling, a fire flashed along the top of the whiskey, and Anyelka's face was badly burned. She was in pain a long time, and now her face was badly scarred.

Tato and Stefan were upset and full of questions. Why had no one told them about their mother's accident? Yustena, crying, couldn't say anymore. They wrote to Michael, and he told him what they wanted to know. He hadn't told them about it before, because he was ashamed that Anyelka had been trying to get the free whiskey going down the gutters. Tato could not understand why he would be ashamed when they were all so very poor. And I still don't know why it was so hard for Yustena to talk to us about the family. Something must have happened between her and Anyelka.

When Yustena was near any of the family children, Zosha, Vladko or my Hanya, she would look sad and sometimes cry. But all of us were sad then. We had only worried words to speak between us after each sad letter from Kozova.

During the early post-war twenties, Mama brooded endlessly about returning to Kozova. When she quarreled with Tato, or when the trouble-filled letters came from her sister, Katerina, her resolve hardened. She made an envelope labeled 'Ticket'. Tato reminded her he really had no land of his own over there. When Tato's father died, his fields were divided between Anyelka and the brothers and sisters who had not gone to America. And Mama's Mama had only the smallest of fields. Mama would be a burden to feed. He forbade her to even think of taking Hanya to such a place of suffering.

Mama got a letter one day, from her brother, Petro. She was ecstatic as she recounted his arrival to me.

I couldn't believe he was in Canada! And he was coming to Boston to see me! Tato told me Canada was still letting Ukrainians in. The hard part was getting out of the Polish part of Ukraine, for some reason especially the men. No one at all was getting out of the Russian part. And, America, at that time, was only letting a few Ukrainians in. It had changed from when Tato and I came. So my brother was taking a big chance of being turned back at the border between Canada and America, but somehow, somewhere, he managed to sneak through.

Then there he was at our door. We talked late every night, even though it made me tired at my new restaurant job in the day. I finally found out everything I wanted to know about the war years. He told me all about the fighting he had to do in the beginning of the war. But, his good luck was to get the flu, though he almost died with it. After he was out of the hospital, he was sick in so many ways, they didn't put him back on the front. He worked in an Austrian hospital until Austria lost and he could go back home.

He told me that our wonderful pear tree in front of our house was destroyed during a battle. They often had to run to the forest to get out of the way of the bullets. He said that Mama at seventy, was hanging on, but everyone was hungry much of the time. Both my sister, Katerina, and he were often sick. I was so sad to hear how much harder it was under Poland. More taxes on the farms. No chance to do anything but farm.

He told me that you hardly heard Ukrainian anymore. Only Polish in the schools and in the courts. Our family still spoke Ukrainian to each other, but had to speak Polish everywhere else. Anyelka and the two young girls by then were speaking nothing but Polish. Of course, when I told Tato what Petro said, he was furious. He got so red in his face I was scared. He wrote a long angry letter to his young sisters, as well as to his brother, Michael. He told them they should continue to talk Ukrainian like their father had. No use to send a letter to Anyelka. She couldn't read. Nobody answered, maybe because the Polish Post Office didn't deliver it. Petro said the envelopes always arrived with the flap opened, sometimes with a letter inside, sometimes not.

You know, Tato always said he is 100% Ukrainian. He believed that because a boy was what his father was, so then, the girls believed they were 100% Polish because they had a Polish mother. So what good was all this quarreling? For what? Why do ordinary people have to suffer so the 'patriots' can have their way? But, I know people like Tato never can accept what they don't like. He's like a pot always sitting in a fire.

But, anyway, Petro got a job washing dishes at my restaurant. I told him he should have brought his wife and stayed, but Petro said no, she was too afraid to be sneaking from Canada to America like he did. He was only glad to be able to earn some money to bring back to his wife and our mother. Of course, we all gave him as much as we could when he was ready to return a few months later. Then I asked him to take me back with him, but he said it would be too dangerous. I told Tato I wanted to go back with Petro, but Tato became very angry at me. He said that when I married him, I promised in the presence of God to be with him, and not with my mother and family. So I said goodbye to Petro, and somehow I knew I would never see him again.

It was soon after that, in 1924, that Stefan and Yustena had a little boy, your cousin that you play with so much now. He was another Vlatko, like Marena's son, but we all called him Ladju. Stefan was so happy to have a boy. He had been sad for so long over little dead Hanya, and, of course, over the horrible story about Yustena's baby, Katerina. She was still over there with Anyelka, and we all wondered if Stefan would ever want her here. I suppose you know Tato really wanted a boy very badly when you were born two years later. I don't know why men want boy children so much.

89

She had told me this often, so it wasn't exactly news to me. Each time I felt the same sorrow at having disappointed him so deeply. I almost asked Mama if she also had been disappointed that I was a girl as well, but she had other irritations to examine.

I was always bothered that all the family here in Boston was Tato's family, not mine. I had Petro for a little while, but he was gone now and I had no one else. When Tato's next-to-last sister, Zoshka, came to Canada, I was angry. If she could come why couldn't my sister, Katerina, come?

I suppose, because Zoshka had married a Polish man, they were allowed to leave now that Kozova was under Poland. Anyway, she was only fifteen, maybe sixteen! So young! She probably wanted to get away from Anyelka. Far away, because almost immediately after they married, they left for Canada; somewhere out in the empty, western part! We didn't see them for quite a few years, but knowing she was in Canada, made me want my family all the more.

And of course, besides all that, we were always busy moving from one part of the city to another. We tried East Boston, South Boston, West End, looking for something cleaner, maybe not so many cockroaches and bedbugs and rats, but nothing was much better. I wondered how could we ever be happy again?

Conquering English

Many nights, Tato expounded on the shock of coming to a place where the language was so difficult to learn. Somehow, he had easily absorbed the German and the Polish as a boy, but English bore no resemblance to anything he knew. And besides the impossible language, a whole new way of life had to be learned.

All of us immigrants needed so much help when we came. It was not like there was a special place to go to learn about everything. When we gathered at the church, we could only share our troubles because we didn't have solutions yet. Our poor Ukrainians had been farmers from quiet little towns, and now they were living in a busy, noisy city. Things like electricity and elevators and streetcars and finding jobs were all new and frightening to them.

But then, the few Ukrainians who had come earlier, who knew English already, began to tell us how to find a place to stay, how to find a job, and most important of all, to explain how much pay we could expect for the different kinds of jobs. They told us to ignore the people who called us Greenhorns, Hunkies, and Foreign Trash. 'Fighting back gets you into jail, that's all,' they said, and that was good advice.

My sister and I were luckier than most. We had Stefan and Yustena and our father's much older, half-brother from my grandfather's second marriage. They all were able to tell us these many things we needed to know. Stefan found me a job and took us to the church.

But we had to learn the impossible English all alone inside our own heads. Now, if we had had some professional, English-speaking Ukrainians around, or maybe just a Ukrainian-English dictionary, it would have been so much easier to learn English, but somehow those professionals seem to have gone to New York and Chicago, not Boston, and I never saw such a dictionary.

Fortunately, I didn't really need to know English for my first job here. I swept floors and washed toilets at one of the big department stores on Washington St. where a Ukrainian man also worked. The boss told him to tell me what to do. But I really knew from my short time in St. Louis that if I could speak English, I could get a better job. I was jealous of Stefan. He already could talk very well. He had a good paying job. He had even bought himself a bicycle. You know, I tried, but I never could learn to ride that bicycle! He said he went to night school, so I decided to go to night school too and study English with a real teacher. I told myself that if I had been smart

91

enough to be a stenographer in three languages at the courthouse back in Kozova, surely I was smart enough to learn another language now.

The teacher spoke only English to the students, all immigrants like me, so we began to feel like we were in some kind of a windstorm that had taken all the leaves off the trees and were spinning them around us. I had so many questions, but there was only wind in my mouth.

At least I knew the Roman alphabet from learning German and Polish when I was a child. But for the rest I am thinking that English is the devil's own language. I had to twist my tongue and lips all around trying to make the words sound like the teacher's. When I would read out loud, I would make her smile, and I knew I wasn't pronouncing the words right. I was not happy that Marena seemed to learn faster than me, she who was only fifteen! I had never realized she was so smart.

But then, she had made friends with the American girl who worked with her in a restaurant. They went together to those new movies, and she learned to read the words they put there to tell you what the actors were saying. She stopped going to night school long before I could.

But, slowly, I began to speak well enough to got a job in a department store as an elevator operator. I was proud that the people understood me when I recited what was sold on each floor. Later, when I got my job at the Walworth Factory, a pipe-works, I was even more proud that I could answer my bosses in English. I was paid much better than for running the elevator. Later, I studied to get a fireman's license, not for putting out fires, but for keeping the big furnaces going in the factory.

But, not everyone let me feel like I belonged in America. Once when I was working at Walworth, I heard some of the workers talking angrily to each other while looking at my friend, Anton, who was sweeping the floor. One man said, '…and what are we gonna do with the goddamn Greenhorns? There's all them Jews and Gypsies and Pollocks and Hunkies and Syrians and God knows what all else and they all should go back where they came from. Why did the government let all those stupid people in? They're taking good jobs away from God-fearing people like you and me. And they don't even try to talk in English.'

I went to them and said in a quiet voice, though I was roaring inside, that every man was the same in the eyes of God, and I was proud that America had taken us in from our troubled countries. I was surprised that I could say all that in English, and they looked even more surprised, but they also looked like they might spit in my face, so I went back to my work, but after that English words seemed much easier to say.

But it was true what they said, some of the people at the church never tried to learn English. They went to the Ukrainian Church. They sang and prayed in Ukrainian, and no one spoke a word of English there. They had only Ukrainian friends and only worked alongside other Ukrainians, so why even try to learn that impossible English.

Oh, they learned to recognize the signs for the different subways stops, and picked up words here and there. They got by, but also, they got only the lowest paid jobs.

After many years, I felt ready to study to become a citizen. I got the little study book from the government office, and with my little night-school dictionary in hand; I began by reading what Emma Lazarus wrote, which was on the cover. 'Give me your tired, your poor, your huddled masses yearning to breathe free, the wretched refuse of your teeming shore, send these, the homeless, tempest-tossed, to me: I lift my lamp beside the golden door.'

So, right away, I knew I was in trouble. I knew only a few of those words. I looked up the word 'huddle', and found the word 'bunch'. OK. Then I tried to look up yearning, masses, wretched, refuse, teeming, and tempest. Only 'masses' was in my little dictionary, so I bought a larger dictionary, hoping it would help me. But I found so many different words I didn't know for the words that I was looking up, that I felt like I was swimming in a whirlpool. And I had thought that I knew English!

The questions and answers in the citizenship pamphlet were a little easier to understand. Still, it took me a long while to learn it all. I memorized every single one of the answers, just in case I would be a little excited when taking the test. When I got my citizenship papers, I was very proud.

So, I decided to help my Ukrainian friends become citizens too. I taught classes at the church for those who knew English. I told the ones who didn't know English to go to night classes, and I would help them later. A few did. But you see, that is how we had to struggle together in this strange, new country."

Mama herself never felt the need to apologize for her slower acquisition of English. She knew what had been in her heart from the beginning.

No, no, no! I was not going to go to night school to learn English. Why should I? I was going back to Kozova as soon as the war was over. But then, when the war was over, Poland wasn't letting anyone go back. But, someday, who knows? So why should I learn English, anyhow?

When I started working in the restaurant, there were Ukrainians there to tell me what to do. And, you know, words had started coming into my head even when I didn't know it. Tato helped me a little bit to read and now look!

I could not, seeing the pride in her face, begin to tell her how painful it was to listen to her talk in her English. How I dreaded the times she took me with her to the local stores on Saturdays. When she spoke her garbled English to bargain with the storekeepers, they would look puzzled, and small as I was, I would have to try to tell them what she meant. If they used a word she didn't know, I had to go in the other direction. I could not tell her how many times I had to endure the taunts of the Irish bullies in my neighborhood when they mercilessly imitated her calls to me from out our kitchen window. 'Stel-la, Stel-la, vye you no comit home. You comit home nudder minute, you gonna getit."

By late elementary school, to my relief, she began to go to the stores alone. She was able to read the newspaper well enough to worry about all the accidents described in the city newspapers, and when we got a radio, she became addicted to the soap operas.

Still, her grammar and pronunciation remained uniquely hers throughout her life. I tried not to laugh when she called Little Orphan Annie, 'Lil Awful Annie,' and Mickey Rooney, 'Macaroni.' She would say, 'I gotta lose my way', when she meant to say, 'I've got to lose my weight.' But, by and large, she was right. Time had been an adequate teacher for her.

My father told me I spoke only Ukrainian to him and my mother when I was first learning to talk, but very soon thereafter began to speak English to Hanya and my cousins. He was amazed at how effortlessly I went between the two languages, not realizing perhaps that my Ukrainian vocabulary was limited to household concerns. When I was exposed to more abstract words during the priest's sermons and Tato's speeches at the church, they only slid in and out of my consciousness.

I felt no real need to learn their meanings for my own use, so my Ukrainian vocabulary remained very small. Later studies in our primitive Ukrainian School were half-hearted at best, and so, while I could understand a good bit of adult speech, I never talked much better than I had as a child. Later, I was always a little jealous that Hanya spoke her Ukrainian so easily and had such a large vocabulary.

Hanya didn't feel that acquiring English had been all that easy for her.

When I turned six, I started the first grade in an Irish Sister School nearby. We didn't call them Parochial Schools then. To pay the tuition was hard for Mama and Tato, but since they had to leave early for their jobs and the Sister School started an hour earlier and ended an hour later than the Public School, they just had to find the money somehow.

I didn't speak English then. Mama was too afraid for me to play out in the streets, so I had absolutely no exposure to English except when we walked to the Public garden or went to a beach. The sisters just ignored my problem and I was supposed to follow somehow. They gave us slates to write on. Mama gave me a little rag to wipe all my mistakes away. One day Streychu gave me a little squirt bottle. The sides were pretty cut glass that made little rainbows when I turned it in a sunbeam. With water in it, I could spray the slate before I wiped everything clean. I loved that little bottle. One day the sister told me that the little bottle would be a wonderful gift to the Blessed Virgin

Mary. I wasn't sure what she meant, but I had learned what the words, 'Blessed Virgin Mary' meant. When she reached out for the bottle, I understood she wanted it. Very reluctantly, I gave it to her, but I was sad for a long time.

That winter, I switched to the German Sister School, because we had moved again. I didn't have to wait in the cold entryway after school because the sister 'let' me clean out the votive lights in the church after school. She pointed to the picture of Jesus and to the glasses we were cleaning out and smiled, so I knew I must be doing a good thing.

The German sisters were really strict about messiness. Even in first grade, we wrote with a pen dipped into an inkwell and if you made a blot, you had to go up to the sister's desk and open your hand for a slap with a ruler. Of course, you had to go up for every mistake you made, as well. After the slap, you had to say, 'Thank you, Sister.' Since I was only just beginning to learn some English, I had a lot of slaps. Hardly half a year later, we started learning German. Most of the kids spoke German already, so I was really behind in that as well. My right hand was always sore.

A lot of my trouble with writing came because Tato had already taught me the Cyrillic alphabet, which Ukrainians use. That had been pretty easy to learn. One letter-one sound. The problem, as you well know, was that some of the cursive letters in the two alphabets are written the same but have totally different sounds, so when you write a small letter g, in Ukrainian it is pronounced like a D. So I'd write gear instead of dear. Same with a cursive m, which is pronounced like a T in Ukrainian. Sister would dictate take, and I'd write make. The teacher scolded me because I was so stupid. I cried a lot that year. But I really did work hard to learn everything they taught me. Maybe the ruler kept me trying so hard, I don't know. I remembered how hard school was for me when you were little, and that's why I taught you to read English before Tato taught you the Ukrainian alphabet. I didn't want you to go through what I did.

I sure didn't learn much in those dirty slum streets. All the kids seemed to be talking a different language, though a few spoke English. I slowly began to understand them and that felt good. But I never really made any friends because we moved so often. It just wasn't the same to play with our baby cousins, Zoshka and Vladko.

But the streets could be fun anyway. When it was hot in the summer, we kids chased the ice wagon and tried to get the chips the iceman made whenever he chopped out a piece for someone's icebox. We all had strap-on roller skates, those same ones I gave you, and it was great fun to hold on the back of the wagon while the horse clopped along the street. Unfortunately, when Mama saw me doing that, she wouldn't let me use the skates anymore. In the winter, I had the strap-on skates for the little pond in the Public Gardens.

All in all, I always did whatever Mama and Tato and the teachers wanted me to. I was sure that any kid that knew English was much more important than me. It was only at the church that I felt equal to anybody.

95

But when I started going to the Settlement House near one place we lived, I began to change. I was ten or so. Some very nice Boston ladies gave all kinds of classes to immigrant children there. I learned how to model clay, how to weave on a little loom, and I got to be a champion Jacks player. On Wednesday nights, a man from the Art Museum came to tell us stories. I loved to listen to him. I began to understand him more and more easily.

Then came the day when those nice ladies at the Settlement House gave me a paper to take home explaining about a camp that I could go to that summer. I was twelve by then, and the only time I had been away from Mama and Tato was when Streychu and Streyna took me to a farm with them for a couple of days. Anyway, I translated the paper from the Settlement House for Mama. Of course, she said 'No!' right away. I begged and pleaded, but all she could say was that no one would comb my long hair everyday and put it in braids. I was crying when I told the lady at the Settlement House what Mama said. The lady told me that the camp counselor would be happy to comb out my hair and braid it every day, so Mama very, very reluctantly let me go.

The two-week camp was the Lincoln House Vacation Camp in West Gloucester. I was homesick only a little at first, but then I began to feel almost for the first time in my life, like a real, adventurous American girl. I slept in a tent with another girl and woke up to bugles every morning. Regardless of whatever else we did, we always spent some time jumping the waves on a private beach. I really loved that beach and the water.

We did crafts and had adventures hiking around the camp, but the best was when they took us on a moonlight boat ride on Gloucester Bay, sailing around Cape Ann. We had a long, beautiful hike home in the moonlight. The last night, we had a costume party. English was coming to my tongue with hardly any thought at all, and I found myself chattering away to everyone. I couldn't remember ever being any happier. I was sad to be going home, but I was happy I could make Mama happy with the quart of blueberries I had picked. But, after that, I felt that I truly had become a real American girl.

Being Ukrainians

For many a new immigrant, the church building became the hallowed
space for being completely and satisfyingly Ukrainian. A very small
portion disappeared into American churches and clubs. The rest formed a
variety of small, non-religious Ukrainian organizations. At first, the
various Ukrainian groups did not interact with one another, but that
changed in time. The only ones that always stayed apart, were a group of
hard-core Bolsheviks. The movement didn't interest their children, and
the organization died off.

Tato, Mama and Hanya felt the church to be a second home, though each
experienced it in a different way. For Tato, the church was the promise of
a patriotic, political and cultural center for his fellow Ukrainians to keep
their identity alive in this new, seductive land. A place to work for
Ukraine's freedom. With the Chytalnia of his youth in mind, he kept a
steady series of events going to foster Ukrainian pride.

For Mama, the church was the place to hear her language, the rituals of
the service, and the music and dancing of Kozova, though here, all was
compressed into a small church and basement. But, for now it was
enough.

For Hanya, the church was a relief from the daily struggle to be American.
She often told me about her Ukrainian world.

*Church was a comfortable place, a happy, busy place. I sang church music upstairs with
the choir, and then I'd sing folk songs downstairs with the same choir. I loved singing
all that beautiful music at Tato's concerts. I wanted to be one of the dancers, but by
then I was taking violin lessons, and I had to play in the orchestra. Still, I learned the
steps. I always wore the costume Mama made me.*

*My real friends were there, because we did so much together. Ukrainian classes three
afternoons a week, choir rehearsals one evening, orchestra rehearsals on another evening,
Tato's play rehearsals. I started by sitting on his lap on stage sometimes, and when I
was older, he gave me some child's part to act, and then even some leads, and I was
never afraid of doing it. Then he began teaching me how to make speeches.*

*I don't know why Mama saved some money to buy me a violin. I never asked for one. I
don't know how Mama knew to take me to the Peabody School of Music for lessons.*

It was a really important music school in the city. I wasn't much interested in violin lessons, and I didn't take to it easily, but I worked hard at it because I knew we didn't have much money left over for the lessons. You should remember that money is even tighter now, so remember that when you decide not to practice your piano sometimes. Mama works very hard to pay your teacher.

Some things we did were really exciting. Once, the famous teacher of Ukrainian dancing, Avramenko, came to Boston to give lessons to our dance group. He was a fantastic dancer! Oh, how I wanted to dance after watching those lessons, but I had to be in the orchestra with that violin I didn't really like. The next time Avramenko came, he brought his own enormous dance troupe with him, along with a big choir from New York. They performed at Symphony Hall. I had never been in such a beautiful place before. And another time, another incredible choir came from New York, directed by the famous Alexander Koshetz, again at Symphony Hall. Our whole family, and everyone from church who went, wore costumes, and you know, the audience wasn't just Ukrainians. I was uncomfortable to be dressed differently, but at the same time, I felt proud to be a Ukrainian. But of course, I didn't try to explain any of this to my American friends.

While Mama was happy to be surrounded by Ukrainian friends at the church, her anger was always there when she talked about Tato's activities. I couldn't share her anger, because I felt a great deal of pride to see him on the stage giving a speech, or acting in a play. I wanted to argue with her, but I knew that it was only my ear that she wanted when she talked, not my opinions.

I wouldn't have minded if he did a few little things at the church. We could have taken walks when he came home from work like we did in the first year or so after I got there. We could have visited friends together, but no! Why did he think that he was the only one there who could make all these things happen? Was he the only one who could make the speeches? Was he the only one who could put on the plays? The only one who could be the funny actor?

Now, I know that Poland was arresting priests for writing official papers in Ukrainian and more 'bad' things like that. But what good was our little protest, and why did Tato have to do all the work that ended up with me working hard too. I had to get Hanya's bed ready for the man who came from New York to give the speech, and then take her over to Marena's house to sleep overnight. On top of all that, I had to make breakfast and dinner for the speaker. And did Tato give me money to buy the extra food?

And of course I had to sew costumes for his plays and take my turn boiling the perohe for the lunches after the church service. If I told him that I wish he didn't do so much, he usually wouldn't answer. When he did, he would be yelling at me. I always thought of Anyelka then. But, I was just talking into the trees. Nothing changed.

And then, when he did have some free time, he would do things I didn't like. Once, he and his friend, Danelo, found out that some of the Ukrainians had joined the Holy Rollers. You know, at their service, they scream and roll around on the ground. So, Tato and Danelo went to the service and watched the Ukrainians rolling around with the other people for a while. Danelo told me that Tato began to yell at them in Ukrainian that they were all fools, and they should stop acting like fools and come back to the real church. Nobody stopped, of course. So what was the use of him doing that?

But that wasn't the worst of what he did. Sundays, after we were done eating lunch at the church, if it wasn't snowing or raining, Tato would say we should go to the Commons before we go home. He always wanted to go to that place where men could get on boxes and talk to anybody going by. Every time, I would say I wanted to go home and start making our supper. He didn't listen to me, of course. I would then tell him these men were crazy, and we should go home. But no, he always did what he wanted to do!

I could sympathize with Mama, because I had my own memory of one such event. I was seven or eight years old. Tato's sister-Marena was walking with us.

"This is such a beautiful day," Tato said that Sunday, "we should all take a ride on the Swan Boats." I was ecstatic, still young enough to think such a ride was an adventure. When we came back to the little dock, I begged to go again, but Mama was already well ahead on the path toward Park Street Station. Tato took a different path toward a crowd, probably as he had planned from the beginning. Mama looked back and angrily turned around to follow him. I was frightened to hear her yelling that she wouldn't come to get him out of the jail when he was arrested.

I felt a stab of fear, as always, when I saw several policemen standing on the edges of the crowds. Mama had used them to keep me in line for years. I held tightly to Tato's hand. A tall, scarecrow of a man standing on a little box was pumping his arms and pointing left and right at the various people around him. He wanted us not to eat meat and to chew our food fifty times before swallowing. The man on the next box was fat and bald and was talking in a singsong voice. "We are now at a moment in time when the stars in the eastern sky are trembling and changing their places, and soon you will see that they will fall into a line and at that time a great darkness…" Tato laughed, and moved casually past a policeman to the next box where a bearded, soft-spoken man was describing the bloody slaughtering of cows in Chicago. I shivered. The next man was ranting about why prohibition was a good thing because of all the evils that came with drinking alcohol. A drunk shouted, "Shut up you old piece of shit!"

Another laughed, and then yelled, "And did ye ever taste any real Irish whiskey?" Another man in the back shouted, "That's tellin' 'em boyos." A policeman moved closer to him, and the man shrugged his shoulders and waddled away.

I began to think that Mama was in her usual, baseless fear mode.

The last man on the row had thicker crowds around him. His face was moist with sweat. I heard the word, 'Russia', and suddenly Tato pushed forward through the crowd. Mama, her eyes on the nearest policeman, grabbed the back of Tato's suit coat and gave it a tug.

"Please, Hilko, please, please let's go home. I'm afraid." He pushed forward until he faced the speaker. Mama, tugging me with one arm stayed right behind him, holding to the back of his coat. The bushy haired man pointed toward the gold dome of the state house and shouted,

"And where has capitalism gotten us, I may ask? It has gotten us into this Depression. The greedy capitalists and government officials have been allowed to do what they pleased, with no concern for the common man. They have been allowed to suck out his every penny in any way they can. No, there is a better way, a very much better way. But we are blind. We listen to the propaganda thrown at us from this American government and the newspapers that things are getting better. And yet, we know that our whole country is suffering, downtrodden. And why is it that we don't really look at how Russia is addressing these problems?

"Look, look and see that the great Marx has shown us a new way, a better way, a way that ordinary men and woman can be equal, giving to the state in proportion to the talents they have to give, and the state in turn sees that all receive in equal measure. All we need to do is just look at the wonders that have taken place in Russia under Lenin, and now Stalin."

At that Tato shouted, "And forget that this Stalin is killing priests, and sisters, and brothers, and starving millions of Ukrainians peasants who want to keep their land. Forget all that."

Mama's tugs increased and her face twisted in anger. "Stop, stop, right now!"

Other people began to shout, some supporting Tato with their booing, a few supporting the speaker with applause. The police began pushing into the crowd. I felt myself engulfed by people, and cried out, but neither Mama nor Tato heard me. Sister-Marena, who apparently had been right behind me, leaned down and said into my ear,

"You are all right. Nothing will happen. Stop crying. It doesn't help."

She was right. Tato continued his yelling about the starvation until his face had turned a deep, frightening red color. The speaker raised his voice louder. The police stood with their billy clubs raised a little higher, telling the audience to calm down. Suddenly, the speaker was done, leaving quickly by merging into the crowd that was listening to the star-man. Someone else stood on the box and began to speak for positive thinking. Negative thinking would bring all kinds of ills to your body. The boos stopped. The crowd thinned.

All the way to the subway, Tato continued to rage. If everyone was as timid as Mama, then where would we be? Were we to let the Bolsheviks, the communists, the anarchists take over the world? And why wasn't Roosevelt speaking out against the starvation of millions of Ukrainians? Didn't he know of the atrocities that were happening under Stalin? Mama rolled her eyes heavenward and went silently into herself. His rant continued all the way home on the subway: yes, we had a Depression, but following the empty ideals of the Communists was not the answer. On the streetcar, he finally began to calm somewhat. He spoke about the wonders of American democracy that incredibly allowed stupid men like that Bolshevik to talk out in public. All this time he spoke in Ukrainian, but his usual, eloquent gestures held several of the other passengers' attention. A watery-eyed Irishman who had been sitting behind him, muttered as he passed us on his way out, "God-damned foreigners."

Church Troubles

As the ties with the Old Country slowly loosened, Ukrainians began to try to look a little more like Americans. Throughout the First War, the women wore their dark, full and floor-length skirts from home. They wound their kerchiefs just as tightly around their heads as when they were first brides. When the heavy skirts began to disintegrate, the women made new, more slender, floor-length skirts with softer, lighter cloths. When the twenties roared in, they were shocked to see American women in the streets showing ankle, calf and knee, but soon, they themselves were trimming their hemlines. The old kerchiefs looked awkward with the new skirts, so they were folded into a drawer and hats, small and large, began to cover their hair, now grown long and twisted into buns. Sister-Marena, was the first to discard the bun and give her hair a modern cut, and the first to get a short flapper dress, both of which shocked the parish one Sunday.

The men's transition was less noticeable. Their fur caps disappeared quickly, exchanged for rolled-brim, dented-top felt fedoras or for jaunty, visored caps, and not long after, thinner, smoother suits replaced their Old Country, coarse, wool pants and jackets.

Still, though their clothes had changed, they did not change into English at the church. Ukrainian prevailed. And except for a movie now and then, all their entertainment was at the church. Sons and daughters were expected to marry another Ukrainian and stay in the tight community. Tato, though, worried that too little was being accomplished in Boston. He didn't stand at the stove when he talked about Ukrainians in America. He just sat glumly at his place and talked without much drama. I usually grew restless at these assessments.

Reading my Svoboda, I see that Ukrainians have been building full-time schools in New Jersey, New York, Pennsylvania, and many in Canada. They have professional teachers, not like the drunk that teaches you. The new churches are large and decorated in gold and bright colors with big church halls. Well-trained choirs and dancers are being developed.

The Ukrainian writers, doctors, lawyers, and all such professionals seemed to have gone to bigger cities than Boston, while the poor, uneducated Ukrainian farmers ended up here. Of course some of the farmers went to Pennsylvania to work in the coalmines, and I heard that many went even farther west to Colorado and Montana to gold and silver mines. But, Boston doesn't seem to have a proper share of the Ukrainian leaders. I sometimes feel very sad about Boston.

Out of the maybe three or four thousand Ukrainians in Boston, the majority belong to our church, but, of course, half the people who belong to our church never step foot in it. Then there is the group we call Bolshevecke, because they like what the Russians are doing, so of course, none of us want to have anything to do with them. The Socialisti, who are not such hotheads as the Bolshevecke, also don't want to be part of a church. And there are other small clusters of people. How can we do anything significant for Ukraine with such a mix?

But maybe we aren't so different from the rest of the Ukrainians in America. Our quarrels here sometimes get hot between the groups, but generally they are small. In other big cities, the quarrels are big. I always thought we all needed someone like that Polish pianist, Paderewski, who could unite the Polish people and make the whole world interested in Poland. Unfortunately, we don't have such a person.

Now, our Boston people are simple folk. The problem of Prohibition is deeper in their thoughts than how we go about keeping Ukraine alive in America. In the basement of the church, they argue about how they made their liquor back in the Old Country and how hard it is to make whiskey or beer in their small flats. They agree that at least the smell of making beer is no problem what with all the bad smells around all the time. They complained a lot when we stopped having our shot of hard liquor after the church service. That habit was hard to give up, even for me. But then, good old Chichko brought it back for us.

Chichko was our church janitor. I avoided him when we were in the church basement. His face, always a fierce scowl under his mat of curly white hair frightened me. The bright, cheery white and navy striped shirt with white garters on his upper arms holding up the sleeves did not convince me that I had nothing to fear.

"One day, not really such a long time after Prohibition started, we were all surprised to see Chichko standing in back of the half door under the big stairway going up into the church. And just like before Prohibition started, he had a bottle of hard drink on the little shelf that stuck out of the bottom half of the door.

His money jar and some small shot glasses were also on the shelf. We men lined up, and sure enough, it was good, strong, hard moonshine! So, everyone was happy again. Chichko, being Chichko, answered no questions. You could ask him whatever you wanted, but if it needed more than a yes or no, forget it. And if he didn't want to answer even yes or no, that was that. But we didn't really care where he got it.

Many years later, visiting my family from our home in New Mexico, Tato told me how old Chichko died and what he had read about his death in the newspaper. I had been aware of his death at the time, but missed out on the details.

I thought you knew how he died, but then maybe you were too small for me to have told you everything. Not so very long after Prohibition ended, he began to have a lot of trouble with his legs, maybe his heart, I don't know. He said he couldn't do any more for the church and so we only saw him now and then. He had no real friends. The new janitor just went and bought the liquor in a store. Then one day, I saw his name in the newspaper. He had been found dead in his room. The police said he had been dead for maybe a week. The paper also said the police found ten thousand dollars sewn into his mattress. I am still wondering how they knew to look inside the mattress! I would never have guessed that he could pile up so much money from making moonshine and beer, but I suppose he made something from lending money to people. Anyway, because he hadn't made a will, the money went to the city of Boston. That was terrible to hear. It should have gone back to the Ukrainian church, at least.

Tato threw his head back, laughing.

But then we found out what a smart man Chichko was. Danelo and I were crawling under the stage looking for somewhere to put some leftover scenery. We saw a small door. We opened it and saw a narrow ladder going down into a hole. We squeezed ourselves onto it and at the bottom, we saw, and smelled, a moonshine still! A big pipe went up from the top of the still through the wall to the outside of the church wall that was on our back alley.

Now, on the other side of the alley, there were the back doors of some speakeasies. Every now and then, during prohibition, the police raided these speakeasies. We heard the noise of it in the back alley. If the police smelled anything coming from that pipe, they must have thought it came from the speakeasies, certainly not from our church, so no one ever bothered us. We were all amazed at Chichko's clever thinking. But, though it would have been good for the church to get his money back, our family did benefit from his money. What would we have done without his loan, when we started building our house in Mattapan?

Mama, talking of those times during lunch, sneered at the problems Prohibitzia had made for the men of the parish.

I tasted vodka once in Kozova, and I could hardly swallow it down. My head began to feel funny and then my stomach. Yet men want it so badly. Do they really like to feel this way? I know it makes some of them laugh more and start to sing, but I know others start to cry, and some usually peaceful men begin to fight. I never could understand how feeling this way was so important that they would take a chance to be arrested and go to jail for making that stuff. She threw a sharp look my way. I know Tato hides the beer that Stefan makes and gives him, down in our cellar.

When they talked to me as a child about the time when the church changed from Catholic to Orthodox I would be confused. It wasn't until Tato was working at rebuilding a Catholic parish and I was in my teens that I began to understand the sequence of anguished events. As always they told the story with their own distinct viewpoints. Mama focused on the dramatic details of the events.

Now that the Ukrainians were in America, they began to think they were more important than they really were. In the Old Country, only the priest ran the church. He might ask for some help, but everyone knew his place. But here, committees of ordinary people were running our churches! Just before you were born in 1926, everything began to be turned upside down. Our new Ukrainian Archbishop sent us a priest with no wife. The last place he had been, there was some kind of bad trouble. Those people came up and told us not to let him in. When he came, the church leaders locked the church. This priest called the police and they broke the locks. The parishioners changed the locks; the priest changed the locks, back and forth. When it was time for a mass, and the people saw him coming down the street, there was a big fight! The women stuck him with their umbrellas, and some even threw eggs at him. Next day it was all in the newspapers. He must have told the newspapers, because the parishioners never would have.

The church committee wrote letters to the Archbishop to send us another priest. When they got no answer, they became very mad at him! Now what was a small church like us doing fighting with the Archbishop of all the Ukrainians in America? This was crazy! But the committee wrote one letter after another to him, and they still got no answer. I told Tato to stop. Enough! But did he ever listen to me? Never!

After a big time of arguing, then lawyers and all kinds of tricks, the people came to own the church and not the Archbishop. A few families decided to stay with the Archbishop, so they rented a house on Beacon Hill. The priest went with them. I thought I would have liked to go with them, but Tato was too much in the whole thing. Next thing I know, we have another priest, who used to be a Catholic, but for some reason, decided to leave the church too. And that was that! No more Catholic Church! Now we are an Orthodox Church!

The first priest didn't say much against the Catholic Church. Everything seemed just like before. He was the one who baptized you. But after him came another who thought because he sang well, he could be a priest. How could I think I was in a real church with that kind of a priest? And he was always talking against the Catholics. Even Tato was mad to hear him. But, Tato always said that the Archbishop was to blame for the mess, and now it was too late. I didn't know what to think of changing my religion, but then, you know, I believe in everything, but not too much.

I tried to listen carefully to Tato because he was always agitated when he spoke of this time. I knew that meant it was very important, but I couldn't understand more than the outline of the problem until I was an adult.

When the Archbishop finally wrote to us, he told the committee to hand over the deed to the church. Only the parish priest could run the church. He must have thought we were still peasants in the Old Country. But now we were Americans who had learned that each one should have a voice, maybe only a little voice, but a voice!

I guess we were supposed to act like the Irish in their Church. We should go in, bow down, pray, and then leave. Oh, and our priests should be like the Irish priests and not be married.

It was true that we Ukrainians needed a place to pray together in the way we have prayed for about ten centuries, but, as Ukrainian-Americans, we needed more. Besides the Holy Service, we needed a place where our children could learn how to be Ukrainians in America. We needed a place to keep our Ukrainian music and dancing and poetry alive here in America. We needed a place to remember our Ukrainian history and to work for Ukraine's freedom from the ambitions of other countries.

I don't really think the Archbishop was opposed to all of that. He just wanted churches to be only churches. We could have built a separate place for all those things we do as Ukrainians besides the Holy Service, but we were poor people here.

But, I was also angry that the Archbishop was telling us not to have events in honor of Ivan Franko. This poet is one whom I revere. He wrote not only poetry, but also history, philosophy, and politics, all with a strong patriotic love for Ukraine. But because Ivan Franko didn't believe in God, we were to forget him. This, I could never do.

And so it happened that, after many months of fighting, we took down the gold-lettered sign by the entrance of the church and put up a new one with the word Catholic changed to Orthodox. During the prayers after the Consecration, the prayer for the Pope of Rome and the Archbishop were left out. So, except for the sign and not hearing about the Pope, you would think you were still in a Catholic Church. I was angry though when the Orthodox priests talked against the Catholic Church. This really wasn't about religion.

A Home of their Own

The entire furor about changing the church from Catholic to Orthodox didn't drive off Mama's anxieties about their day-to-day life. In the ten years since Mama's arrival, they had never found affordable, verminless rooms that didn't have shared bathrooms. As soon as Mama had learned the relative value of the money, she took over their finances. She counted the bills and coins into labeled envelopes to pay their expected expenses. Whenever there was any leftover money, Mama would make a trip to the bank. She watched to see that the clerk counted the bills and coins correctly and that he wrote the number correctly into her little passbook. She always told Tato a lower sum than was actually in the passbook, because she knew he would be too generous the next time he was collecting at the church for some Ukrainian cause.

One Sunday, a friend asked Tato to help him dig his cellar the next Saturday. He had just bought a lot out in the perimeter suburb called Mattapan. His wife was going to make some food and they would have a picnic at noon. Mama and Hanya were welcome to help serve the food. After several treks to Mattapan, both Mama and Tato began to feel the lure of the silence, the trees and the sweet air. Each began to make discreet inquiries into the cost of the land and building.

One Saturday, having said their goodbyes to their friends at yet another work party, they took a roundabout way to the streetcar. The streets had a few two-story homes widely spaced between wooded patches. Turning a corner onto a maple lined road, they saw a portly man tapping a 'FOR SALE" sign with a hammer. The man turned to them, a quick smile widening his face.

"Anything I can do for you fine folks?"

Tato hesitated, and then asked, "The lot… is it still for sale?"

"You bet, mister, you bet. Real fine lot. Corner, bigger than most. Could make a real fine home for you and your missus."

Mama searched his face for any hidden meanings, since the man was talking too fast for her understanding. She kept a frown on her face, so the man wouldn't think them too eager, but Tato was all smiles as they negotiated the price and arranged a meeting.

Mama and Tato talked excitedly all the way back into Boston, and suddenly she was faced with telling him exactly how much they had saved in the last ten years. She prepared herself for an argument over her lies, but he just nodded and said,

"That's a good amount, I think."

Apparently, once Tato had put their money matters in her hands, he was unconcerned about the details.

Mama made lists of the various costs as Tato determined them. She added the columns carefully. Tato talked to a few people who might have some money to lend. Finally, all the talking was done. The corner lot was purchased, and they took on the challenge of what kind of a house to build in America. Mama oversaw and authorized every transaction. When she told her story, though, I could hear that she was both energized and saddened by the implication of owning property in America.

So, in 1925, Tato and I were the first of our family to buy a piece of land in Mattapan. A friend of ours from church, Helyena, who had been in America a long time and who worked in the statehouse, loaned us enough to buy the lot. We had a hundred and twenty feet on Harmon St. and maybe fifty feet on Greenfield Rd. We decided that a two-story, two-family house would help pay the mortgage. We would live on the top floor and rent the first floor.

The friends we had helped came and helped us dig the cellar, and then we hired people to help with the framing. I was strong and worked right beside Tato. I helped with the carrying and did whatever he asked. Later, if you can imagine, I even sat on the second floor scaffolding and caught the bricks he threw up to me to stack up for building the chimney.

When we used up our money, and the money from Helyena, we borrowed from Chichko, the church janitor, and finally, we got a mortgage for the rest from the Wildey Savings Bank. Of course, Tato was too soft to boss the workers. He was mostly like his father, Ivan, though sometimes he yelled at me just like he was Anyelka. So, I watched over the workers myself. I stopped working at the restaurant for a while and was on our lot every day. I told the workers when they were not working hard enough. I watched the clock and put down exactly how long each one worked. I would count the nails they had put into the wood at the end of each day, then check how many nails were still left to be sure they didn't take any. When once I found out they were short, I fired them right there. I couldn't say everything just right in English, but they understood me, all right.

By the end of winter, we didn't need workmen anymore. For a while, Tato would go to the house by himself on Friday night, sleep on a cot and start working very early on Saturday morning. But, just as soon as there was water and electricity, and Hanya had finished seventh grade in sister school, we hired a mover to take us out of the city to live in our new house. I was glad to be out of the city, but I knew it would not be like being back in my beautiful, little, straw- covered, whitewashed house in Kozova.

The house on the corner of Greenfield Rd and Harmon St.

And so Mama's third life began in their new, big and bare house. The meager slum-flat furniture left large empty expanses. Mama started a new envelope to save for a table and chairs for the dining room and a few chairs for the living room. The kitchen, however, was complete and without rats or cockroaches. The newly purchased wood and coal burning Black Beauty stove with the gas burners to one side and flanked by the kindling and coal scuttle on the other, filled an entire wall. Two deep soapstone sinks and a narrow counter filled another. And best of all, water faucets! One for cold water, and one, amazingly, for hot. After carrying water buckets into her kitchens her whole life, she could not believe this miracle was her very own! The metal-topped table and four high-back wooden chairs they had carried from flat to flat in the city, fit nicely between the two kitchen windows. When she sat to her lunch, she could look across Harmon Street to a stand of birch trees and remember the birch trees by the river in her beloved Kozova.

The huge cellar became Tato's domain. The furnaces and coal bins took one corner, a walled off storage room for the tenant took another. Mama's laundry room filled a third corner at the bottom of the stairs, but all the rest was his to fill with a worktable, boxes of tools and nails and screws, and small stacks of wood and pipe that had been leftover from the building of the house. The empty attic awaited any excesses that Mama might someday need to be stored, though she had no expectation that might happen.

Mama had a hard time explaining to me her conflicting feelings about the new house.

I knew I should be happy in the new house. Greenfield Road was wide and had a nice sidewalk. Harmon Street had trees in a row down both sides. I liked how it looked like a tunnel. But then, Tato was a real American citizen now with a new house and mortgage, so I knew for sure that he would never, ever go back to the Old Country. Could I go back without him? So, I was sad to know I was going to stay in America for the rest of my life. Maybe someday I could go back for a visit, maybe not. When I thought maybe I would never see my mother again, I would just cry and cry, but I tried to hope that maybe, maybe, someday, she could come here.

Then again, how could I not be glad to be in a quiet, bright place that only smelled of new wood and fresh paint? A place, when you looked out the windows, you saw trees, not just somebody else's windows. Tato always asked me if I was happy to be here, and I tried to say 'yes' though I didn't really know if I was happy or not.

Tato tried to make things easier for me. He made the laundry room and put in the two big sinks with faucets: one hot, one cold like in the kitchen. Now I could just put the plug into the drain of the sink, turn on the hot water, scrub the clothes on my washboard and crank them through a pair of rollers he clamped onto one of the sinks. For a while, I took turns with the lady renter downstairs using the clothesline in the back yard. Tato said he could make another clothesline in the back yard just for me or put a rope from our upstairs piazza[1] over to a tall tree in the far corner of the yard, like they had in our flats in Boston. I didn't want to use up the backyard space that I was planning to make into a garden, so I told him to make me a line off the piazza. But, going up that extra flight has been hard for me with those heavy, wet clothes. Tato put some clotheslines up in the attic for wet days, but I try to wait for dry days, because I can't carry those heavy baskets that one flight more.

---

[1] The Boston pronunciation is P'YAZ-a. The Italian pronunciation is Pee-YAT-za.

Mama soon found a relatively unscratched dining room set and two stiff black leather chairs for the living room at a second hand store for the exact amount in her savings envelope. Much later, Tato found a floor-standing Philco radio that cost almost as much as the furniture Mama had bought, but he wanted it so much that she dipped into her bank account. He tried sitting in the stiff black chairs in front of the radio, but finding them uncomfortable, he asked her for a rocker. With a rocker, he could position himself directly in front of the radio right after supper, rock a little and listen to the news. She told him to look hard for a really cheap one in the second hand stores in Boston, because she couldn't go into the bank account again.

She had mixed feelings about the back yard.

I was thinking about our black, soft dirt back in the Old Country that needed only some old cow manure before planting in the spring. But here! When my new fork first hit the ground, I heard the stones ring. Stones and more stones, hard like everything I have found in America. So, Tato made me a sifter to fit on the wheelbarrow.

Mama at work in her stony garden

I knew right away I would be lucky to clear even a small piece in time to plant. I would get up before Tato on Saturdays and dig until he called me in to help him do some painting or varnishing. I only planted a few potatoes and beets, but I kept digging all that summer, and by fall, I was sure I could have a fine garden the next spring. I didn't know it then, but I would be digging stones out of that dirt for many years.

Tato bought two cherry trees and two pear trees. He didn't explain to the tree man that we wanted sweet cherries like we had in Kozova. I still can't forgive him whenever I taste the sour cherries, even though they make good pies. He made a little house for our chickens and put a big wire cage in front of it with a gate, so we could go in, but the chickens couldn't go out, and later, he made some frames for grapes. But, even with the sour cherries, it was good that he did all these things, because when the Depression came, we had food I couldn't afford otherwise.

Hanya never talked to me when I was a child about how she felt about her new life. I asked about it in later years and was surprised that it hadn't been a happier time.

I never saw anyone my age outside on the streets, so I was pretty lonely and bored. I wished I had a way to get books. One Sunday, we walked way over to Blue Hill Avenue to get a streetcar to the Franklin Park Zoo, and I saw a library right by the stop. I got very excited and asked Mama if I could go there the next day to get books. It wasn't even a ten-minute walk from our house, but Mama said 'No', because I would have to cross Blue Hill Avenue, which had streetcars, automobiles and horse wagons, and besides, she said I might get lost. I was a good little girl and wouldn't have dreamed to sneak over to there like you always did, so it was a very, very long summer for me.

I was so glad when I could start eighth grade at the old Trescott School where you went to kindergarten. I couldn't believe how easy everything was after Sister School! But, there was no library there and not much homework, so I was still pretty bored. Our class had a reading club after school, and the teacher gave us one book a week to report on. That was great, except that it didn't last very long for me.

The Big Surprise

It was just before Hanya started school that fall that Mama came to a stunning realization. While telling me this part, she would look even harder into my eyes, and feeling strangely guilty, I would bite my lip.

At the restaurant, I was throwing some dough down on the big marble table. It was hot. Nickolai, the head chef, looked at me and said, 'Marena, are you having a baby?' I laughed. 'No, I couldn't be. I'm too old. I'm thirty-eight. Hanya is fourteen. No, I couldn't be!' But you know, he was right. I was already in my seventh month.

Whenever she got to this part of her story, her face would be full of a fresh surprise. In later years, having had a child myself, I had to ask at this point in her constantly retold story,

"Didn't you feel me kicking?"

"I thought it was gas."

"Didn't you notice that you were getting a large stomach?"

"I thought I was getting fat."

"What about when you were pregnant with Hanya in Ukraine."

"Well, of course I knew I was pregnant then. I always knew everything then. I was somebody then. But in America everything was so different that I knew nothing anymore. I was a nobody."

When telling this part to me as a small child, however, after the 'No, I couldn't be!' she only shook her head and wiped tears from her eyes. After I had tried to understand how Nikolai could tell she was having a baby, and didn't dare ask, the questions of the whys and wherefores of babies returned.

The neighborhood boys had gone through several explanations, each with absolute certainty on the process, but if they knew absolutely, why was the story always changing? And besides, I knew without question that Mama and Tato would never do such things. And of course, besides never telling me how I got into her belly, Mama never told me how I got out. The boys told me that babies came out of your belly button.

She had no worries about telling me about how she felt on the day of my birth.

Oy, it was so hard when you were going to be born. I started feeling the pains early one morning in October. Tato went up to Chocha and Vuychu's[2] house to tell them to get the Russian lady who helps women have their babies. Vuychu had just bought a car. When the lady came and unpacked the big scissors from her black bag, I was screaming and screaming. All during the day, she pushed me here and there, and nothing happened. Finally, late that night, she said that I needed to go to the hospital. Hospital! I was never in any hospital in my life. I yelled, 'No hospital!!!' but she packed up her bag and told Tato she didn't know what else to do. So Tato ran back up to Vuychu's through the rain to get him to drive me to the hospital.

The vision of the big scissors that the lady brought for my birth haunted me for many years. Was the lady going to use them to cut into Mama's belly button? I never dared ask her. I probably couldn't have interrupted her story anyway. She would become agitated while telling this part, a fresh distress on her face.

Vuychu drove me to the hospital. The rain came down so hard, Vuychu couldn't see, so he had to go very slowly. I did not know what to do with the pain. I didn't remember that it was so hard with Hanya. But when she was born, all of the women of my family were there to comfort me. My Mama was holding my hand. But here, only men, well, one lady nurse.

So, we walked through the rain from the car and into the hospital, and you know, I could barely walk. A nurse put me on a bed with wheels and told Tato and Vuychu to go somewhere else. I was alone and so scared. A doctor, a man, comes in and I cannot tell you what he did and what I was feeling, because you are too young, but I was thinking all this cannot be happening to me. I was thinking that America was as bad as the priest in Kozova said it was.

I was wheeled into a white, shiny room and the doctor says something to me I don't understand. They put something over my nose, and I begin to feel like I am falling into a dream. When I woke up they told me I had a girl. Tato was disappointed it wasn't a boy for him, but what are you going to do?

---

[2] Chocha was the name used by Hanya and me for Tato's sister, Marena, our aunt. Vuychu, was the name we used for her husband, Hilko. We called Tato's brother, Stefan, Streychu, and his wife, Yustena, we called Streyna. I will use these Ukrainian equivalents of Aunt and Uncle hereafter.

Apparently, the night of my birth had not been easy for Hanya either.

The night you were born was worse than anything I can remember. I was so terrified. Of course, no one told me what was happening. I guess, those days, you didn't tell children anything like that, even if they were already fourteen years old! I thought Mama was dying with all her screaming. And that strange Russian woman that stayed with her! When Vuychu took Mama and Tato to the hospital, leaving me home alone all night, I was sure I would never see her again. Tato didn't come home in the morning, so I couldn't decide whether to go to school or not. I went, but I couldn't concentrate. When I came home for lunch, Tato was there, and he told me I had a sister. Of all the horrible things I had been imagining, I had never thought she was having a baby.

They chose the name, Stefania, for my baptism. Tato called me the diminutive, Stefchu, while Mama, having heard the name in the slums, called me Stella. Tato corrected Mama now and then, saying that there were no Stellas in Kozova. Mama said this was an American baby, not a Kozova baby. Everyone else in the family called me Stella, so Tato eventually did as well. I always hated the name.

Mama just shrugged when I asked her why I had been called Stella instead of my real name, Stefania. "That time, I couldn't even tell you my own name."

As if I had not been bad enough to give Mama so much pain at my birth, I continued to be difficult when I was brought home. I'd try to avoid her eyes when she told me of those early days, but I couldn't avoid the guilt. She sighed a lot as she spoke.

I thought you would be as peaceful as Hanya had been, but no, you really were an American baby. When I took you home, you cried day and night, even the doctor didn't know what to do. I didn't sleep in the night. I didn't sleep in the morning. I stayed home from work for a while, but we really needed the money, so even with you still crying, I went back to work. We had to pay the Morrgach.

Streychu and Streyna finished their house on the next block, so Streyna and I went to work at the restaurant together around four o'clock every afternoon. We worked until around midnight. We didn't make as much money as Chocha, though. Since she could talk such good English, and she could work in the day because her two kids were in school, they made her a waitress. We were jealous because she got lots of tips.

Those days, Tato and Streychu worked all day, so Hanya had to come home right after school, so I could go to work. She had to take care of you, and baby Ladju, Streychu and Streyna's little boy, who was two years old by then, until Tato and Streychu came home. This was hard for Hanya, because you cried so much, and of course, sometimes, she wanted to stay and do something in school with her friends, but what could I do? You can't imagine how hard it was to have a fussy baby to worry about.

The new baby: Stella, Stefchu, Stefania

Hanya agreed vehemently.

I hated having to come home right after school to take care of you and Ladju, but that was that. I had to stop my reading club, and it wasn't until I went to Hyde Park High for ninth grade that I was finally near a library. You really don't know how lucky you were to always have had books.

Mama did plant her first garden that second summer. She and Tato gradually finished the painting and varnishing and felt pride in the house they had built. Now and then, they took the time to enjoy Carson Beach, a half-hour away by streetcar, or some nearer public park. The money in Mama's envelopes lasted comfortably to the ends of the weeks even with the mortgage payments. The numbers in her little bankbook went up. She didn't smile exactly, but her face was calmer when she talked about my first year.

Everything was good for a little while. I began to think that maybe I could stay in America after all. You weren't crying so much, but right away you started to walk and talk, and then we couldn't stop watching you for even a minute, because you would be almost falling down the stairs, or climbing on the bed and falling off. Still everything was good enough.

During this relatively peaceful time, according to Hanya, Mama finally began to take some interest in actually learning to read English. She first sounded out signs and words in newspapers according to the sounds of the corresponding letters in the Polish alphabet, which she had learned in school as a child. Hanya patiently showed her how they should sound in English. By the time I was reading, Mama could read about some horrible accident in the newspaper to me so that I could understand most of her words. Improvement in her speech came much more slowly, however. She never lost the need to use her hands whenever a word eluded her.

She must have been feeling fairly confident with her reading abilities when she announced, in the summer of 1929, to Hanya's and Tato's shock, that she would like to try to take the citizenship test. She insisted that she still wanted to go back to Kozova some day, but for now, she should be a citizen along with the rest of the family. Hanya told me later that Tato, trying not to look skeptical, brought out all the booklets he used for his citizenship classes at church. He and Hanya took turns having Mama repeat over and over the answers to the list of questions.

Finally, she said she was ready, and Tato should make an appointment for her to take the test. On the appointed day, Tato took a day off from work and went with her to the State House. She had already told Nickolai she wouldn't be coming to the restaurant that night. Either she would be celebrating, or she would be too nervous and sad from not passing the test. Hanya said that she had never seen such a smile on Mama when she came up the stairs that afternoon. She propped the certificate of citizenship against the sugar bowl on the table and continued smiling throughout supper.

"I did it. I really did it. I never thought I would pass, and neither of you did either, but I passed! See, I didn't really need to go to night school like the rest of you. I was smart enough to do it all by myself."

Section IV

1929-1934 The Bitter Years

And who will watch the little ones?

Three months after Mama became a citizen, and a few weeks after my third birthday, Tato read of the crash on Wall Street in the newspaper to Mama. They didn't understand why the headlines were so large, but when some parishioners at the church lost their jobs and couldn't find new ones, when riots broke out in the North End in front of some factories, and when a 'Soup Kitchen' opened its door near the church, a new fear lodged behind their eyes. A new word, Depressia, flew around the church basement.

The family was lucky for a while. Vuychu, Streychu and Tato were kept on at their various factories, but everyone's salary was cut. When the foreman told Tato about his cut in pay, he told him to look for another job, because they could close any time. Tato toured the factories, just in case, but he couldn't find anything. Mama began to have a hard time putting enough money into her envelopes to last from week to week.

At the restaurant where Chocha, Streyna and Mama worked, they also were kept on, though others were laid-off. Mama noticed that more women were kept than men. She guessed it was because the women had never been paid as much as the men.

When Mama and Streyna began to leave for the restaurant at four in the afternoon, faithful Hanya, now called by her English name, Anna, by everyone but Mama and Tato, came home promptly after school to take care of our five-year-old cousin Ladju, and three-year-old me. Tato made two small desks for the little room at the top of the front stairs, and Anna pretended to be our teacher. She began to bring picture and story books from the library. Ladju waved off the books, preferring to play on the floor with his toys. He sat at his desk only when Anna asked him to read something aloud. This he did with a dramatic flair. Though I liked the picture books, I wanted to be able to read the storybooks like Ladju did. Anna began writing a few letters at a time for me to copy and sound out. Eventually, I learned them all. Then she wrote words. When I was able to read along with Ladju, he became annoyed, and refused to read unless I shut up.

Sometimes when we got quarrelsome, she would declare recess and take us outside to play hopscotch, or maybe take us down to Mattapan Square for an ice cream cone with some money Streyna had given her.

Ladju, Lidgy, Walt, Walter at five.

One afternoon, Anna was allowed not to come home to tend to me. Anna's French teacher, as a reward for some excellent work Anna had done in her class, took her to a restaurant for an early supper one afternoon. Ladju and I went up to Chocha's house so Cousin Zoshka, now called Sophie, could take care of us. Her brother, Vladko, now called Walt, was in junior high, and Sophie was in high school. They both disappeared into their rooms so Ladju and I went out onto the porch to look at Walt's stack of comic books until Chocha came home from work.

Chocha was small and thin, not stocky like Streyna and Mama, and she wore fancier clothes than they did. Sometimes Mama called her the 'Amerikanka' with a little raise of her eyebrows. Though Mama thought Chocha, and women in general, were crazy to be doing such a dangerous thing, Chocha was proud of being the first, and for a long time, the only Ukrainian woman in Boston who had gotten a license, or whose husband had a car for that matter. Vyuchu had bought his Chevrolet just before the Depression hit, and seemed to worry more about losing his car than his house if he lost his job.

When Chocha called Walt and Sophie and announced that we were all going to a movie down in Mattapan Square, Ladju ran whooping down the stairs. I followed more slowly, a bit apprehensive because I had never been to a movie. I clung to Chocha's hand when we entered the dark space, but once the movie began and I saw Charlie Chaplin's face that spoke without words I relaxed into happy laughter. I laughed with every stumble and bump of his body. When I got home, I begged Tato to take me some time again; he said we had to save our money now. The Depressia, you know.

That night, when Anna got home, she told Tato about the dinner with her teacher. Rather than enjoying the reward, she felt uneasy from the time she was asked what she would like from the menu. None of the food was familiar to her. How could she choose? Then, which fork to use? She had never used more than one. And finally, Anna had ordered tea and the teacher had ordered coffee, so Anna had no clue as to where she should put her tea bag. Should she leave it in her cup while she drank the tea? Should she put it in the saucer? Or on one of the dishes still on the table? Tato shook his head and told her gruffly that if she was polite and tried to be neat, she didn't need to worry about silly things like where to put a tea bag.

During the time Anna was getting ready to graduate, I would overhear Mama and Tato and Anna talking softly, like they did when something important was happening. Now and then I caught the name, 'Katerina' and 'only thirteen.' I hadn't yet been told the stories about the young left-behind Katerina, or about Streyna and Streychu's dead baby, Hanya. All those stories would come later, when Mama felt I was old enough to understand them.

One day, Ladju didn't come to our house after school. Anna said that his sister, Katerina, had just come from Ukraine, so she would watch him now. My three-year old mind couldn't understand how Ladju had so suddenly acquired a older sister. On the next Sunday afternoon, I was excited by all the activity before supper. Chocha and Vyuchu and Sophie and Walt arrived, and Vuychu helped Tato put leaves into the dining room table, and carry the kitchen table all the way through the large opening into the living room. When they put the two tables together, there was room for twelve chairs. Chocha spread several tablecloths to cover all the joints. Then suddenly, Streychu, Streyna, Ladju and a thin, blond, pretty girl stood stiffly in the kitchen door. Tato and Mama embraced the girl first, and then Chocha and Vyuchu embraced her, and finally Anna and Sophie. Walt stayed in the dining room. Tato took my hand and drew me from where I was hiding in back of Anna.

"Stefchu, this is Katerina, your cousin, Ladju's sister. She just came from Kozova on a boat across the wide ocean." I stared at her, but she kept her eyes down. Mama and Tato took turns asking her about the family in Kozova, but she answered with only a few words. The adults talked a little more noisily than usual during dinner.

Now, I was sent to Ladju's house when Mama and Streyna had to go to work. Ladju was out playing with a friend, Katerina said. I followed her into Ladju's room, and noticed that his toys had been pushed to one end of the room. A new cot was on the wall opposite to Ladju's bed. Katerina sat in the middle of the floor and one by one, picked up a ball, his jacks, the cards, the comic books. I told her the names in English, and she nodded, repeating the word after me. I opened the box of erector set pieces and showed her, as best as my three-year old fingers could, how the pieces fit together. She smiled and tried herself. When Ladju came home and saw our construction he yelled,

"I don't want you to ever touch that again. It's mine and you can't play with it!"

Katerina stood quickly and went to the kitchen to make supper. Ladju slammed the door behind her, then turned to me and said, "I mean it!"

In June, Anna graduated from high school. Mama and Tato listened proudly to Anna's speech on Andrew Jackson. The subject had been her civics teacher's idea and though Anna wanted to change it, she didn't dare. Mama wiped away tears when Anna received her diploma. Her civics teacher, Mr. Sherlock came up to her after the graduation and told her he thought she'd make a fine lawyer. Anna shook her head. "I just want to be a secretary," she said.

At home, Mama made a fine chicken dinner and invited the whole family again. Anna gasped when she unwrapped the Brownie camera everyone chipped in on. When we were eating the rice pudding for dessert, Anna told everyone at the table her Valedictorian story. According to her grade point average, she should have had that honor, but the principal chose another girl.

"I was pretty shocked to be passed over, but then I found out that girl's father owned a bank. My Civics teacher, Mr. Sherlock, was shocked also. He went to the principal, and later told me the principal wouldn't change his mind. He told Mr. Sherlock that the program wouldn't say that she was the Valedictorian, but he would announce it. At least he had four others including me give speeches after her. I thought maybe the principal would say that I had the highest grade point average of all the graduating seniors, but he didn't. It was so unfair! "

While her tears flowed, Chocha shrugged, Mama bustled about, and Tato shook his head briefly, then poured drinks for everyone. Anna told me later that she figured they just didn't understand how important it had been to her.

Anna applied to many companies, before finding one that allowed her to sign up for an interview as one applicant among a hundred. The salary would be ten dollars a week. Shaking a little during the first interview she'd ever experienced, she came out feeling quite hopeless. She left Chocha's telephone number just in case. Chocha came down to our house a week later and told Anna that she had been the one chosen out of the hundred other girls, and that they wanted her to start the next day. Tato told Mama, "You see I was right about coming to America. If you are smart, you can become someone here, even with this horrible Depression."

Tato now left the house at four in the morning, returning at four in the afternoon, replacing Anna as our new caretaker and teacher. He immediately began to teach us the Ukrainian alphabet. Ladju complained bitterly but Tato ignored him. Tato started with the few printed letters A, K, M, O and T, which were the same in both languages. Then came the letters like B, H, P and X, which we found out were pronounced like V, N, R and the strange, gutteral Kh. Finally, we learned the rest of the alphabet which didn't look like any English letters at all. We didn't know what he meant when he said it was similar to the Greek alphabet. We thought we were done with the hardest part, but then he began to teach us all those impossible letters in cursive.

But, by the time summer was over, we had learned all the letters and their sounds. With the wonderful realization that there was only one sound for each letter, we were excited that we could read every word of Tato's Ukrainian newspaper. Of course, we understood none of it. Finally, Tato ordered a couple of primers from Ukraine. The stories were about as dull as the Dick and Jane books our children read, but to our relief, we understood every word.

That summer, Streychu registered Katerina into a summer English class for immigrants. He carefully taught her the streetcar, trolley, subway route to the school and everyone in the family praised her for learning English so quickly. Her name remained Katerina amongst the adults, and became Catherine with the younger ones. After the summer classes, Streychu registered her into eighth grade, and though she struggled at first, by the time she finished high school, she had almost no accent at all. Tato and Mama observed that Streychu became very involved in her problems. He helped her with homework and went to talk with her teachers. Streyna on the other hand had become cold with her. We didn't often see them talking to each other.

1930, From left: Catherine, Streychu, Ladju, Tato, Me, Mama.

Kindergarten and Dancing

In the fall of 1930, yet another change in Mama and Streyna's work schedules put me at Streyna's house in the early morning. Since Ladju was now in second grade, I would have to play alone. I didn't mind, because I knew Streychu was always buying him exciting toys. But Streyna stopped me at the door to his room. "Ladju said you should only play with these things," she said pointing at some comic books, a pad of paper and crayons, and a few broken tin soldiers. I was furious and probably cried.

Every day, I objected a little more strenuously as Mama pulled me by my hand down the street to Streyna's house. "There's nothing to do there!" I wailed. At the end of the second week, as Mama finished scrubbing my face in front of the bathroom sink, she put her hands on her hips and stared at me. I stared back making my evil face.

"Nu," she said. "We won't go to Streyna's today."

"Where are we going?" I protested as she pulled on my Sunday dress. She didn't answer. We started in the direction of Streyna's house, but turned onto the first side street then crossed to another. She stopped in front of the Trescott School, the big, old wooden building tucked into some dark woods that Anna had shown me once.

I followed Mama quietly through the big door, and into a hall, paneled with dark wood and lit with dim lights hanging from the high ceilings.

"Where Principal?" she asked me. "You lookit for sign."

I saw a little sign on the wall beside an open door that started with a PR, but Mama had whipped past it too quickly for me to sound out the rest of the letters. I tugged at her and pointed hesitantly to the little sign behind us.

Mama ignored the questions of the lady at the desk and only said, "Principal, principal." The lady shrugged and opened a door behind her. Mama pulled me in and sat me in the empty chair. She stood in front of the desk and wiped her eyes with her large handkerchief.

"Stella, she gonna be four in Hoctober. I vannit she go to school. I gottit to vork all day to pay Morrgach hinterest. My…" she turned to me in

Ukrainian "how do you say what Tato is?" I shrugged, "Father?" She turned to the principal.

"So she fadder he vork daytimes too, also Hanya."

Back to me, "How do you say Streyna?"

"Aunt?" Back to the principal.

"So, Stella, she is yelling 'no' for haunt, I don know vat to do! I gottit to go to vork. So, please, you takit her, please!! I no care she goes kindergarr two years, just you takit her, pleess" She blew her nose loudly.

The principal was quiet a while. He stared at Mama, confused, then at me, then maybe touched by Mama's obvious distress, told her that they would take me, but since I was so young, I would have to stay in kindergarten for two years, so that I would be the same age as the rest of the students when I entered first grade. Mama said, "Ya, ya," and then told him she needed for me to go to both the morning and afternoon sessions. The principal sighed, and looking at me with a frown, said that if I was too restless to stay all day, I would be sent home and Mama would have to choose whether I'd go morning or afternoon.

"She behave, don you vorry." Mama glared down at me, then said in Ukrainian, "You go with Ladju to Streyna's for lunch today."

Mama then asked him where the 'kindergarr' was. The principal rose from the desk and led us down to the end of the hall. The big room stunned me with its large windows looking out onto the inviting woods. The children, sitting around several circular tables, watched the teacher come to us, smiling. The principal explained everything to her, and turning to me said, "Stella Chopek, this is Miss Campbell." Mama gave me a little push and left. The principal followed her out, telling Mama he needed to know her name and address. Mrs. Campbell took me to a place around one of the tables and told the class, "This is Stella Chopek."

I sat with my feet dangling, excited, my face almost hurting with a smile that wouldn't fold down. I was in real school at last!

Miss Campbell clucked happily to find that I was already reading. She had no trouble with me being there both morning and afternoon, though she had to remind me now and then that I needed to sit down and not be bothering the other children. The question of holding me back from first grade never came up at the end of the school year.

Stephanie M. Sydoriak

Kindergarten picture just after my fourth birthday

I walked to Streyna's after school with Ladju, but after some milk and a cookie, he went out to play with his friends. I begged to go with him. I think I even cried, but Streyna told me that Mama said I had to stay in the house with her. I asked Catherine to play with me, but she said she had to do her homework. She went into the room she shared with Ladju and shut the door firmly behind her. At home, I whined to Anna that I had nothing to do there, so she began to get library books for me again. After that I was satisfied, though not particularly happy, with a corner of Streyna's kitchen, where I could sit on the floor and read until Tato or Anna picked me up after work. To my delight, Ladju played with me whenever it was raining. Those were the best afternoons.

In the late spring, when Ladju told me he was going to be sleeping out on his piazza, I begged Tato to let me sleep on ours. Mama objected a little, but she knew that Anna would be happy to have me out of 'her' room and 'her' bed. Tato brought Anna's old cot and mattress down from the attic, and Mama covered it with the feather perena that she had brought over on the boat. I tucked my books and my jacks and ball under the cot, and was overjoyed to have a bed all to myself. Mama told me to come in and go to Anna's bed if I was cold, but I only came in if there was a lightning storm. For years, I slept out on the piazza from early spring to late autumn, going from perena to blanket to sheet and then back until finally the perena couldn't keep out the cold. I was never scared. The sound of the crickets, the frogs and the night birds, and even the howl of dogs and cats were my happy lullabies. I dreamed of someday being free to roam out in that world that sounded so entrancing.

Though Mama disapproved of much that was American, she admired the bathtub, especially the one in her very own house. Unlike the slums tubs which she had to scrub at great length and fill from water heated on the stove before she could use it, the new tub in our house could be cleaned quickly, and best of all, just like the kitchen sink and the laundry sink in the cellar, it could be filled from the faucets to just the right temperature. On Saturday nights, Anna bathed first, because her hair was heaviest and took the longest to dry. Mama would let out a little of her cooled water, add some hot, and I would be next. Another addition of hot water, and Mama would be last, unless Tato wanted a bath too. He did this only once a month, because he felt sink washing was good enough. He was happy that Mama enjoyed the tub, however.

While waiting for Anna to finish her bath, Mama gave me my weekly dose of cod liver oil with the juice of half an orange. Mama said the doctor who gave me my small pox inoculation, told her it would keep away a terrible sickness. I objected, as always, because the orange juice had little effect on the awful oily taste of the codfish. Mama would then catch my shoulder and stare me into stillness. She then took my chin with one hand and held the glass against my mouth with the other until I had gotten it all down.

Then finally, the dreaded question; "You gottit hard or loose?" No matter what the state of my insides, I said I was fine, because if I said 'hard', she'd give me Ex-lax, and I hated the way I'd have to hurry to the bathroom the next day. If I said 'loose,' she'd bring out a bottle of some brown liquid that she had brewed from leaves her mother had sent. I always gagged on the swampy smell, so I learned never to say 'loose' either.

When Anna came out of the bathroom, I rushed in and pulled myself over the high edge of the tub. I protested a bit when Mama came and made me stand, so she could scrub me with a soapy washrag. She always made my skin hurt and turn red. Then she pointed me into a kneeling position and dunked my head into the bath water, so she could wash my hair and rinse it under the faucet. I could hardly breathe with my neck crooked so far. When she was finally finished with me, I grabbed the edges of the deep tub and sunk back until the water tickled my chin, and everything that had been swirling in my head went out into the air around me.

Occasionally, Mama made us bathe on Friday night while she was at work, so we could all go to one of the Saturday night 'Balls' at Oakland Hall. She'd thrust some coins at Tato, saying, "Let's see if you can eat and get drunk on that much!"

To get to Oakland Hall, we had to walk the long block down Harmon Street, then a block and a half up Cummins Highway. The Socialist

Ukrainians, who had recently bought the building, ran the dances. Tato and Mama did not actively help the Socialists with planning or food or help in the kitchen, so they were free to buy a dish of perohe, the tasty little potato or cabbage filled dumplings slathered with sour cream or maybe some holubchi, the cabbage wrapped fist of rice and meat, before sitting down. Mama sat at the table of women and Tato with the men.

I didn't stay with them after I ate. Though I hoped that one day I'd see Mama dance like she said she danced in Kozova, I knew that she never would. She always stayed with the women singing their endless songs. The men around Tato spent their time toasting and treating each other with little glasses of whiskey and big glasses of beer. After Anna and I ate, we went up to the dance floor where Al Halatyn's band was playing furious polkas and fast waltzes behind a big bass drum painted with a moon and stars. When, occasionally, the musicians played a slow fox trot, most of the dancers rested. Once in a while, Anna would join the players with her violin.

Children congregated on the wall benches close to where Kuzh would be dancing. Kuzh, a short, sweaty, round man with a bushy, grey, handlebar mustache on his red face wore a perpetual smile. Mama said that people talked a lot about Kuzh, because he had never seemed interested in getting married. Some of the gossips said Kuzh had left a wife behind in the Old Country. Others said no, this wife had died in the war, leaving several children behind as orphans who couldn't join him here, so he was too heartbroken to marry again, and still others said, with lifted eyebrows, that he was just one of those men who never marry. I didn't care about any of that. I just waited eagerly for Kuzh to choose me to dance.

Kuzh liked to chose a younger child who didn't know how to do the polka or the waltz yet. He held them by both hands and stepped the rapid, hopping one-two-three, one-two-three of the polka, urging, with his bushy eyebrows, that the child to do the same. If the band played a waltz, he would do a slower, gliding, one-two-three, one-two-three. With an older child, boy or girl, who had already learned, he would grasp the waist and whirl rapidly around the dance floor, smiling, always smiling.

Kuzh took us all in turn, and I squirmed impatiently on the bench while I waited my turn. I was ecstatic when he clasped me around the waist and spun me round and round the other couples until the room was spinning faster than me.

At the end of the couples dancing time, Al signaled the drummer to start a beat for the beloved Kolymeyka, always the grand finale. Everyone on the dance floor rushed to join hands in a big circle to begin the fast triplet running steps. Sometimes they ran forward, and then with a hop would turn to run in the opposite direction. When the next refrain began, each man put one arm around a woman's waist, and she around his, and round and round they'd spin, until another refrain told them to go back into a circle again. When the dance tempo increased, a man would put himself in the middle and do his fanciest knee-bends and kicks. Then another man would take over the center and do a more difficult variation. The contest would go on to the end of the music, which ended with a loud thump of the bass drum and a clang of the cymbals. Then everyone stopped and cheered and clapped with the joy of it all. It wasn't until the end of summer that Kuzh gathered me up when the Kolymeyka started, joined us to the circle of dancers, and let me begin to feel it all in my own body and heart. The difference between watching and doing was immeasurable.

Tato and Streychu would walk home with their arms slung over each other's shoulders, talking loudly and laughing. I loved to hear Tato laughing. He didn't laugh much at home these days. Mama seemed annoyed, though. She would mutter to Anna, "See, it happens every time. Everyone keeps treating him after he runs out of money. They like to see him drunk! I don't know why men are so stupid with their drinking!"

At least once during a summer, we would be invited to a wedding reception at the Hall on a Saturday night when there wasn't a Ball. The women did what they could to follow at least some of the old rituals, all the while, bemoaning the loss of the streets and various houses of their villages to do them properly. One ritual they tried to keep was when the women friends took the bride to her home, and with the mother, sang the songs for cutting the bride's hair and binding it with a kerchief. The songs that followed told of the bride's grieving for her mother, and the mother for the bride. They had to leave out the actual hair cutting, of course, but at least they could sing the songs. They had to be content to have the bride sit with her mother at the head table, and surrounded by the women, sing the saddest songs I had ever heard. 'Bind my hair, dear mother, nevermore will it flow free' would make half the women sob, then 'Mother, mother, hold me yet another moment,' threatened the rest. By the time they got to 'Who will feed my little red hen?' the words of the song alternated with choking sounds as they all clasped their hands into their rayon bosoms.

At last the grieving bride was separated from her grieving mother and was offered to the groom and his family. As both families sat at the head table, happier songs began with the food and drink. At the other tables, women hovered over their husbands, trying to slow down the rate of the toasting songs to the bride and groom, but to no avail.

When we children finished eating, we slid along the slick dance floor behind the tables and held jumping contests from the stage, until someone inevitably knocked over the clarinetist's spare sax. Once I hid under the floor length tablecloth at a table where men were alternating between singing their own songs and laughing helplessly. The words of the songs didn't seem at all funny. I wondered if I understood the words right.

Eventually, the head table would be moved up against a wall. Helpers cleared the other tables and folded them away into closets. The band tuned up, and the rest of the evening was devoted to drinking and dancing. The bride could not refuse to dance with anyone. By the end of the evening she could barely move. The groom couldn't help her. He would be stretched across some folding chairs by then, completely drunk because he was not allowed to refuse to drink a toast with anyone.

Mercifully for the bride and groom, the three all-day celebrations in the Old Country were cut to two short evenings at the parents' homes after work in this inelastic American world. Just as after the Balls, Mama would berate Tato all the way home, but he and Streychu would be laughing so hard, he never heard her.

Our Ukrainian World, Upstairs and Down

Sunday mornings, the routine moved quickly. Mama fried eggs for breakfast, if the chickens were laying, constantly admonishing us to hurry. The curling iron was hot on the gas burner when I was done eating. She combed out a hank of hair at the top of my head and wrapped it around the hot rod. When several such curls were accomplished, she put a rubber band and a ribbon bow around them all. Now and then, she might trim high and straight around my head and leave only a tuft of bangs. As I grew older, she finally gave in to my pleas to let my hair grow down over my ears.

Once I was out of the way, Anna propped a mirror on the back shelf of the Black Beauty stove and heated the crimping iron hot enough to make an impression on her front hairs. Then she carefully wrapped her hair into a bun at the back of her neck. By nine, dressed in whatever was washed and ironed, she and I would be in the parade going down Harmon Street: Mama first, walking rapidly, Anna and me next and Tato at the end. My three Irish classmates were usually just ahead of us. The dresses were usually frilly with lace edges. Their fathers walked first while the mothers and children straggled behind. They were walking to Saint Angelus, a nearby large, high-steeple, brick Catholic Church.

We waited for the streetcar on Cummins Highway. Chocha and Vuychu got on a block ahead of us and Ladju's family got on a block past us. I asked Anna why Walt and Sophie hardly ever came to church with Chocha and Vuychu. Anna said that Chocha didn't make them come if they didn't want to. Ladju and I would stand in the back of the streetcar and holding a pole, laughed as we were tossed back and forth.

When we emerged up the subway stairs at Park street, after a couple of transfers from streetcar to trolley to subway, we joined the small parade of Ukrainians walking from the subway entrance down Arlington street towards the church. Mama usually found her friend Ksenya to walk with. I was surprised to see Mama laughing with her occasionally. Mama never seemed to laugh at home.

The vari-colored brick buildings made a solid front along the street. Signs over the doors said 'Electric Supplies', 'Plumbing Supplies', 'Truck Parts',

'Ball Moving Company,' though more than half the windows and doors were boarded over. The windows not boarded were so grimy, I couldn't see inside. The church, also of brick, stood grandly at the end of the block. Its façade was broad, tall and flat. Two recessed double doors were set into two brick arches on either side. Higher on the wall, was a large arched stained glass window, flanked by two smaller ones. The multicolored glass designs couldn't be seen from the outside.

The Church on Arlington Street

People arriving at the doors immediately began sorting themselves out. The women, carrying bags of the food they would heat and sell after the service, went through the first set of doors and down to the basement.

Tato and Mama, unless she was doing the food that day, went in the first set of doors as well, but went immediately up to the church. Young men and older boys walked past the church toward the huge, windowless wall of an elementary school across the side street to play handball. Ladju and Streychu leaned against a black iron fence to watch them play. Anna and the other choir members went through the other doors where there was a tight, iron, spiral staircase up to the choir loft.

The rest of the people made a large semicircle the width of the church and halfway into the empty street. They stood in women's groups and men's groups talking in loud voices that echoed off the church wall. All stood slightly apart to leave room for their wide, expressive gestures.

When the bells rang in the church, the men continued to argue while the women turned to go inside. They straggled in over the next ten minutes or so. The men and boys playing handball made no move toward the church whatever. The general agreement seemed to be that they could join the congregation at any time they wished as long as it was before the blessing of the bread and wine.

The women went into the pews on the left side of the church, the men on the right. Little boys sat with their mothers, but around the age of nine or ten began to show up on the men's side. Some of the children raced up the narrow spiral staircase to the choir loft, draping themselves over the rail. Once I conquered the steepness of the narrow twirl of stairs, I took the only space left, which was in front of the alto section. The director ignored the children as always. We could sing or not, as we wished.

I enjoyed the music behind me, and the view of the church and people below. The walls were austere, though a trim ran along the upper edges. Tato said that you could pray anywhere, so the bareness shouldn't matter, but Ukrainians had a way of painting Holy Figures that were their very own and that inspired them to be better people.

"We call our pictures of Jesus and the Saints, Icons. They are painted in deep, bright colors and everywhere possible, there is gold. When you are in a real Ukrainian church, you feel that you are in the presence of God himself." he told me. "Maybe someday when this Depressia is over, and we all have a little money…"

This Ukrainian, Sunday world was as much known and understood by me, as the American world was a mystery. The service would play out exactly as it always did, long and sung from start to finish, interrupted only by the short interval of the priest's spoken sermon. I knew every person who came to the church, not always by name but by their faces or backs, as well as the sound of their voices, both singing and speaking.

The words and music that the altos sang had long ago become a part of me. At first, I couldn't separate out the alto sound from the rich harmonies coming from the other singers, but gradually, I could hear their musical line. Learning to sing the words came more slowly. The first time I found them on my tongue, all the voices were singing the same words at the same time. A little later, I could even find the words when the different voices were chasing each other. I never made a decision to sing. I just couldn't keep my mouth from opening to let my voice join the rest. I was mesmerized by the inevitability of the way the harmonies always worked themselves out.

Tradition forbade the use of any musical instruments, so the Holy Service was a four-way singing conversation between the priest, the deacon, the people and the choir. For a large part of the service, the priest or deacon intoned the prayers and the people made short responses in three or four parts: Hospode Pomeliu, Podai Hospode and many Allelluias and Amens. The choir sang the longer, more complicated pieces in four parts. But, actually, everyone sang everything. The choir sang softly during all the responses the people were making, and the congregation sang along softly in whatever part they liked during the choir pieces.

When the director raised his arms and set a lively beat for the opening hymn, I eventually could sing out boldly, following carefully the starts and stops of the altos. When the back-and-forth prayers began, Mrs. Bondarevich, in the front pew threw her screechy voice into the discussion. She sang her Hospode Pomeliu's vehemently and slowly. No one waited for her, so her voice was still two syllables away from being done when the priest started singing the next prayer. The choir director turned around and glared down at her, but since she was facing the altar like everyone else, she never saw him. When the priest turned from facing the altar to finish that set of prayers, he also glared at her, but she avoided his look by meditatively examining her clasped hands. She would be just as slow for the next set of prayers.

When all the litanies had been sung, the deacon's turn came. Standing at the front of the choir rail, holding a large Bible with gold edges and several red satin ribbons hanging down, he chanted the long Bible passages in his high tenor voice. Sometimes he strayed from the simple melodies and embroidered them elaborately in his own style.

Just before the Gospel reading and the sermon, the priest turned to face the people with his censor. The sight of the men coming up the stairs from their game in the schoolyard, creeping toward their seats, crossing themselves and bowing low so as not to have to look the priest in the eye, inevitably twisted his face in anger. Ladju and Streychu, wiser than the rest, stood down by the doors to the street, out of sight. They didn't go up the stairs until long after the priest was done with his sermon and his back was to the people.

Staring at the latecomers, the priest would shake the censor with rapid jerks, setting up clangs and clanks and turning the air above the altar an angry blue. He kept his frown throughout his sermon, and when he finally resumed the service, he sang out in a furious, high pitch. The sopranos and tenors pulled their brows up into their hairlines with the effort to match his tone for the response. The director stood shaking his head in disbelief. At every exchange the choir flatted down, but the priest held almost to the end of the litany when he faltered and the half tone was secured. The congregation split its loyalties. Old Mrs. Bondarevitch and the women around her, held to the priest's pitch, even after he had conceded it. When the next litany finished, the choir was clearly the winner. Even Mrs. Bondarevitch had slid down to join the rest.

The choral music was sometimes fast and joyous, sometimes grand, sometimes unbearably sad. Depending on the mood of the moment, I might mount a horse, and join the Kozak's sweeping ranks, my sword gleaming over my head, or perhaps become a black-browed maiden, braids coiled around my head like a crown, looking with tear-rimmed eyes at my handsome Kozak astride his white horse, disappearing toward the horizon. Would he ever return?

When the last Amen shook the walls, the priest retreated and I moved quickly to be first down the tight spiral of stairs from the choir loft, leaving the sweet incense cloud for the stronger aroma of cabbage, the garlicky sausage called kobasa, all mixed up with the sharpness of Chichko's beer and whiskey. Desperate for the toilet by then, afraid I might wet my pants, I pushed myself between everyone's legs and was always the first to enter the little room beside the kitchen.

By the time I was done and out of the toilet, having wiped myself tentatively with the cut up pieces of stiff newspaper stacked up on the floor, the people had sorted themselves out again. The food preparers had come down before the Service was over. Some were busy at the stove in the kitchen, others stood behind the big half-door handing out plates of the boiled perohe that had been slathered with fried pork fat and onions, or fragrant plates of holubchi that had been baked in a tomato sauce. Another lady offered thick slices of steaming sausage, which we called kobasa, along with a dollop of the red, horseradishy xhrin. The last server would shake a big spoon of sour cream on top of the food. The women usually first got a dish for their husbands, putting the coins they could afford into an empty jar on the flat top of the half door and then took the dish to a long table spread out in front of the stage area. Then they would go back to fill a dish for themselves and their children. The money all went to the church, though the women donated the food.

The men, meanwhile, lined up in front of the space under the stairs where Chichko, the church janitor, was ready with his moonshine whiskey and homebrew beer. Again, there was a flat-topped half door, but a narrower one. Each man in turn threw a few coins into a jar on the narrow counter and watched Chichko fill a small glass with the whiskey. The man would throw it back, swallowing with a grimace. Then Chichko would fill a tall glass with foamy beer, and the man, his eyes softer now, would take it and go look for his wife and family. The money in the jar went to Chichko.

I had overheard Tato and Vuychu and Streychu talking on more than one occasion about Prohibitzia. Anna told me it was the name of a law that said you could get arrested for making beer and whiskey or buying it. I felt frightened to hear that, but then if making it could get you arrested, why was Streychu making beer for the family in his cellar and Chichko selling beer and whiskey in the basement of the church? Anna said they were all crazy to do it, but they probably figured they wouldn't get caught. There weren't enough policemen to go down into every cellar in the city to see if someone was making liquor, and unless someone tattled, who would think to go into a church?

In the summers, on some Saturday afternoons, the Church would put on a picnic. Tato usually was the one in charge. He would first talk some farmer-parishioner into letting the church use his farm for a picnic. If there was no willing farmer, Tato would reserve some picnic tables at nearby Houghton's Pond, or in desperation, a little open space near Chocha and Vyuchu's house, called Sallie's Rock.

Then he'd ask the parishioner with a truck to load the folding tables and chairs, and assign all the rest of the work as best he could. I helped Tato make raffle tickets at home. Anna would buy some prizes at a Five and Dime, with the dollar or so of church money he gave her. Mama and Yustena and others of the churchwomen spent Saturday morning making big batches of perohe.

Tato always brought the oilcloth he kept in the attic. He had painted it years ago with different colored circles the size of nickels, dimes and pennies. If you tossed a penny and it landed on a penny circle, you would get two pennies' worth of candy. A nickel landing on a nickel circle got you a prize worth a dime, and a tossed dime got you a prize worth twenty cents. It was a favorite game at the picnics, and Tato always collected more than he gave out in prizes.

If we were at a farm, Ladju and I always ran first to the barn where a spotted horse might be waiting to be stroked. We chased squawking chickens and geese, and then might watch some pigs eating their slop at a trough. As the afternoon wore on, the young adults started a softball game, while the younger kids made a Dodge Ball circle. The men threw horseshoes, and the women kept a careful eye on the whole scene, especially the spot where the illegal liquor was dispensed, as well as the road where police might come roaring down.

Sometime in the afternoon, Mrs. Bidak would begin singing softly. Other women set their folding chairs around hers and began harmonizing her melody. Mrs.Bidak sang a little louder, never faltering on the words of the verses. Soon some men would join. The younger people sat out the outer rim of the group on the ground. Only a few people sat without singing. Among the rest, some took the lead voice, others took various harmony parts. The men sang with extra verve from the whiskey and beer. Mrs. Bidak led them through a wide range of sad love songs, happy love songs, comic love songs, wedding songs, songs of the consequences of listening to your mother, or of not listening, songs about drinking and drunks. Songs about the heroic deeds of the Kozaks inspired the men to sing in full, soldierly voices. When the women sang out sadly about the beautiful women the Kozaks left behind, the men hummed the harmony. Tears flowed when the songs were about leaving their beloved homeland. I sang along, the words coming evermore easily out of my mouth and slowly becoming understood in my brain.

When the picnic was at Houghton's Pond, the children ripped off their clothes down to the bathing suits underneath. It was necessary to hurry into the water as soon as you arrived, because after you ate, the strict rule of staying out of the water for an hour was enforced. I fussed loudly while Mama pinned long thick stockings onto my bathing suit.

"You no vannit blut-sucker to grab you leg and suck out you blut!" I also fussed at the heavy sneakers she laced tightly onto my feet, so the broken glass on the bottom of the pond wouldn't cut me. With the extra weight, there was no possibility of trying to swim like the older boys and girls. But, once in the water, I enjoyed the boisterous splashing with Ladju until he swam out with windmill arms to join some older boys in the deeper water. Tato and Streychu and a few of the men swam across to the other side. Mama tried to forbid Tato from crossing the pond, but as usual, he ignored her.

When all else failed, Tato had the picnic at Sally's Rock not far from our house. The tables had to be crammed into a small flat area at the base of a massive rock. The restless younger folk complained about the lack of space for a ball game. Someone set up horseshoes in the weeds. The singing started early and the smaller children played tag between the tables and various stones and boulders. When I twisted away from an impending tag, I tripped and fell elbow-first to the ground on the backside of the boulder that had been used by former picnickers to smash bottles. I could not suppress a scream of pain. Mama flew to my side.

She lifted me, adding her shrieks of *"Oy yoy yoy!"* to my howls. When she wiped at the blood, I screamed even louder. The women offered their overlapping opinions.

Dip it in water. Don't dip it in water. Keep wiping. Don't keep wiping, there might be glass in it.

Tato arrived, and held my elbow closer to his face.

"I think I do see glass in the cut. See how deep it is." The advice came faster.

Does anyone have any tweezers? Maybe take her to Mrs. Kazhik, she would know what to do. Well, of course it would take almost an hour to go in a car. Remember that little girl that died of lockjaw when she was cut by a rusty nail. That won't happen with glass. Yes, but you might not find all the pieces of glass. She should go to the hospital. No, she shouldn't. It will cost a lot to go to the emergency room.

Tato lifted me into his arms and carried me to Vuychu's car. Mama followed, crying. Between my loud sobs, I began to worry about what was coming next. In the emergency room, they dipped my elbow into a bowl of iodine. My scream shook the walls of the room. Mama responded with an even louder scream. A nurse guided her out of the room. Tato held my head to one side while the doctor adjusted my elbow under a magnifying glass and picked out several pieces of glass. Tato held me even tighter while the doctor sewed up the gash and wrapped a huge wad of bandage over it.

When we got back in Vuychu's car, Mama began to chastise me,

"You are a wild child who never listens to her Mama, who does whatever she wants no matter how dangerous…"

"Stop." Tato said. "She needs to rest. Save your speech for another day."

Mama glared at him, but stopped. Once home, Tato put me gently onto my cot on the piazza. Mama gave me a dish with two large pieces of kobasa, instead of the one small piece I usually got. Tato sent Anna to Ladju's house for the Sunday funnies. Tato sat next to me on the cot so I could look at the pictures while he read to me. He had never done that before. When he was done and he had left, I puzzled over how wonderful I felt, in spite of all the pain of that afternoon. Sleep came softly and easily.

Carson Beach, First Grade and Law School

On the Sunday before Labor Day, Tato announced the church would join with various non-church committees and hold a rally in late September at the Oakland Hall. A speaker would tell us about how Poland was arresting our priests for not using Polish in their official church documents and about the time of terror that the Poles called 'pacification' when they beat men, women, children and priests. He urged that people tell all their friends outside of the church to come. Mama looked sourly at Tato. The speaker would likely stay at our house and would need a special supper. As if there was enough money in her envelopes for that after the expense of the Emergency Room!

At home after church, sitting out on the piazza, Mama argued only listlessly with Tato about the rally. The heat and humidity outside was just about the same as inside, but she said maybe it might get cooler out there as it got dark.

All during that hot and sticky night, I wrestled with my sheet. When I came to my final waking in the pale sunrise light, the top sheet was on the floor, and the bottom sheet felt damp. It felt almost too hot for our usual Labor Day trek to Carson Beach. I hoped that tomorrow, when I would be starting first grade in the newly built Chittick School, would be a little cooler.

Mama, moving slowly around the kitchen, a thin sheen of sweat on her face, complained that some night bird made noises in the tree that was closest to her bedroom window and she didn't sleep.

"Such a squawking," she said. " At least if it sang like the nightingales in Kozova, maybe I could have slept. Oh! If only I could hear those nightingales again!"

The kitchen was already oppressively hot, even with the door opened to the piazza. Mama pushed some kobasa into a cloth bag along with a jar of bright red xhrin. I had mixed feelings about the xhrin. If Mama put too much horseradish in to the sweet and sour mash of beets, my eyes would water and I'd need to breathe through my mouth awhile. When she put in a little less, I could enjoy it. She tossed her head at Tato.

"I hope there's no Bolsheviks on the beach, so you won't be yelling at them all day." It had been a few weeks before that Tato had been yelling at that Bolshevik speaker on the Commons. I shivered with the memory of the police.

Then, "I don't know why you have to be so crazy sometimes."

Then, "Why do you think you have to do all the work at the church? Is there somebody making you? Does anyone even appreciate how much time you spend, and for what!!! And do they know how much it will cost me to feed the speaker?"

Then, "You collect money for Ukraine with the priest and you go back to the church with only a few coins. Don't you know you can't get blood from beets?"

Tato went to the stove and poured water for another cup of tea and said,

"I am only one thin piece of hay. By myself I could not start a fire, but there are many thin pieces of hay all around America and Canada. When they bundle us all together, we will burn with such a heat that no one will ignore us." He took his tea out to the piazza. Mama turned to me and said,

"You get dressed in some old clothes. Put your bathing suit on first."

She continued to fill her stash of cloth bags with more food and jars of water. Finally done, she turned to packing the other things we'd need. Mama pointed at me.

"Go get four towels from the bathroom, thin ones, so they won't weigh so much."

Anna helped her fill the cloth bags with our rubber caps and wide-brimmed hats, old shirts to protect us from sunburn, and finally a threadbare blanket to sit on. Mama pounded everything down hard, so as not to have to take so many bags, but couldn't fit my tin bucket and shovel. These I would have to carry myself.

Mama distributed the larger, heavier bags between herself and Tato and Anna, and gave me the smallest one. We made a slow parade to the streetcar stop. Ladju, Catherine and Streychu were already at theirs. Streychu said Streyna had another one of her headaches and couldn't come. I dragged behind during each streetcar transfer, watching the bags over Mama and Tatu's shoulders bumping into any nearby person. I wished we had a car like Chocha and Vyuchu.

Sweat poured from Tato's face as we walked through the wet heat from the station to the bathhouse. I hated the hot, moldy, darkness of the bathhouse. The women's voices echoed so harshly against the hard, wet walls, my head began to hurt before we had finished changing our clothes. Once outside, the gentle, salty breeze coming off the ocean soothed my temples. I began to feel impatient to get into the slap-slap of the little waves. I didn't learn until much later, when Tato bought a car and we could get to heavy-surf beaches on the open shores, how pathetically small the waves were at Carson's inner-harbor beach. At the time, however, the gentle flaps were exciting enough.

Mama strode ahead to search for a spot for our blanket, zigzagging around the thick scattering of blankets, towels, umbrellas, chairs and pinkening bodies. Chocha and Vyuchu poked their umbrella into the sand next to their blanket, and Streychu spread towels for himself and Ladju and Catherine.

Ladju and I usually raced to the water's edge immediately. We would have gone out to where the cool water came a little past my belly button, even though Mama would be screaming that we had gone too far. But this time, Chocha's Walt, who was six years older than Ladju and didn't usually pay him any attention, took him out to jump the waves at the point where Ladju's chin scraped the water. Anna, Sophie and Catherine ran out to join them. I started to wade out in their direction, but Mama yelled that I should wait for Tato. I stopped, staring out jealously at Ladju and Walt. I looked back for Tato. When he came by, I reached for his hand, but he told me to stay with Mama, because he and Streychu and Vuychu were going out to swim where it was deep. I howled,

"Not fair! I want to go now." He frowned at me.

"Stefchu, you be a good girl. I am going to swim."

He splashed some water on himself and joined them. I sat down and slapped the water hard with my palms so the water splashed up to my head. Mama, who had been right behind me, stepped back a little to avoid the sheets of water. She waited until I stopped and sat down beside me. Chocha was the last to get into the water. As she passed us she said to Mama.

"She couldn't drown here, even if she tried. What do all your fears accomplish?"

Mama glowered but said nothing. I rose and tried to reach for Chocha's hand, but she strode past us without looking behind. I sat again. Mama's eyes followed the three men. Tatu was swimming straight out with

Streychu, while Vyuchu floated belly up. When Tato disappeared briefly behind a swell, Mama stood up and startling the other children around us, screamed,

"Hilko! Hilko!" She walked into deeper water.

"Hilko, Hilko come back, come back!"

A man who was splashing himself with water before going in said,

"Lady, they can't hear you out there. You're wasting your breath."

Mama glared at him. He shrugged his shoulders and marched into the water.

At long last, all the swimmers began to straggle back. Mama strode back to the blanket to open the bags of food. I jumped up and down until Tato reached me. He took me out to where the water was around my shoulders, so I could feel the water pull me up with every little swell. The water flapped a little higher and got into my nose and stung my eyes. As I choked briefly, Tato grasped me at my waist and holding me high, went a little further to find some higher waves. Holding me horizontally, he gradually shifted his hands until only one was under the small of my back. He urged me to relax and let the water hold me up. For a half a minute or so, I felt the amazement of buoyant water supporting me, but a tiny splash of water on my face curled me upright in fear. As we were coming back, I saw Mama back at the water's edge.

"Vassa matta vit you, you take her so deep!!" Mama's face was red with the sun and her fear and her anger.

Tato spoke back in Ukrainian,

"You don't trust me with my own daughter? I don't understand why you torture yourself with all this fear. You were not afraid of anything in Kozova."

"There was nothing to be afraid of in Kozova," she answered.

I ran ahead to get my pail and shovel. I didn't want to hear them argue. I didn't want to hear the bad things Mama was going to say to Tato. I did not want to hear his anger. When I glanced over to Chocha's blanket, Walt and Ladju were playing cards. Ladju always played with me! It was not fair! I caught my toe and almost fell as I turned to run back to the hard wet sand at the waterline.

My tears stung as the old thought rushed through my head. Why hadn't I been born a boy instead of a stupid girl? I bet they would have played with me if I were a boy. I jabbed my shovel into the hard wet sand and threw the sand as far as I could, watching it plop into the lazy water. Mama yelled,

"I ready, you commit eat now!" I washed my hands in the water, just beyond a dead, slimy jellyfish that was entangled in newspapers and candy wrappers, and moved slowly through the mass of people. Mothers pummeled, poked, greased and fed their kids. Fathers snored. Children raced through the bodies playing tag. No one seemed to be speaking English.

While munching on the kobasa and xhrin, which Mama, thankfully, had skimped on the horseradish, Tato and Vuychu argued about Hoover and Roosevelt. Streychu as always avoided their heated, political discussions and joined the boys' card game. Anna stared out over the water. Catherine sifted sand through her fingers. Mama fussed with the food. Sophie and Chocha argued. I heard Chocha's voice rising.

"No, your name is Zosha! Sophie, in English! I don't care if you want to be called Mimi, I will not call you that, and I will not go to your school and change it to Mimi!" Vuychu nodded his head vigorously. Sophie sat straight and lifting her chin, said, "Well, if you don't change it, I don't care, because I'll just tell everyone that I am Mimi." She went to sit in the silence between Catherine and Anna.

After the requisite hour's wait, everyone went back to play briefly in the water which had begun to recede into low tide, leaving a wide swath of wet, hard sand. Chocha and Vuychu left for home first, then Streychu, Catherine and Lidgy waved goodbye. Mama, carrying an empty bag and a small trowel walked toward the far, low tide, water's edge ahead of Tato, Anna and me.

"I don't know why they are all too lazy to look for clams," she said.

Near the water's edge, Anna and I stomped the wet sand until a thin spray erupted. Tato dug down to the spitting clam with the trowel and Mama plopped it into the bag. When the bag was half full of clams, Mama, looking up to the sky told us to hurry, because the sky was beginning to turn a strange yellowish color. Within a few minutes, she made another scan of the sky and declared we had to go home.

We carried all the restuffed bags, now damp and sand covered, back into the bathhouse. I took my bathing suit off carefully, because my skin had become tender and rosy, even under Tato's big shirt that I had worn all day. The shower water felt too cold on my hot skin, but at least the scratchy sand was off. We walked quickly under the blackening clouds to the station.

Once home, Mama picked four ears of corn out of the garden and boiled them in one pot while steaming the clams in another big pot. We ate the fragrant feast on the piazza. I reached eagerly for the melted butter to drizzle on both the clams and the corn.

"Don't use too much. There isn't any more," Mama said.

She shook her head, and looked at Tato.

"I hated clams when I first tasted them. Remember, you took me to some beach that first summer I was in America. Someone taught you how to dig for them before I came, and you liked them, so then you tried to show me. I never saw such things in Kozova. They scared me. When you steamed them, I couldn't even swallow one of them. But, when something is free, you learn to like it. Now I think they are very good."

A sudden flash of lightning and an almost simultaneous rip of thunder brought us to our feet, clattering the dishes on our little table. Everyone grabbed something and ran from the piazza to the kitchen. Mama closed the kitchen door behind her and ran to close all the windows in the house, before coming to the table to finish her clams.

I sat back and breathed deeply, taking in the sudden cooling from the harsh rain, the noise of the thunder and the sweetness of the clams and corn. Mama fretted that I couldn't take a bath because of the storm.

"Bad to take a bath when there is lightning. But at least you took a shower in the bathhouse. I hope we got the salt out of your hair. Remember, you should sleep inside tonight."

"I'll go out when the thunder stops."

"You wait until I tell you!"

Anna frowned as I followed her into the bedroom. "I'm eighteen years old and I still have to fight for the bedclothes."

I stayed awake in Anna's bed long enough to hear when the rain stopped. I crept quietly out to my beloved cot and exulted in the rich odors from the wet woods. I pulled an extra blanket over me that exactly balanced the warmth of my sunburned body and the coolness of the breeze blowing through the piazza.

In the morning, Mama produced a brown dress, Anna's gift from Streychu and Streyna fourteen years ago. Mama had hemmed it up, she said, because little girls wore shorter dresses now, but it still felt heavy. I was glad the air was cool.

The old, wooden Trescott School had been declared a fire hazard, and over the summer workers had broken it down into a pile of rubble. Tato said the Irish thought Mayor Curley a saint for putting so many people to work building the new Chittick School, but others wondered how it could possibly cost so much to build.

The new, two-story, yellow brick school spanned the whole of the short block I walked from my house. I stood undecided between the two big sets of doors on either side of the wide wall of windows and was grateful that Ladju took me to my room on his way to finding his own third grade room. I took a seat in the first row and stroked the new silken desk and stared through the enormous, clean windows.

The teacher, her dark hair cut in a modern bob, stood by her desk. She introduced herself as Miss Jordan. She told us we were not in kindergarten anymore, so we couldn't wander around the classroom. We had to sit in our seats unless we had her permission to move. We weren't to speak until she asked us to. We had to raise our hand if we knew the answer to her question. Over the next few weeks, my hand waved in the air so much, she called me up to her desk and told me to take my things to a desk in the back. She handed me a reader, saying,

"The other children need to do drills more than you do, dear. They haven't learned to read yet, so until I tell you to join the class again, you should read this reader. And do try to be quiet."

Disappointed, and feeling vaguely guilty, I went to the back and watched the rest taking part in sounding out letters and syllables. My hand would fly up now and then, but she ignored me. Eventually, tired of only watching, I read. She did let me participate in the arithmetic classes, but mostly ignored my urgent arm waving in favor of letting some boy answer, and again the injustice of being a girl burned through me.

She did notice me more often during our handwriting times. "Could you please try to form the letters more neatly?" She'd frown. "Slow down and pay attention to what you are doing!!" I did try, but my stubborn, little fingers continued to twist the letters. But still, I was in school, and I was happy.

I wasn't the only one starting school. Anna announced her enrollment into Portia Law School. No one told me what that meant, though I did see the pride in Tato's eyes when he told his friends at church about her decision, even though they laughed and taunted him about wasting his money sending a girl to school. I heard Mama arguing with Anna that once she was a lawyer, she would be in a different class than the young men of the parish, who obviously weren't going to become doctors or lawyers or such because of the Depression, so how would she ever get married? Anna told her none of these young men had shown much interest in her anyway. She reminded Mama that when she had been asked on a date by a young, Ukrainian man whose father was a Socialist and didn't go to church, Tato had forbade her to accept. And he had been one who was hoping to go to a night school like her. I left when their voices began to rise.

When I was an adult, and fully understood what a lawyer was, I asked her how she choose law to study, and how did she pick Portia Law School.

"Well, Skip Sherlock, the civics teacher, told me after my graduation speech about Jackson, that I had the makings of a lawyer and that stuck in the back of my mind, even though I didn't really know what a lawyer did. At work, I could see that being a secretary was a dead-end job. My ten-dollar-a-week salary wouldn't go up for a long, long time. Then I heard that the men lawyers in my company made three times as much as a secretary. I thought I had to find something better to do than being a secretary all my life.

I couldn't pay for regular college, so I tried to find a night school. I wasn't looking for a law school exactly, but none of the other night school courses sounded interesting to me. Then I read about Portia Law School for women. Portia Law didn't require a college degree to enter. I couldn't afford to pay for four years as an undergraduate and then four years for a law degree, even if I had found night classes for pre-law. You know, only a few years later, all the law schools made you go to college first, so my timing was lucky.

You won't believe this. I chose Portia over Northeastern University, which also had night classes in law, because I would have to pay an extra nickel for the trolley to get to Northeastern from work. A nickel a day less to go to Portia, and I was convinced!

The house on Beacon Hill was really high class. Louisa May Alcott had once owned it. Her Oriental Rugs and drapes and old family portraits were still there. Only six or seven women were in each class, so it was easy to make friends. But, my days were very long.

After an eight-hour day doing stenography, I had less than an hour to eat my sandwich and get to my first class. After three hours of classes, I got home close to ten, and though I studied on the streetcar I had to spend maybe another hour studying at home before bed. It was pretty hard going, all in all."

In late September, the rally that the various committees had been planning took place. On a Saturday afternoon, Tato met the guest speaker's train at South Station and brought him to our house. Mama fed him a tasty meal, heavy on our garden vegetables and our chicken's eggs, on Saturday night. Anna slept on a mattress on the floor of the reception hall. I moved my clothes for Sunday from Anna's closet out to the piazza, so I wouldn't disturb our guest in the morning.

The event took place Sunday afternoon at the Oakland Hall. The seats filled quickly and people had to stand along the walls. The priest made his usual introductory speech, Tato presided and a variety of local Ukrainian dignitaries gave speeches. Our New York visitor gave an eyewitness view of how Poland was persecuting the clergy. He described in great detail the destruction of Ukrainian cultural, religious and educational institutions and the tearing down of some historic Ukrainian churches. He described the many protests taking place in all the American cities where Ukrainians lived. I found myself fascinated by how the men in the audience wept as they directed questions to the podium. Usually, at our regular affairs, no one got so agitated. I saw some of the women crying into their hands. At the end they passed a resolution to protest to Poland, the United States and the League of Nations against religious persecution. The cheers shook the walls. Mama leaned over to Chocha and said, "And what are the chances that anyone will listen to the two hundred people in this hall?" At last, the choir, in full costume as usual, sang the Ukrainian national anthem and everyone went down to the basement for the food. Anna found Tato.

"Tato, I've been thinking. It is one thing to talk to Ukrainians in Ukrainian who know all this, but we should be talking in English to Americans, so they could learn something. There were no ads in the Boston papers, so how could they know to come to Oakland Hall, and if they got here, they wouldn't understand a single word. Next time, we'll have to do some advertising, and we should plan so our speakers can speak in English." Tato nodded thoughtfully. "Of course, you are right."

Before the speaker left with Tato to catch his train at South Station, he bowed low over Mama's hand and thanked her for her hospitality. Her lips made a small smile as she shrugged the implication that it had not been a bother at all. That night, Mama told Tato once again, that while it was good for the people to hear such a man, she did not know why she had to do the work? Couldn't he ask someone else in the parish to give a bed and a meal? Wasn't she working hard enough? Tato shrugged and said he would try.

Laid Off

In January, the fears Mama and Tato had had since the Depression started came to pass. The pipe company closed. Tato was laid off. Mama wept. Anna said she would drop out of Portia temporarily. She would keep the credits she had earned, and she would give Mama the tuition money she didn't spend. She would go back when Tato found a job. Tato said no. They wouldn't need her money for a while. Mama wrung her hands.

I listened to their heavy, worried voices in the kitchen from behind closed doors, filled with a dread I could not understand. When Mama said the bank might take the house, she began the wailing of her mantra, "Oy, morrgach, morrgach!" For the rest of the Depression, I would hear those words as she went down the back stairs to work, or was dividing coins into her envelopes. She hadn't started explaining things like that to me, because she was still working in the day, and our lunchtimes together were yet to be.

It was later that year, when Mama began to work two night jobs and was home in the day, the stories that colored my lunches throughout elementary school began.

I enjoyed whatever form the potato took, sometimes boiled, dotted with butter and sprinkled with dill, other times baked whole and served with sour cream, or perhaps sliced and baked in a cream sauce, or grated into latke, pancake style, which was my favorite. She sat opposite me at the table, and in Ukrainian, began contrasting her life in Kozova, in the slums and now in Mattapan under the weight of the Depression. She ranged through her life experiences: her early childhood, teens, marriage, immigration to America, and finally coming to Mattapan. With each passing year, I was better able to make the connections between all these stories and what I had been seeing for myself. But what was happening to them as the Depression deepened, she told with the heaviest sighs, the most tears, the most despair.

It was like being in the fields and you saw lightning strike very close. You knew it would strike again, and you realized that you were the largest thing around. With no jobs, how could we live without a farm like we had in Kozova. My little garden could feed us only a few months. Tato tried to cheer me up. He said Boston was different than a lot of American cities. It had all different kinds of businesses and factories and not all of them were shutting down, but still, what if Tato's pipe factory shut down?

On the day Tato found out that he was laid off, oy, yoy, yoy, he was like a wild man. He cried all the time, going crazy with all the worry about the house, and how will we pay the Morrgach! Every day he goes out, looking all over Boston for a job, any job. And what does he see? Everywhere, long lines of men all looking for work. And then the most horrible day of all came, that day when we didn't have enough money for what we owed the bank that month.

Tato was afraid that Anna would have to stop law school, so he went to Helyena, who had lent us some money when we built the house. She said to forget the principal for a while and only pay some interest. She could wait. She had been smart and taken her money out of the bank before the banks closed, and she still had her job with the city. Chichko surprised us by saying the same thing as Helyena, but then he was making good money with the moonshine for the church.

The bank was a different story. They said they were going to take our house. We went crazy for a while. We asked Vuychu and Streychu for a loan, because they were still working, but they could only give us a little bit. Then, crying together, we decided that when they take our house, Tato will move in with Chocha and I will go to Streychu's with you, and Anna maybe will go to Tato's cousin, Marena, in the West End.

But then, a miracle! Somehow, between Roosevelt and the banks, they saw how many empty houses they would have from all the people who couldn't pay the Morrgach anymore. And what would they do with so many empty houses? So, the bank tells us, just like Helyena and Chichko, that we can pay only the interest, no principal, but every year we have to go tell them how much money we are making from our jobs, just to make sure we still couldn't pay the principal. Oh, but even to pay just the interest was hard.

I am already careful with every penny I earn from my job. I have chickens, I grow our food, I don't buy anything we don't really, really need. And then, we had to come down on how much rent we charge, because after our last tenants moved out, we couldn't find anyone to move in for a long, long time. I knew I had to take another job. When Varvahka, from church, told me about a cleaning job at the Metropolitan Life Insurance building where she works, I took it.

I start working with her at six o'clock, and we finish at midnight. Nickolai, at the restaurant, lets me come after that and I work there until four-thirty in the morning. And that's why I am home now in the day, and I can make you lunch. But, I never have enough sleep anymore.

But you know, the hardest thing about all this is to be so afraid. Always so afraid. There is just me and Varvakha in that big, dark, empty building. When the light comes into the offices from the streetlights, it makes black shadows on the glass office *doors you can't see through. On one door, the shadows looked like a man standing on the other side, and I thought I was going to faint. Later, Varvakha told me that the shadows came from a dentist's drill stand. How was I to know that?*

Sometimes when I look for a light switch in a dark room or hallway, I shake so hard I can't turn it on. When I roll the big cart with my mops and buckets and brooms and carrying the big bunch of keys, I am sure I won't be able to hear someone coming around the corner or up the stairs behind me. Sometimes I can't even move or breathe. I don't know if Varvakha is somewhere too far away to hear me if I screamed for her help.

When we finally finish, Varvakha goes home on the subway, and I walk to the restaurant on Dover St. Oy, you don't know how it is to walk on those streets. I am afraid even worse than in the building. On Dover Street, real men, not the shadows at the insurance building, sleep in every doorway, stinking with the moonshine they drink all day. Some of them are awake and swearing on the cold cement. Someone else is having a dream and screaming. I never walk on the sidewalk. I walk in the middle of the street, and just move over if a car comes once in a while. I shake all the way to the restaurant.

Oy Bozhe, Bozhe, What have I done to deserve this from you?

I wondered if God could really be punishing Mama and Tato? What bad thing could they have done? After some vigorous blowing into a handkerchief, Mama went on.

When I get to the restaurant, I feel better. It is warm there and everyone jokes a lot. I start some bread dough for Nickolai and then make whatever kind of cake he wants, or maybe some pies to fill the glass cases for the customers coming at breakfast.

But, when I am back in the street, going home, I am afraid again. Once, on the trolley car when I couldn't keep my eyes open, a man sat beside me and I felt his heavy head on my shoulder. I screamed and he rolled off the seat saying many swear words at me. The conductor looked up into his mirror and shouted to the man to sit somewhere else. After that I always make myself stay awake.

Tato always comes up Harmon Street to Cummins Highway to walk me down Harmon Street. There's no streetlights, so except for the winter when there are no leaves and you can see the moon, it is dark. Even with Tato beside me, I am afraid. So afraid.

When she made a crook of her arm on the table and lowered her head onto it, I tried to leave quietly, so she could sleep, but often she opened her eyes, and without lifting her head, she would say,

And then, I can't fall asleep when the sun is coming up, and if I do fall asleep, the noises everyone makes in the kitchen wake me up.

She would really fall asleep then, and I would tiptoe out of the kitchen.

With only me and Tato at the supper table, Tato told me his own stories of what he did after he was laid off. He sometimes spoke sitting at the table, but more often he took a story-telling stride in front of the black stove, occasionally blowing his nose into his overused handkerchief.

Hundreds of men looking for jobs! I stood in lines with them all over Boston, North, East and South, even knowing we wouldn't be hired anywhere. I heard about a possible job on the Quincy docks, so I left the house early one morning before even Mama came home. I began running as soon as I got off the streetcar. I was so sure I would be the first one there! But no! Already a couple of dozen men were standing pressed like sardines to the door. I pressed myself to the last one. He smelled like the dead fish on the beach just beyond us. What a look he gave me!

Oh yes, already we hated each other. The only good thing about standing so close was that we didn't feel the wind off the sea, cutting us like a fish knife. When the first morning light came, there was no end to the line, no line really, just men squeezed tightly together as far back as you could see. When the sun was maybe at nine o'clock, the magic door opened and six men were pulled from death into life. The rest pushed against the door like one body. I yelled with the rest. We could hear the closest men beating on the door.

Suddenly, policemen, horses, firemen, hoses! Water hit us. Some began to fall, some of us from the force of the water, some from running away from it. I tried to step over a fallen man, but was pushed. I lost my balance and stepped on someone else on the ground. He screamed. A policeman drove his horse into the crowd just ahead of me. I could not turn away. I could not move. The crowd carried me.

The policeman leaned down and began to hit men on the heads with his billy club. I saw his horse's hooves come down on the skull of a man who was on the ground. It split open like an egg and I saw his brains. I don't know how much time passed before I could move by myself. I began to run. I ran until I couldn't breathe any more. I fell to the ground and wept.

I thought, when I was coming to America that life would be better than in the Old Country. I was coming to a place of freedom and justice and men with maybe a little love in their hearts. Now, I find myself an animal among animals.

This is America, Stefchu, not Poland, not Russia. Yet, I read in the newspaper that men in white sheets were hanging black men in some place they call the South, and policemen turning their eyes away. And then, to see, here in Boston, a policeman killing a man no different than me! I suppose I should be glad it was only one man, when the Bolsheviks are murdering millions of Ukrainians, just because they are stubborn Ukrainian farmers. But to see this in the holy city of Boston, where the idea of America was born, this I cannot understand.

But, I was not ready yet to give up. I still walked the streets, and then, two months ago, a miracle happened. As you know, I got a job at another shipyard. That time, I came even earlier, and I was in the front of the line. I thought maybe our troubles were over. I was so happy to put my first pay into Mama's hand. But I had only worked a few weeks when it happened. Do you remember?

Oh yes, I did remember. I was following Ladju, who was playing Tag with his friends on the way home from school. We had gotten to our corner, just as a car drove up to my front door. Ladju and I were shocked, first to see a car at my front door, and then to see Tato emerge with his head looking like he was wearing a huge white helmet. He walked unsteadily up the stairs and rang the doorbell instead of using his keys. Ladju and I left the game to follow him into the house. When Mama opened the door, she screamed,

"What happened to you? What happened to you?"

She held his arm up the stairs, Ladju and I following on his heels. She took him to my cot on the piazza and made a pillow pile under his head. He seemed dazed and spoke slower than usual.

" I was on a scaffold with two other men, about half way up the side of the ship. We were painting when I felt something hit my head. I fell over, and someone grabbed me, just as I almost fell off the scaffolding. It's a good thing I didn't fall off, because it was many, many feet down to the water. I don't remember, because everything turned black. When I woke up, I was in the hospital, and I was told what had happened.

"Someone working high above me dropped something, a big rivet maybe. The doctor had to sew up my head. He said I should stay in bed until he sees me in two weeks to take off the bandages. I am pretty dizzy."

His eyes filled with tears, and he stopped speaking.

"Oy, yoy! Hilko! What will we do! Will you be all right?"

"I think so, but now, I have no more job there. They let me go, because I am injured, and they will hire someone else tomorrow. They paid the doctor's bill for today. I guess I should be glad of that."

Mama told us to go to Ladju's house and tell Streyna what happened, and that I should stay there for the night.

I was still seeing Tato on the pile of pillows, when Ladju and I got into his bed. Ladju got up on one elbow and said softly that maybe Tato could die. His friend, Frankie, had once told him about his uncle who died when someone hit him on his head with a baseball. I struggled to understand what it meant to die, and what it would mean if Tato died. A new terror filled me. Ladju told me the next morning he didn't want to sleep with me ever again, because I kept talking really loudly in my sleep.

Eventually, the bandages came off of Tato's head, the dizziness went away, and I didn't feel so afraid he might die. One Saturday night at supper, he said, staring at his plate, "I am done looking for work in the city. There are no jobs there. If I was Irish, I might have a chance to find a job, but for a greenhorn immigrant, no, there is no job for me in Boston." Mama began to weep. Tato looked up at her. Tears began to stream down his face.

"I went down to Mattapan Square to talk to Mr. Feltstein at his hardware store today. He told me once, before I started to work at the shipyard that people sometimes ask him for someone to paint a few rooms, or maybe put on some wallpaper. And I have the plumber's license from when I was building the house, though I don't know if I can pay to renew it next month.

So, he told me to come in the afternoons before he closes, so he can give me a name and address, if he gets one that day. Also, I will ask Ksenya from the church, if the people she works for on Beacon Hill need any work. I might also go door to door, maybe in the rich places like Newton or Milton and ask if they need any work done.

My mother would have said that it was the hand of the devil on me. But, no, bad things fall just like the raindrops. They fall in the same measure on the rich man and the poor man, the good man and the bad. But it doesn't matter. All I know is that my hope is dead. It has been put in a box and buried."

The Woods and Streets

When first grade was over and a new summer began, Mama insisted I go down to Streyna's after breakfast, so she could sleep. Ladju went out to play with his friends as soon as I arrived. Catherine, now fifteen, left for her job stocking shelves at a department store. I began to fuss at Streyna. "It's not fair. Why can't I play outside with Ladju? I'm five years old now!" Streyna, finally told Ladju at lunch that he had to take me with him. Ladju said "No." Streyna took him aside and some stern negotiations took place.

On the way out Ladju said that I wasn't to call him Ladju anymore. The gang called him Lidgy, and I'd better remember that! First thing he said to the group of boys was that he was stuck with taking care of me, so "nobody better say nothing." I said, "Yah!" and tried to look threatening. They looked disgusted, but said nothing. I followed them over a winding path through a scratchy patch of blackberry bushes into a bright little field of daisies and buttercups. They almost disappeared down a thick, ferny path, but I pushed through and caught up. We came out at the edge of a wide, black-water swamp out of sight of any of the surrounding streets. I followed them, jumping from rock to rock, to the rusted, open model T that was sunk up to its hubcaps in the middle. Standing on the sieve- like running board, I saw a granite cliff beyond a scrim of trees.

Soon, the curly-mopped Danny started inventing a story involving a fight between American and German planes. He pointed to Tommy, the redhead, Sully, the plump one and Andy, the short one. "You will be the German pilots." Frank, who had shiny black hair and Lidgy, the tallest of them all, were to be American pilots like him. He gave me no role. The Germans went buzzing around the swamp, firing at the old Ford. The Americans, crouched below the rusted doors, stood from time to time to aim their guns at the other three. I crouched behind a tree, unsure of what I should be doing; unsure exactly what the commotion was all about.

Later, Tommy, Sully and Andy ran off, and Danny, Frank and Lidgy, still shooting off their imaginary guns raced through the paths looking for them. I trailed after them, happily imitating their ack-ack noises.

When Mama undressed me for my Saturday night bath time and saw my legs scratched with blackberry thorns and lumped with mosquito bites, she asked angrily how this had happened. I told her about Streyna's arrangement with Lidgy. She exploded out of the kitchen, and from the tub, I could hear Tato telling her not to go to Streyna's.

"Stefchu isn't a baby any more. I'll talk to Ladju about taking care of her." Mama did some more yelling at him, before coming back to finish my bath.

Mama made sure to yell at Lidgy in the subway going to church on Sunday. She went on and on about how many ways I could fall or get hurt by their thrown balls, or maybe bitten by some unknown animal. She was especially ardent in demanding that he take me indoors before the mosquitoes started to bite. Lidgy listened, expressionless.

But of course, Mama was right not to trust Lidgy. One day, a week or so after I had begun to play in the woods, I woke to a violent itching over both my legs. Large watery blisters had formed from my ankles to my hips. I thought to wake Mama, but the inevitable scolding scared me too much. I lay on the cot all morning, trying to scratch only between the blisters. When I heard Mama making lunch, I came into the kitchen. She didn't notice anything until I was done eating and stood up.

"What happened to you?" she screamed. "I don't know," I answered. She wrapped my legs in long, wet cloths, and then ran down to see if Streyna knew what it could be. Streyna came to look and told Mama that Ladju had had the same thing when he first went into the woods. He rubbed against some bad plant called 'poison ivy.' Tato, who had no work that morning, heard the commotion from the cellar. When he came up, Mama shook her finger in his face. "See, see what comes of trusting Ladju!"

Tato took me down to Lidgy's cot on his piazza every morning for the next two weeks, so I wouldn't bother Mama's sleeping. Streyna spread calamine lotion on my legs and wrapped them so I couldn't scratch the fat blisters. I went home for lunch and stayed on my cot during the afternoons. Anna's stream of library books could not take my attention away from the burning and itching.

When my legs finally healed, Tato took me into the woods and pointed to the shiny, red-tinged leaves in sets of three. He walked with me down all the paths, making me identify every plant. One of the paths was so completely overgrown with the ivy we didn't even go in.

"Did you ever go down this path?"

"Yes," I said.

"Did the boys go down it too?" He asked.

"No, but they told me to use the path as a short cut into the swamp."

"Well, you see that's why you got the poison all over your legs. The boys knew better than to use this path. You've got to learn to be smarter than them. You also must remember that they wear pants, and you wear a dress, which leaves your legs bare. Did Ladju ever show you poison ivy?"

"No," I said hesitantly, sure I would be getting Lidgy into trouble.

"So, let this be a lesson. Learn to depend on yourself."

I tried, but I had to learn to accept my itchy, sore, summer skin, which always had a blister or two of poison ivy, long scratches from the brambles, myriad bumps from the mosquitoes, black and blue spots from falling off rocks, and patches of sun burn. I begged Mama for some pants like Lidgy wore, but she just shook her head sternly, "Girls wear dresses," she said, "You just can't do everything the boys do!"

During the rest of the summer, I spent many happy hours playing out Danny's plot lines, which apparently came from Saturday matinee movies. I desperately wanted to go with them to the Oriental Theatre to see these stories for myself, but Lidgy refused to take me. He was responsible for me only Mondays through Fridays, and that was that!

Danny's stories sometimes had us whooping like Indians in and around the old Ford, sometimes lurking about like gangsters. Sometimes the Ford was an airplane, a get-away car, a boat, a bunker in a war field, a tank. When they needed props like a spear, Frankie used the penknife he had snitched from a box of odds and ends in his father's cellar to whittle a point at one end of a thin stick. Andy made a green limb into a bow with string he scrounged from his cellar.

Making a flag was a little longer project. The boys scouted the back yards of the houses on Harmon Street for laundry pinned to the lines. Andy, because he was small, crept behind a nearby bush and listened for the sound of any one coming from inside the house, or perhaps someone out on the street. Satisfied that no one was coming, he signaled to tall Lidgy, who darted to the clothesline, unpinned a handkerchief and raced back. Danny produced a couple of safety pins. Tommy folded the edge over a straight stick, while Lidgy pinned the handkerchief tightly. Danny carried the flag as lead-man.

Inevitably, the stories took us running through the winding paths, past the swamp, and sometimes up a crack to the top of the granite outcropping, which they called 'The Rockies.' I thought we were on the top of the world up there. I could see wide Cummins Highway, draped down the middle with the sagging electric lines that powered the streetcars on their rails. Turning slowly, I saw through the frothy tops full of noisy birds into the second story piazzas of the houses on Harmon St.

Sometimes, we'd all sit on rocks in a flat circle tucked halfway down the cliffside and play cards or listen to Andy who specialized in scary stories. He usually fixed his eyes into mine and would lower his voice into an ominous whisper.

"Once they found a dead man right over there, half in and half out of the water."

"What's it mean to be dead," I interrupted. The boys snickered at my stupidity.

"You don't breathe any more, and when they bury you inside the coffin, your body goes green like rotten old meat. It stinks real bad, way worse than garbage." I had more questions, but Andy went on.

"They had to haul him out of here, and then put him into a coffin at the funeral home. They didn't know he wasn't really dead, you see. So they took the coffin to the cemetery, dug a deep hole and dropped the coffin down into it. Then the men shoveled dirt onto the coffin, and the noise woke the man up. Everything was black dark around him. He felt around the sides of the box, and began to claw with his fingernails. He screamed, but no one heard him. He screamed a long, long time, until finally, his screaming stopped. He gagged and couldn't breathe, and this time, he really died."

That night, and off and on for a while after, I woke screaming. My hands were in fists and somehow my fingernails seemed to hurt. Tato came out to try to wake me up. Once, waiting at the rock circle for the boys, Danny showed up. I was excited to be talking to him alone like that. He asked me if I had seen Mrs. Loughlin across Greenfield Road from my house. She had a really big belly now, and he heard his mother say that she was going to have a baby. I hadn't noticed, but I told him the boys told so many different stories about where babies came from, I was all mixed up. He said he knew where the place between my legs was, and if he were to put a seed in there, I would probably get fat like Mrs. Loughlin, but I'd only have a doll. He told me to take down my pants so he could show me. I clapped my hands over my crotch and said, "No sirree!" and ran toward home. My thoughts about babies and boys grew more complicated.

When the adventures in the woods waned, the boys took to the streets on their trikes. I rode on the back of Lidgy's, holding him around the waist, both terrified and exhilarated at the speed he would acquire on the slight slope of Greenfield that went all the way down to where it dead-ended at the railroad tracks. The screaming caravan went straight down the middle of the street, because there were never any cars.

Lidgy, tired of my weight slowing him down, told Tato I needed my own trike. Tato found one on a trash heap and took it down to his cellar to scrape all the rust off. He painted it green. I was always the last, since my trike didn't go nearly as fast as theirs, no matter how hard I pedaled. Best of all was when I bumped over the manhole covers. I always let out a scream. The first time I hit one along its edge instead of the middle, my trike tipped over, and I made the mistake of crying. Lidgy came back to me and thumped my head hard with a couple of knuckles, and said, "Shut up, sissy girl." The bunch waved goodbye as they walked their trikes down muddy, unpaved Harmon Street. I didn't know if they meant to leave me alone or not, but I stopped crying immediately and ran to catch up to them. After that, only the most serious pain could make me cry.

Tato also found Anna's old, slum-street roller skates and showed me how to clamp them onto my sneakers using the big key. He had collapsed the skates along their axis, so they were only a little too long, but my five and three-quarter year old fingers had great difficulty coordinating the shoe and the clamps and the turning of the key. I didn't actually skate with them very much, because frequently I didn't tighten the clamps enough. If the rollers caught on something, the skates would come off and I'd have another purple bump and another struggle with the key. The boys would make two or three passes down Greenfield to every one I made.

So as not to provoke a long harangue from Mama at lunch time, I would move swiftly to the table when she was in the pantry or stirring something on the stove, and try to hide my purple bruises under the table. I envied the boys their pants more and more. I was also envious that boys were so much more skillful than girls. I never considered that they were all two or three years older than me.

Now that I was relatively happy with the gang, I became reluctant to go home when Mama would call me from the piazza before she had to leave for work. I'd climb a tree and watch her run a little ways down the overgrown paths into the woods, yelling all the while for me to come home, or see her head down Greenfield toward Lidgy's house in case I was there. Then through the one thin slit between the trees where I could look out onto Harmon Street, I'd see her marching angrily toward the streetcar line on Cummins Highway, yelling as she went, "You go home now. Mosquitoes coming."

Next lunch time, she might say "Vat's the matter vit you? Vy you such a vild kid? Vy you no come home when I call you? Vy you gotta alvays run in the voods vit dose boys?" But, surprising even to me, my little rebellion remained firmly in place.

After a while, she would only shake her fist into the woods. The conditions of the pact had settled in a routine. She would holler for me once or twice as she walked toward the trolley, and I endured her brief, next-day scolding. With no other consequences, I saw no reason to change. Tato, if he was aware of my rebellion, made no mention of it.

Once the sound of the bucketing trolley told me that she was safely gone, the boys and I might play a little longer before dispersing toward our homes. We didn't want to be out in mosquito time either. After supper, the mosquitoes calmed down a little, and we could go back out into the early evening streets to start the games.

Kids gathered under our streetlight from many blocks around. Besides the Harmon Street gang, girls who lived nearby, but only played with dolls on their piazzas during the day, would show up along with rival boys from other streets. Someone might start with Tag, or Capture the Flag, but we always ended with the favorite: Hide and Seek, or its slight variation, Scatter. I did more hunting than hiding, probably because I was a girl. But I did like the drama of leaning against the pole with my eyes closed, counting by fives until I got to a hundred, then shouting in my loudest voice, 'Allee allee umphree, here I come!' I didn't so much like searching into the darkening shadows behind the bushes and trees. Eventually, the parents began to call, and one after another, we went home to bed.

Baseball and Movies

Occasionally, that summer, Lidgy and I slept over together. Of all that I did with Lidgy, sleeping over was the best. In the dark, he talked more than he did otherwise. He might wonder how cowboys learned to lasso steers, or whether actual gangsters lived in the North End or West End. I pretended to know what gangsters were, or even cowboys. Movies were still in my future. He was sure he had seen some when we were visiting one of Tato's and Streychu's cousins, because they dressed just like Jimmy Cagney.

He was usually quiet when the boys were talking in the rock circle about how babies were made or how they came out. I hated it when they stopped right at the most interesting part, tilt their heads over to me and say something like, "Let's talk about it later, when she's not around"

But in the dark, he didn't seem to care that he was talking to the sissy baby. Remembering Mama's account of my birth, and the Russian lady's ominous black scissors, I told him I really wanted to know if they used scissors to get the baby out of the belly button. He said he wondered too, but he thought the belly button just opened up by itself. But he said he did know for sure that a man and a woman had to be naked in a bed together to make a baby. "How do you know that?" I asked indignantly. "Mama and Tato would never do that! " He just said, "You'll see."

Then, in a soft whisper, he said he finally figured the whole thing out. He knew the real scoop. "I used to think you put an apple seed or maybe a watermelon seed into the girl's belly button, but now I know that you have to stick the seed on your thing and stick it somewhere between the girl's legs, and you have to be naked for that." I didn't tell him that Danny said you used a finger. I wondered which one was right.

At least I knew what the thing was. I saw Lidgy naked once when Streyna had put him in their bathtub, and I figured that men had the same kind of spout, because I saw them standing up against bushes at the church picnics with a stream coming out.

"How do you really know all that stuff?" I asked.

"I know things that would curl your hair." Then he rolled over and went to sleep.

As my eyes began to close, I decided he was more like a brother than a cousin and even better; he was my best friend in the whole world.

Though I kept hoping the boys would talk more about all this, it didn't seem to happen. They played in the woods less and less. Now it was marbles on Harmon Street. I learned the difference between Aggies, Shooters, Immies, and Milkies, and finally got in the game after a lot of foot stamping. Anna bought me a small bag of marbles one day. She said they were on sale. I knuckled my big Cat's Eye well enough to play, but not well enough to keep my bag full. When Streychu bought Lidgy new marbles, Lidgy gave me his chipped ones, for which I was very grateful.

At some time of the day, the boys inevitably headed down to the field by the tracks at the bottom of Greenfield Road. Some boys from the other side of the tracks hung around, practicing throws, waiting for someone to show up to start a baseball game. I begged to play, but Danny told me I couldn't because I didn't have a mitt. Besides, it was more important that I kept the two pitchers of water filled so they could drink when they were thirsty. Whenever a pitcher was empty, I was to run up Greenfield and look for water faucets on the sides of houses and come back with the pitcher filled.

When I tried a house close to the field, the lady came out and shook her finger at me. A man was sitting on a piazza right above the faucet on the next house, looking right at me, so I went to the third house. I couldn't find a faucet there. Finally, I ran up to Lidgy's house and ran, panting, back to the field. The other pitcher was now empty, so I had to run back. When the game was over, I realized I hadn't even seen them play.

When I saw Sully emptying a pitcher just as I was returning, I understood. I told Sully that was it, and he said, "well, we were going to take you with us to the movies, so if you don't get the water, we won't."

I wasn't sure I believed them about the movies, but just in case, I kept filling the pitchers. That Saturday, I followed the gang from Frank's house to the movies, expecting to be shooed off, but no one objected. Lidgy paid five cents for himself, and holding my hand told the ticket taker he had to take care of me and he didn't have another nickel. He said I was four. Outraged, I almost said I was five and a half. The man shrugged, and I walked in with the rest.

"I can't pull that two times," Lidgy said. "Next week you have to get your own nickel." That night, I started three different ways to ask Tato for a nickel for the movies. He was always good for a penny, but I hadn't ever asked for a nickel. He didn't say no. Instead he looked into my eyes for a long time and said if at all possible, he would have a nickel for me at lunch next Saturday, but it wasn't for sure. But somehow he managed to have either a nickel or five pennies for me almost every Saturday after that.

I soon understood why the boys had let me join them that first Saturday. They took me around the side to show me a set of doors high up on the back wall. A fire escape came down from the door and stopped just above our heads. Andy said those doors only opened from the inside of the balcony section. Danny said that the bottom of the fire escape dropped down if there was an emergency, but they kept it bent up, because they didn't want anyone getting in for free. So Lidgy was going to let the boys climb up onto his shoulders and get into the fire escape and go up. My job was to pay for my ticket, sit beside the doors up in the balcony, and when I heard a tap, I was to open one quickly for them. Danny glared at me as though I was sure to foul it up.

I did as I was told and sure enough, I heard the tap. When I pushed open the door, Danny, Frank, Sully, Tommy and Andy rushed in, closing the door quickly behind them. The brief brightness alerted the ushers to rush up to the one-way door, but by then the boys had crawled away rapidly along the rows of seats. They sprawled flat and the ushers didn't see them. Terrified, I remained in my seat. The ushers asked angrily if I had seen what happened? Did I open the door? I had enough sense to lie. I told them some boys were here but I didn't see what they did. I felt myself shaking. The ushers left, sliding their flashlights up and down the rows. Soon Lidgy arrived the regular way by getting a ticket. I joined him and the boys almost at the top of the balcony. Each of them gave Lidgy some of the ticket money they had saved. I asked if I would get any for opening the door, and they said, "No." Though that was the only time they tried that stunt, they let me follow them to the movies every Saturday after that.

The movie house was a hot, ten-minute walk down Cummins Highway to Mattapan Square. A long neon sign, glowing on the front of the canopy over the sidewalk spelled out 'THE ORIENTAL' with ornate letters. We'd go to the end of the ticket line, usually a block-long, noisy bunch of kids, whacking each other as they wove themselves in and out of the line. Once inside, we pushed our way through the black velvet curtain into the soothing, air-conditioned blackness. The gang usually tried to lose me at that point, but they were successful only once when my attention veered over to an usher nabbing a kid who had tried to sneak in without a ticket.

167

After that, I didn't look to the left or the right, but stuck close to Lidgy's heels until we were in our seats.

Safe now from abandonment, I would rest my head on the back of the seat to watch gossamer clouds slide down a velvet, midnight sky that was magically pinpricked with stars. Then, I'd take a long look along the walls broken up by shallow nooks and tiny balconies all at different levels. The nooks held glowing lanterns. Meditating Buddhas sat on the balconies in front of filigreed windows framing distant curled pagodas. Hidden lights gave a sense that a hidden moon was shining through the windows and glancing off the Buddha's shoulders. With all the children running up and down the aisles, I could believe I was on a real Chinese street.

Much as I enjoyed tracing myself in and out of the little balconies and around the Buddhas, I always returned to the sky. I wondered how it was night up there, and day outside, and how there could be a cloud indoors moving from the back to the front. I was a little sad to learn from Lidgy that there was a black cloth, probably velvet, on the ceiling and probably a movie machine that projected a cloud moving across. He said it was pretty obvious that the stars were just tiny electric light bulbs.

We always sat up when the lights dimmed and the crashing music pressed us into silence. We waited with mild interest through endless previews and the Newsreel with pictures of President Herbert Hoover or later, Roosevelt, talking earnestly into a microphone, or maybe men in bread lines looking sad. Sometimes the Newsreel was exciting. They showed a train derailment, or some swirly dust and dirt from some storms on what they called the prairie. The last event on the Newsreel always involved something funny like a dog with bows around its neck jumping through a paper hoop, or women in bathing suits holding a five-foot hot dog, or a man trying to fly with some wings he had made.

Then, at last, the weekly serial. Last week, Tom Mix maybe would have been left on the ground, his gun out of reach, an Indian holding a spear to his neck. Now, the opening scene was the same as that final scene, except that the gun was closer to Tom Mix's hand and suddenly, the Indian is falling back with a bullet through his heart. I always had a brief sense of being cheated, but would be distracted by the close-ups of thundering hooves, arrows whistling and blazing guns. After a little bit of story, Tom Mix is racing his horse, belly-flat, to the edge of a steep precipice. He pulls hard on his reins, but surely the horse cannot stop his momentum. A collective groan rose from the seats when the inevitable words, "To Be Continued," broke through the blackout end.

The first of the double features might be a Laurel and Hardy comedy, maybe Charlie Chaplin, or a new musical. When it was a musical, the leading lady would be a platinum blond, who sang and danced throughout the picture. The leading man also sang and danced. A story came through now and then, but not so often that I could really follow it. Just as I thought I had something figured out, a huge set of stairs would appear covered with white-blond ladies dressed in what seemed total glitter, swaying, waving feathery things, singing and looking very happy. My feet hanging from the seat danced with them, and it didn't seem so important to understand the story.

At that point, the lights would go on and a short intermission was announced. The gang went out to buy some more popcorn or candy. I went too, even though I had no money, because I worried they might just go find some other seats. The buttery smell of the popcorn made my stomach churn with jealousy.

When the lights dimmed again for the second feature, violins began to sing a different story, a story heavy with the weight of tragic love and courage. The swelling music pressed me low into the seat. Now, coming into focus, a beautiful woman stood in a luxurious room. She moved in flowing chiffon, summoning a butler with a little bell. I ignored the giggles of the gang. Eventually the handsome leading man appeared on a dark street lit by a single streetlight. Throughout the movie, his face registered a state of rapture, because either he was looking at her or thinking of her. It seemed that his problem was that he was poor, though I couldn't tell because he seemed to have nice clothes. The story twisted and turned between them and events they couldn't see coming. When they kissed, the boys moaned. The chiffon lady often wept to no avail, her yearning face shown behind one or another of rain-covered windows. It all ended badly with the leading man staring out over the dark waters of the city bay, still completely in love and completely defeated.

The cool air of the theater lasted just to the exit doors. Outside, the weight of the hot, wet air would settle on my shoulders. I didn't care then that the boys ran ahead and disappeared. My body was carrying the story home, barely aware of the heat. I was walking in chiffon, the leading lady's words forming silently behind my lips. I felt the power of her lover's yearning surround me. I looked through her eyes into his and felt his long and lingering kiss.

When the intensity of the images began to evaporate, I began to wonder whether ordinary men could love ordinary women like in the movies. I certainly never saw Tato and Mama kissing. Had they ever kissed? In the neighborhood, school and church, I saw clearly that boys hated girls, and men didn't seem to be much different. Around my house, I saw men smoking together on the front steps, while the women chatted from across their porches. In my Ukrainian world, couples were hardly together at all. When walking to the church, the men stayed with men, and the women stayed with the women. The same when they sat in the pews or talked down in the basement. But then, I remembered that men held women and danced together at the Oakland Hall dances. Sometimes the men smiled down at the woman in a way that was a little like the men in the movies, but mostly they just smiled at the walls as they spun the woman around. Did that mean anything, I wondered? I'd have to watch it all more carefully.

When I turned down Harmon Street, I saw the boys had already gotten to Danny's porch stairs. Tommy had a hand on his hip and was walking with an exaggerated sway. The rest were writhing with laughter. Would these boys ever become like the men in the movies? How could they, when they hated girls so much?

Beacon Hill and Funerals

Tensions in the house increased throughout that summer of 1932. Mama's lack of sleep, Tato's lack of luck with finding enough odd jobs and the lack of enough coins for Mama's envelopes, edged the days with sharp words. In the pale light of sunrise, Mama and Tato's steps coming up the stairs would wake me. When Mama disappeared into her bedroom, Tato and I had some tea and toast together out on the piazza. We spoke in whispers though Mama couldn't possibly hear us out there.

Tato poured my tea into my Ovaltine cup with the faded Li'l Orphan Annie and her dog, Sandy, on the side. I wished I could tell him I was too old for that cup, but he thought it was still special to me. We had ordered it together, just before the horrible day that he lost his job at Walworth's in January. I held the dime to the label he had cut from the cereal box while he taped it on. I read the address, spelling out each line. I licked the stamp and flap, and we went down to the mailbox together. When the cup came, I was excited to drink my Ovaltine from its thin, silky plastic lip. Between sips, I loved to look at the colored decal on the side. Mama shook her head against the expense of that 'Lilla Awful Annie' cup. But now, the picture was almost worn off and the edge was rough against my lips.

If I woke too late, Tato would be gone. I didn't eat anything then, so as not to wake Mama. I went down to the cellar to see if Tato was there. If he was not, he was probably off doing a painting, wallpapering or plumbing job, or just going door-to-door in some wealthy part of town, asking if he could mow the grass. More often, these days, though, he was in the cellar, repairing something for one of Mr. Feltstein's customers or fixing some discarded, broken thing he found on the streets on garbage day before the garbage men were collecting. Mama would then try to sell what Tato had fixed to the ragman who came around on Saturdays, but he never gave her more than a few coins.

Down in the cellar, Tato would have me step up on a little step stool, and if he were making a hole, he would hold my hands on the drill and help me turn the handle. When he put in a screw, he held my hand on the screwdriver, so I could feel how hard to push and turn. I hoped Mama was wrong, telling me all the time that he had wanted a boy when I was born. He never said that, so maybe he didn't, but I knew I wasn't doing as well as Lidgy would. After a little bit, he would open a box of small pipes he had greased so they would screw together easily. Another box had Tee and Ell joints, also greased. I sat on the floor and happily screwed the pieces together into different configurations.

Then, before the end of that summer, I began to notice that he made more noise than usual with his hammering, and was quieter than usual when he was measuring. His face was tight, as though he was holding something behind it. He no longer held my hands on his drill, or gave me a nail to hammer in. He only pushed the pipe boxes in my direction. One morning, I stood looking down the cellar stairs. Was he realizing I would never be the same as a boy, whether I learned how to drill or screw or not, or was it that he still didn't have a job? Either way, it wasn't fun anymore. I turned slowly and went out the back door to find Lidgy and the gang.

But, still, when he happened to be going out to a job, he would ask me to come with him. We'd walk down to Mr. Feltstein's hardware store and I'd get fidgety while Tato and Mr. Feltstein talked about what supplies Tato would need. Sometimes they'd talk about whether Mr. Roosevelt would get elected. When a customer came in, Mr. Feltstein would write Tato's purchase into a book and finally we'd be out. Tato would hand me light things like brushes, while he carried the paint cans.

I always liked exploring the strange houses we went to, but only if the owners weren't there. Otherwise, I would sit near Tato with a book, or go outside and sit on the curbstone to watch a line of ants. I might then hop around the sidewalk cracks, playing 'break your grandmother's back.' If I remembered to bring my ball I would bounce it to 'One-two-three-O'Leary, I spy Madamazery, looking through the dictionary. One-two-three O'Leary.' That, with all the possible bounces between the hands, spin-arounds, and throwing my foot over the ball at certain places in the rhyme, could keep me occupied most of an afternoon. If a child or two occasionally joined me, so much the better.

One rainy morning, Tato told me he had a job at a special house on Beacon Hill.

"Ksenia told me in church yesterday that the people she works for up there need someone to paint the kitchen. Do you want to come?"

Nodding, I tiptoed through the kitchen to the bathroom, leaving the toilet unflushed, lest I wake Mama. Tato took an umbrella.

Once we were rocking along in the streetcar, Tato began to talk. "Can you imagine how ignorant people are sometimes? I was waiting last night, to get my few dollars for wallpapering a room on Commonwealth Avenue. It was a big room, in a big apartment, in a big and fancy building on Commonwealth Avenue. The apartment of rich people, of educated people!"

He tapped the back of one hand down onto the palm of the other.

"Though this lady had a fancy dress and fancy hair, she counted out the money very carefully. At the end she said, 'you have an accent. You are an immigrant. And where is it that you come from?'

I told her, 'Ukraine.'"

Sarcasm tinged his voice. "So she says, 'and could you tell me where that is?'"

His hands went up in a gesture of disgust, then he pointed at different spots in the air, as though on a map.

"I told her that it is south of Russia and Poland, and east of Hungary and Czechoslovakia, and she said, 'but there is no country there besides Poland and Russia.'"

He shook his head back and forth.

"I said 'No! No!' and I tried to tell her that Ukraine began its own language at the time of Christ, and that within eight or nine hundred years we had a prince and a kingdom that lasted until the thirteenth century. After that, we were invaded by everyone, Turks, Tatars, Mongols, Swedes, Russians, Poles..."

I watched the double-deckers slide by and felt my lids lowering with sleep. He didn't notice.

"I had gotten to the part where Poland in 1795 had to give up its rule over us by giving half of Ukraine to the Russians and half to the Austro-Hungarians, when she put up her hand and stopped me. 'Well, you see it isn't really a country after all.' I was so angry, I almost started shouting at her, but I knew that she still needed some painting in the kitchen and bathroom. She wouldn't hire me if I got her mad, so I just said nicely, quietly, 'In my heart, I know that I am a Ukrainian, not a Pole, not a Russian, not an Austrian and not a Hungarian.' And I bowed low. Bowing gave me a moment to collect my words. When I stood straight, I said, also quietly and calmly, 'Thank you for asking me to do your wallpaper. I hope you will call on me again. If you do, you may call Mr. Feltstein at Feltstein's Hardware Store in Mattapan. He will make an appointment for me.' I gave her Mr. Feltstein's little card with his telephone number on it, and I left.

"Oh, I had tears in my eyes on the subway and streetcar coming home. How is it that Americans do not know who we are? Hah, I do know why. It is because we have been hidden for so long, behind so many different powers. These foreign powers are the ones who have written our history with whatever lies they want, swallowing our very existence. They write about our famous writers and artists and musicians and thinkers as though they were Poles or Russians or Austrians. So, of course, no one knows about us."

His voice had come up almost to a shout. A passenger across the aisle looked up, startled out of his doze. Tato lowered his voice.

When he wagged his finger in my face, I knew the usual reminder was coming.

"So Ukrainians everywhere, me, your sister and you, young as you are, must always tell the world about us. We must show the world that we exist, that we are a people with our own language, our own customs and have our own beautiful land. We must tell them how many of those Russian writers, musicians and intellectuals are Ukrainians from a country called Ukraine, not Russia, not Poland! "

"My teacher said we are Americans." I offered.

His eyes widened. I looked up to see if I had angered him, but his face showed only a quiet determination.

"Oh, yes! And I am very glad that I am an American and not still over there under Poland or Russia's heavy feet. But still, but still! Remember, that you are 100% proud Ukrainian and you are 100% proud American. You must never forget that. Never!" When I finally got to percentages in school, I pondered this skeptically.

At Park Street, we took a winding path through the Public Gardens under a sheeting ran. I could not have explained why we needed to be silent as we stepped onto one of the Beacon Hill cobblestoned streets. I felt that perhaps we were trespassing, and maybe a cop would come and chase us away. We passed steps, doorways and black-edged windows at regular intervals on the unbroken wall only a few feet away from the sidewalk. Heavy lace curtains blocked any view of the rooms inside. Tato checked the number over a doorway; pulled on something brass hanging there, and we heard a bell tinkle inside. Ksenya's broad smiling face greeted us.

"Dobredeyn, dobredeyn! Come in." Down in the kitchen, she asked, "Would you like some coffee, Hilko?" and then looking to me, "Some milk for you, Stella?"

While we sat at the large wooden table in the middle of the room, she pointed to the walls that needed painting. The kitchen was more than twice the size of ours in Mattapan, with a real refrigerator and not just a box with ice. Long counters lined both sides of the room. Pots and utensils hung on the walls and even from the ceiling.

"You, Stella, should go upstairs to my room on the top floor It's really just the attic, but it is my room and I like it. I have a comfortable chair where you can read. The windows are opened a little, so it won't be so hot, though with the rain it won't be too bad. The mister and missus of the house are down on the Cape for the summer. Just go up those stairs all the way to the top and remember, don't touch anything!"

At each floor, I stepped into every room, opening the doors very slowly so they wouldn't squeak, then looked behind me, in case Ksenya decided to come up. In one large room, floor to ceiling, lace-curtained windows loomed on both sides of a large fireplace. I fingered the creamy carved moldings around the pale blue-painted walls, and then sat gingerly on a tall red satiny chair. Kneeling on the floor, I ran my hand over a soft tufted rug patterned with tiny flowers and birds. I tried to see Mama or Anna or Tato in the room, sitting on the sofa or the chairs, lighting the stately lamps, but I couldn't. I parted the lace curtains with my finger and saw that the sidewalk was just a few feet away. I breathed a sigh of relief that no one was on the street to see me.

In the next room, I almost cried to see the floor-to-ceiling bookshelves, with two soft, inviting chairs nearby. A wooden desk with a large golden-brown globe at its side stood in front of the window. I went back to the staircase and looked down to the kitchen, to check on Ksenya. I returned and gently spun the globe, then began to spin myself joyfully round and round watching the books and chairs whiz by.

When I stopped and the room was back in its place, I went slowly up to the second floor into what looked like a child's room. A rocking horse stood in a corner, its pretty colors flaking off in places. I couldn't help rocking a couple of times on the horse, though I was really too big for it. From a bookshelf beside the horse, I took a book called 'Uncle Wiggly's Adventures' and hiding it between my two, went up to Ksenya's room. A bookmark fell out, slender, white, with a delicately painted yellow rose on it. When Ksenya called me for lunch, I put the Uncle Wiggly book back where I had found it, but I tucked the bookmark into my own book and felt myself rich too.

Tato sometimes took me with him in the evenings when he went to visit Streychu or Chocha or some nearby friend. The stories were different than the usual ones. On rare occasions, we'd take the streetcar to a house with a black-ribboned wreath on the door. I had been going with him to such places before my memory had even begun, so I was familiar with the drama of it all, if not the reason. I found out later that the visits to these houses were just another of Tato's self-appointed duties for the church, which Mama uselessly berated him for.

One night, Tato and I walked to a house a few blocks away. Heavy smells of cabbage, carnations and garlicky kobasa, sliced through with the usual smell of beer and whiskey, blew out the door when we entered. As Tato made the slow walk to the long ornate box, he made a solemn bow to the sobbing people in the front row before beginning his big Sign of the Cross ceremony in front of the box with the large frosted doughnut of white carnations at its side.

I stood beside him and tried to imitate his actions. He started with his three fingers of his right hand tightened into a sharp point. First, they went up to his forehead, then down to his stomach, to his right shoulder, to his left shoulder. He bowed deeply then. Slowly coming upright, he repeated the crosses and bows twice again. I was only on the second cross when he sunk to the kneeler, looked into the box, then lowered his head and folded his hands in prayer. Done, he stood and made another drama of the three crosses. A golden-edged book of Psalms awaited him on a little table beside the tall candle. He sat there throughout the night, reading aloud from time to time, leaving only occasionally to get some food from the aromatic kitchen. As always, I sat on the floor beside him where he read, watching the candle flicker wildly in a little breeze from a window. I listened to the drama of sorrow and trust in his soft cadences and copied the occasional tap of his fist on his chest.

One night, wondering if I was tall enough now to see inside the box, I stood on the kneeler and saw the strange, warped, chalk-face of a lady who once gave me some candy in the church basement. Was she dead or alive like the man in Andy's story? I leaned in a little to see if she was breathing. At first, I saw no movement, and then her eyelids seemed to be fluttering. Her soft blouse moved. A sharp shiver twisted through me. She wasn't dead! Why didn't she get up?

I stumbled off the kneeler and clutched Tato's knees. Trying to whisper, I said, "Tato, she's not dead. I saw her eyes move, and she was breathing."

"Shh!" he said, his finger over my lips. "No, you imagined it. She is dead."

I tried to repeat what I'd said, but he held my chin in his hand and I couldn't. "Let's go into the kitchen," he said.

I breathed in the comfort of the kitchen smells, after Tato wiped my eyes with his handkerchief. Helyena nodded to Tato to go back to his place by the coffin and handed me a thin piece of ham and a slice of pickle on a piece of pumpernickel. I told her what I saw and told her Andy's story about how the man being buried was still alive. She patted my hair and said a little bit of wind probably blew in from the window, and maybe the candle was playing a trick with her eyes. "And do remember not to believe everything that little boys tell you," she added.

I thumped down to the floor holding the ham and pickle carefully and leaned against the wall. A man was telling a story. He laughed softly at first, but before he finished it, he was wiping his eyes. Another man lifted his glass to the dead lady. Mrs. Bidak started singing, 'Klechuit, Kru-u, Kru-u, Kru-u,' and the rest joined with different parts.

I had long ago understood the words. 'The gulls are calling Kru-u, Kru-u, Kru-u. In a strange land I'll die, and before I reach the shore, my wings will tear and beat no more. My wings will beat no more.' Only the lady who had started the song finished the song. The rest were crying. She waited a few minutes and began another. This was one that was never left out at any gathering.

'Winds are blowing. Winds are blowing, savage, dark and strong. Oh my heavy heart is breaking, but no tears do flow.' I felt a tightening in my throat with the sadness.

When I was done eating, I sang softly with the rest, until my eyes began to close, and I went to find a bed. Trying not to disturb the fancy arrangement of pillows and a doll, I curled up on an edge. The walls of the room had come toward me almost to the bed when Tato woke me. His voice melted the walls away, but I remained troubled as we walked in the pale pink light of morning to meet Mama at the trolley stop. What if the lady was really alive, and no one was paying attention?

One evening, Tato took me along to a church meeting at someone's flat in the slums. As usual, I had become sleepy over my book and was glad to leave. We walked past a few scabby doors and windows pasted with 'Vote for Curley' signs against a wind that had almost blown Tato's worn fedora off his head. He stopped abruptly at a door with a black wreath on it.

"We lived here once," he said. He took my hand and walked up to the stoop and went into the dark, pee-smelling hallway. He led me, protesting, to another door with a black wreath. He knocked and stepped in. The door opened onto the familiar scene: the box; a white carnation doughnut on one side; a woman on the other, her hair wrapped with a black kerchief, weeping. Other weeping people sat on folding chairs behind her. I pulled on Tato's arm to leave, but he moved forward, shrugging me off. He took off his hat, and began the sign of the cross routine and poked my arm to do the same. I made a quick one and looked frantically into the casket. It was a girl that might have been as old as Anna. She was dressed in white, her face waxy on a puff of white satin. Tato pulled me down to kneel beside him. His prayer finished, he stood and passed in front of the grieving woman. He nodded and bowed slowly. When I passed the woman, I found myself too paralyzed to do the same. I blinked my eyes rapidly, and followed him to the chairs. Angry tears gathered in my eyes, while he chatted softly in Polish, with the woman next to him. He shook his head sadly from time to time. As we left, he dropped a few coins in the bowl by the door.

"Why did we go in there?" I demanded.

"What you all mad about?" he countered. "You think it's so bad to go and pray a few minutes by a poor girl's coffin? Is it so bad to comfort a grieving mother? That girl was murdered, the other lady told me. Can you imagine, murdered!

"That's the same place where I lived with your sister and Mama, not so many years ago. You think I don't thank God we got out of there, out of these bad places in the city. But that poor widow lady how is she going to get out? God! You work and try to keep one penny rubbing against another one so you can begin to live some kind of life and what happens? The country goes crazy, you lose your job, and all that holds you in one piece is people, poor like yourself. So that's why we go in there. Someday you'll suffer and know what I mean, God forbid."

He walked rapidly, then suddenly stopped and covered his eyes with his hands. His shoulders shook. "Oh, please, dear God, have mercy on us!"

Miss Egar and the Bully-Boys

Two days before school was to start, the boys were at the rock circle talking about how bad it would be for them to get Miss O'Donnell for fourth grade. Andy turned to me.

"You know, Old Iron Egar is just about as bad as Miss O'Donnell. If you get her this year for second grade, you will be sorry. She was the worst, the worst-worst of any teacher I have had so far." Tommy leaned toward me.

"She grows hair under her corset when there's a full moon."

"She has to sit backwards on the toilet to pee," Sully said.

"Listen, you'd better take some action pretty quick," Tommy said. If you wait until you find out you got her, it'll be too late."

"I worked on it the whole summer before second grade," Danny said. "Every time I had to piss in the woods, I'd make her picture in the dirt first and then I'd piss all over it until it was wiped out. I don't know why that didn't work."

"I could have told you why," Sully said, "That's kid's stuff. You needed to do the hex.

I told Dougherty how to do it. He made a kaka and took it to the school in a bag and left it beside the school stairs and he didn't get her."

Sully lowered his voice and turned to me.

"See, this is what you have to do. The night before school starts, you gotta promise the Devil you'll do something really, really bad for him, something you gotta think of all by yourself. You gotta be in a black-dark place, and you gotta say it right out loud." They hunched into a tighter circle, and after Sully crossed himself three times to show the devil he wasn't talking to him, he said,

"OK, this is what you do. When you are in a dark-black place, you make a cross going from your right shoulder to your left shoulder."

"But we do it that way in our church!" I said looking at Lidgy, who said nothing.

"Well, so maybe you go to the Devil's church, ever think of that?" Sully said jutting out his chin. My heart began to beat hard.

"So, after you cross yourself the wrong way, you spit into your left hand and say, 'Devil come, Devil come. I promise I will do...' and here you tell him what bad thing you will do. You gotta say it out loud, really loud. That's important! Then you say, 'so I don't get Iron Egar' You cross yourself backwards again and say, 'Devil go, Devil go!'"

Scared and uncertain, I waited until the night before the first day of school to try the hex. The bathroom without the light seemed dark enough, though a distant streetlight showed vaguely on the window. But how could I talk out loud with Tato in the bedroom right next to the bathroom. Maybe I should go to the attic, or cellar, but the darkness there was much scarier than in the bathroom. And what really bad thing could I do? My mind flew around, but brought nothing worse than maybe stealing some money from Mama's envelopes. I knew with certainty I couldn't do that. Besides, which was the wrong way to cross myself? Like Tato did, first to the right shoulder? Or first to the left shoulder, which was opposite to Tato's way, but which is how Sully and the gang did it. My neck prickled and I felt very cold. I turned the light on. This wasn't going to work. I'd have to have Iron Egar.

The next morning, I waited for the gang on the corner. Tommy, of course, asked me if I had done the hex as soon as we turned into Roseberry Road. I knew he'd say I was a 'dumb sissy-baby' if I told him I hadn't, so I told him I had done it. Sully asked me what bad thing I was going to do. Just as I was mulling over my answer, we saw the four Irish bully-boys, as they were called, sitting on the curb of the wooded side of the street. They didn't usually pick on the boys of our gang. They preferred smaller kids like me. If I were alone, they'd throw pebbles at me, or trip me up. I slid into the center of the gang. The bully-boys yelled over to us, anyway, "Look at you sissy bunch with that sissy-baby, greenhorn girl! Ha, ha, ha!"

Before they had gotten the first word out, the gang went into their comic mode Danny pretended to trip, Andy started staggering like a drunk, and Lidgy and Frank accidentally bumped into each other, Tommy and Sully grabbed each other and pretended to be wrestling, all with loud laughter. I did some tripping and staggering but found it difficult to laugh at the same time. The bully-boys looked past us to the next little group of kids. I wondered if the boys had done all that to protect me.

Of course, searching the list for my teacher assignment, I found my name on Miss Egar's list. Tommy shot me a disgusted look. I pulled up my chin and went to my room. Miss Egar, a small, stout woman with a ragged bun of unruly gray hair, stood at the door. Her little nose kept wrinkling up, as though we smelled bad. Her piercing blue eyes scanned the classroom, left to right, right to left, cutting into a pair of child's eyes now and again. I wondered how she could hate us already, before we had even done anything. I felt scared and took a seat at the back of the class.

She was just as unhappy with me waving my hand in the air all the time as Miss Jordan had been, but instead of putting me in the back of the room, she put me right in front of her. She said that if I didn't sit perfectly still, she would keep me after school. I tried to sit very still when I lifted my hand to ask a question, but I had so many questions that year. She answered some, but maybe I asked too many or maybe they were dumb questions, because I found myself spending at least fifteen minutes after school on most of the days of the week, my hands folded on the edge of the desk.

A few months into the school year, Miss Egar told me she wanted to meet with Mama. Afraid of what Miss Egar might think of Mama, I told her that my mother worked all day, crossing my fingers behind me. I hoped Frank was right when he said you weren't really telling a lie with your fingers crossed. Miss Egar said nothing further, but at report card time, she sent a note in the sealed, report card envelope. Mama didn't see the report card that afternoon, because I went directly from school into the woods to look for the gang, card in hand. When I didn't find them, I sat on the top of the 'Rockies' and daydreamed until I heard her calling me on the way to the streetcar. That evening, unsuspecting, I gave the report card to Tato. When I saw him unfolding a note, I knew I was in trouble. Apparently, Miss Egar said that Mama could come in on a Saturday morning, since she couldn't come during a weekday. After Tato read the note, he scolded me for an extended time for lying to my teacher. I sniffled, eyes on the floor. He didn't often scold me, and when he did, I couldn't ignore it like when Mama did. Then, after a little silence, he held up my chin and looking deeply into my eyes, said,

"I think you are like I was. It was hard for me to sit still and behave. I was always fighting with the teachers and playing tricks on them. But I learned that it all worked better when I behaved. You will learn that too. It will be hard, but I'm sure you can." Next day at lunch, Mama didn't tell me any stories. She spent the whole time expounding on my whole, hopeless childhood. I didn't cry, but I felt broken.

When Mama finally came for the conference at the close of school one afternoon, I was sitting in my seat, hands folded as usual. Mama didn't try to sit on our little chairs. She stood in front of Miss Egar's desk and said, "She give me trobber lotsa time." (trobber was her word for trouble.). When Miss Egar heard the accent, she scowled and interrupted. She began speaking as though to a child, slowly and loudly, as to why I was being kept after school every day. Mama stiffened and narrowed her eyes against the insulting tone. She paused a moment, then responded,

"You de teacher, you makit she behave in school. I makit her behave at home." She grabbed my hand and pulled me out of the room. I continued to be kept after school.

One day, when Tato had no work, he came to the school office and changed my registered name from Stella to Stephanie without warning me. I was shocked to hear Miss Egar's mocking voice talking about me.

"Class! Pay attention. This is important! I have been told to inform you that you are no longer to call Stella, Stella. Her name has been changed on the record to Stephanie Chopek. Therefore, you are to call her Stephanie, repeat after me, Stephanie." My heart began to race as I heard the giggles.

At recess, a strong wind brought alternate waves of rain and sleet, so we played in the small basement auditorium instead of on the playground. My classmates kept saying, 'Stella! No! Stephanie!" then fold over laughing. When Miss Egar finally let me leave the classroom after school, the rain had stopped. I was almost at Greenfield, when I saw the four bullies on Patrick's front porch. Patrick was in Miss Egar's class like me. The other three were his older brother and two of his brother's friends. This foursome had long been a problem for me when I didn't happen to be with the gang. Their favorite taunt was a high-pitched version of Mama yelling at me from our second story window.

"Ste—el-la, you comm---mmit home right now, you bad, bad girl." Followed by something like, "You Hunky-greenhorn, why don't you go back where you came from!"

"It's a free country," I'd sometimes yell back if I was far enough away.

Today, they came down from the porch and stood in the middle of the road, so I couldn't get by. Patrick led off, chanting,

"Ugly Stella lost her fella.

Stuck her in the big black cellah.

Ha, ha, stupid Stella,"

His brother took a high girly voice,

"So this is Step-on-me-Chopsticks." Patrick must have told him about my name change. I guessed that this was their not-so-funny joke on 'Stephanie' Chopek.

One of the other boys joined in with, "Why don't you go back where you came from, Step-on-me-Chopsticks!"

Stiffened with fury, I hurled myself at Patrick, my fists punching at his face. I was shocked to see some blood on his nose. I turned, lowered my head and rammed it into the stomach of the smaller of the two friends. He let out a big, "Oooof." The brother grabbed my arm, and while he forced me to the ground, the fourth picked up a stone and holding it in his fist, brought it down hard onto the top of my head. I screamed.

At that moment, I heard Mama, just out of sight of us, yelling those embarrassing words for me to come home, because she had to go to work. The boys, laughing heartily, retreated into their house, and I ducked into the path that came out on Greenfield. I sat on a rock and put my hands over my ears. When she stopped yelling, I lifted my throbbing head and watched through a thin bush until I caught sight of her running down Harmon.

Up in the house, I took off the dress. I saw a smear of blood on the collar. Terrified, I could see Mama finding the drops tomorrow and yelling at me for being a bad girl again. I jumped up once in front of the bathroom sink, hoping to see in the high mirror where the blood had come from, but my head hurt too much to try a second time. I found the sticky place on my scalp and wiped at it with a wet washcloth. It stung.

I wet the dress collar and rubbed the soap bar over it. It was a very long time before the spot faded to where Mama might not think it had been blood. I tried to wring it out like I had seen Mama do with the laundry, but it all seemed too difficult. I took the dress up into the attic and went to the furthest place under the eaves where Mama maybe wouldn't go. I laid it on top of a dusty box. I went to bed right after supper, because my head throbbed, and I needed to be alone to cry.

The next morning, the collar was dry and twisted. I didn't know how to heat the iron on the stove, and besides, it was time to go to school, so all I could do was put it into the middle of Mama's laundry bag and try to prepare myself for her anger. It never came. I didn't know if she just ignored the evidence of the washed collar, or if she had just thrown the dress into the soapstone sink with the other clothes without looking at it.

Feeling increasingly dizzy and nauseated, I debated about going to school. If I didn't go, I'd need a note. I combed a few strands of hair backward over the gash, so Mama wouldn't notice it when I came home for lunch. She made no comment when I sat with my head in my hand and my eyes half open.

That night, the kitchen table seemed to be making circles. I couldn't swallow the stewed cabbage and carrots Mama had left on the stove. I wanted to tell Tato all about what had happened, but I knew that all he would say was, "You should know better than to start a fight with four boys!"

He folded the newspaper and looked at me. He was about to begin one of his monologues and once he started, I knew there would be no way to break in.

He took a deep breath, but before he opened his mouth to speak, I blurted out, "Why can't we be Irish?"

I had wanted to say, the Irish boys and girls are always being mean to me. Why had this jumped out instead!

His forehead creased in puzzlement and his blue eyes bit into mine.

"Irish? You want to be Irish?"

I thought that maybe I could work my way around to the bullies and the girls and maybe Miss Egar, if he didn't get too upset before I could, so I said,

"Well, the Irish boys are stronger and meaner than everyone else." Which wasn't what I wanted to say either.

I dropped my eyes to the carrot circles in the bottom of my bowl and moved them around with my spoon, knowing it was too late now to try to explain anything. Besides my head was throbbing. He sighed, and I heard anger and disappointment in his voice.

"How could you ask such a question? Have I failed so badly in making you proud to be a Ukrainian? You want to be Irish?" Another sigh. "You have to understand something. The Irish came long before we did. They knew English when they came, so of course they have the good jobs now. Now, I came here and I did not know a single word of English. I knew German, and Polish and some Yiddish, but no English. And I'm thinking all the time, 'what would happen to Mama and Anna if I couldn't earn money?' So I did learn English, and I did work myself up to a good job at the pipe factory. I built this house, and for a little while everything was good." He blew his nose into his big handkerchief, and then turned to stare down at the empty street below the window. I looked out of my window. He didn't need for me to add my problems to his. He turned his eyes abruptly to me again, and said sternly.

"Oh no, dear child, you must never wish to be Irish. To be Ukrainian is so much, much better." His voice softened a little. "Do you remember when we went over to the Knights of Columbus hall a few months ago, when Mr. O'Reilly next door asked us to watch their talent show? Do you remember the songs they sang with a piano, only just one voice? Now think, when we are singing, we sing in harmonies, women high and low, and men high and low with no hiding behind a loud piano. Think of how many different songs we have: fast songs, slow songs, holy up in the church and not-so-holy songs downstairs in the church hall, dance songs, so many, many different kinds of songs.

"And oh yes, the Irish boy did dance on those sad little shoes that made a sharp noise, but think of how our dancers dance, the men in their red pants and boots and the women with ribbons flying about their heads. Think of how they dance wildly all over the stage making you leap out of your seat to shout and clap! Did you feel that when you saw them tapping their little shoes? No. How could you?" His face hardened.

"I expect you to always respect our beloved heritage and be proud of it. I never want to hear anything like this from you ever again."

He glanced at the clock and stood to go to his rocker in front of the radio in the living room. He apparently forgot what he was originally going to talk about. I felt too ashamed and too much in pain to join him. I never cared much about what Mama thought about me, but to have Tato so disappointed in me was almost more than I could bear. I went out to my cot on the piazza and lay staring into the darkness beyond the window trying to keep the cabbage from coming up.

The next day, Saturday, I continued to feel dizzy and nauseated. Saturday night, when Mama asked her usual, "You gottit hard, you gottit loose?" I tried to decide once again whether I wanted to sit on the toilet with the Ex-lax, or take her Mama's tea, but before I could answer, I had to run to the bathroom to throw up. Mama followed me and said in the broken English she had begun to use with me most of the time,

"You gettit now to bed, I make the harbatka. Mama's tea goot for trowing up."

I said feebly, "I don't want any!" but she was gone.

I tried not to think how much it smelled like our swamp when I was trying to swallow it, but before I finished the cup, I was back in the toilet throwing it all up. Mama went back to the kitchen to make another batch.

"I won't drink any more of that stuff! Your Mama probably picked the wrong leaves and it's poison!" I clamped my lips shut.

"My Mama knows vat goot, vot bad," she said aiming for my lips.

"Maybe the Polish police took her leaves out and put poison leaves in. You always say the letters were opened."

Mama sat heavily, and I ran back into the bathroom. I stayed on my cot on the piazza all day Sunday. Mama stayed home from church to watch me. I tried to read my books, but spent more time thinking how I could avoid the bully-boys the next time I went to school. I hoped I would be sick a few days longer, but by Monday morning, the dizziness and throwing up were gone.

I wondered why Lidgy never had trouble with the bullies, and then I realized it was because he was a boy, first of all, and he was taller and bigger than they were. Mama often said he was tall like our oversized grandmother, Anyelka. I decided it would be better to ask Saul Feltstein how come I hadn't seen him getting beaten up recently. I had seen Saul, whose father owned the hardware store down in Mattapan Square, attacked by the bullies many times, but instead of mocking his mother, they would say, "You kike, you Christ-killer, you Jew-boy, you deserve to die," and because no one ever came to his defense, they kicked him halfway up the block.

Saul and I had sometimes found ourselves hiding out in the woods together, having escaped while the bullies were working over another small kid. Saul said that the boys picked on him because he was a Jew, the only one in our school. Apparently, his grandfather built their house in the neighborhood maybe forty years ago, when there were almost no houses around. Later, when houses began to be built in larger numbers, the banks decided not to give Jews any mortgage money if they tried to build in or neighborhood. But they couldn't get rid of the Feltsteins who were already there. Saul said he wished he lived in one of the Jewish neighborhoods, because no one would be mean to him there.

After school, on the day I returned to school, I found him in the woods. He said he knew a way home around the bully-boys. I could follow him, but I shouldn't walk with him. He went in the opposite way that we usually went, taking a very long, zig-zaggy route through streets and woods. After a few days I could do it myself.

When the weather turned cold, rainy, sleety and snowy, the boys of the gang, as well as the bully-boys, went straight home, so I did too. Mama was too busy making supper and getting ready for work to ask me to do more than a few dishes in the sink or fold some laundry. With the house all to myself after she was gone, I would twiddle the radio dial with the volume turned up. I zipped by the talking stations as well as the ones with stories that I couldn't understand. When I heard music coming out, I stopped twiddling and sat up in the rocking chair to listen.

The beat lifted my feet, and as I stamped and twirled, I felt myself becoming a witch. Casting spells, I glowered and stirred a pot of boiling toads. I glared down the devil himself, lurking back of the door. When the music softened, rippling with a silky harp, I became a fairy princess, spinning and gliding around the two stiff black chairs, pretending to be oblivious to the witch lurking with the dark woodwinds on the dining room table. When the trumpets, horns and drums took over, I became a room full of soldiers wheeling and strutting. I stared straight into the eyes of the bully-boys, and they melted into waxy blobs on the floor.

Stephanie M. Sydoriak

An Extra Christmas

In December of second grade, I began to realize that Christmas in my Ukrainian world would be extremely different than Christmas in my American world. When I was in first grade it hadn't mattered to me that American Christmas was celebrated on December 25th and Ukrainian Christmas on January 7th. This year, I needed to know the difference. I asked Tato and understood nothing about his explanation that Americans and Ukrainians used two different calendars, the Gregorian and the Julian, and so their Christmases were two weeks apart.

I also wanted to know whether our Ukrainian Saint Nicholas was the same as the American Santa Claus. Anna told me that they were, just dressed differently. Well, If Santa Claus and Saint Nicholas were the same, why did it seem that American Santa Claus was so much nicer than Ukrainian Saint Nicholas? I remembered that Santa Claus brought real toys to my American classmates last year, while Saint Nicholas had only left an orange in my shoe in early December. When he came to the church, he only gave out little bags of candy to the children. Was it because we were 'foreigners' and 'greenhorns'? How could I believe that Santa Claus and Saint Nicholas were the same person when I knew perfectly well that the Saint Nicholas who passed out the candy in the church basement was my own father dressed up to look like Saint Nicholas? I asked Tato as best I could, but he only said, "You are Ukrainian. Our saint is Nicholas, not Santa Claus. Giving presents is American. We celebrate the birth of Christ without them."

Anna had tried to catch a little bit of American Christmas when I was in kindergarten. She gave me a book called the 'The Cherry Tree Children,' It was about robins and squirrels, which totally delighted me no matter how often I read it. When I was in first grade, she had taken me downtown to look into store windows and sit on Santa's lap in Filene's. I had seen a real beard on Mr. Krawchuk at church, and this Santa's beard seemed to be just some cotton fluff. I told him I needed a new ball. He patted me on the head and said "Next." On American Christmas, Anna had a wrapped a set of jacks for me to open. There was no ball. On Ukrainian Christmas, she gave me what became my most beloved book, 'Heidi,' There still was no ball.

This Christmas, I confronted Anna. 'I know you gave me 'Heidi', but you're not Santa Claus and you're not St. Nicholas. I still want to know why Santa Claus goes to everyone else's house with presents and not ours. And why are we having St. Nicholas Day, when it's not Christmas?" Anna just said, "It's complicated."

The celebration of St. Nicholas Day at the church came in early December before anyone at school was even talking about Christmas. Tato got busy right after Thanksgiving fussing with the costume parts for Saint Nicholas, the angel-girl and the devil-boy. He noted that the old bishop-hat was coming apart, the angel wings were beyond repair, and somehow the devil-boy's stick was lost. We went down to the cellar for some old newspapers. Tato made a soupy paste of some kind, while I ripped the papers into thin shreds. He mixed the paper and paste together. With my happy help, he patted the gooey mess over a ball we sometimes took to the beach. He said it was the same size as his head. He stuck a tiny wooden cross into the top of it. When the hat had dried out, he painted it gold and glued colored glass chips on its sides. I put my finger on the chips while they dried. He also needed my fingers to hold the end of the black crepe paper he wound around a stick for the devil-boy.

Another night, I watched him bend two wire frames into the shape of angel wings. He gave me a roll of white crepe paper and scissors and showed me how to make little cuts along one edge of the long, skinny strip. When he wound the strip around the frame, the cut edges looked like feathers. I begged him to let me be the angel, but he told me that it wouldn't be fair to the other children at church for him to choose his own daughter. Besides, helping him with the costumes was the most important job of all.

On a Saturday, Mama washed the year's musty smell from the various robes she had made many years ago when Tato had first become Saint Nicholas. She ironed each piece carefully. On the Sunday before the event, we carried the props and costumes in big bags to the church to stow under the basement stage. The night before the event, Tato gave me a stack of little paper bags to open and line up on the dining room table. I put one roll of Necco wafers into each one and then a coil of black licorice. Tato put in three chocolate coins wrapped in gold paper. Tato told me St. Nicholas must have intended the one leftover gold coin for me, because I had helped him so much.

Right after a very early Saturday supper, Tato and I went to the church to oversee the preparations. Olga, the newly chosen angel-girl, and Andrew,

189

the devil-boy were already there. I tried to swallow my jealousy when I saw Olga standing in the long white dress, while Tato fussed with the straps across her shoulders holding the wings. The wings flopped too much, so Tato had to do some magic with some string to keep them steady. They looked even more like real angel wings on Olga's back than in our kitchen.

Andrew stood shyly in the red suit and red cap with the tiny horns Mama had stuffed tightly with cotton balls. Tato gave him a small bag with a few pieces of coal in it, and then with a flourish, handed him the new black stick. Tato told him to look mean. Andrew tried to rearrange his face, but didn't succeed very well. When Tato, fully dressed in his new, gold crown, red robe and white sash, added the big white beard to his chin and leaned heavily on his silver stick, I could almost believe it wasn't Tato any more.

When the choir started singing a carol from the stage, I went to sit by Lidjy. The colored glass in Tato's crown sparkled under the ceiling lights as he walked slowly down the aisle. Andrew glowered at the children first on the left side of the aisle and then to the right, shaking his stick. Olga reached into the bag and gave each child a bag of candy. I felt a strong pride to see our fine work and wished people knew I had helped.

When Saint Nicholas arrived at the front, the angel-girl held his arm as he climbed the two steps to the stage, where he sat in a chair in front to one side of the curtains. The angel and devil sat at his feet. Soon everyone was singing carols with the choir, including the one I loved the best, the now famous, even to Americans, 'Ring Christmas Bells, Merrily Ring!' Eventually, the choir left the stage and the curtain came down. A few noisy minutes later, the curtain came up on a scene of a mother, father, son and daughter sitting around a table.

The playlet had the father scolding the boy of the family for having run off to play when he should have swept out the stable. The mother scolded the boy when he began to tease his sister. The father said St. Nicholas was listening and the boy might be surprised at what would be in his shoe next morning. The boy laughed and tossed his head. Then the children and the parents stood at the door. The father and mother made wide signs of the cross. The children imitated them. The father and mother each said a prayer, marking every sentence with another sign of the cross. They concluded with a song about the coming birth of Christ. The children arranged their shoes carefully. As they tiptoed towards a backstage bed, the lights went out.

A single light suddenly focused on St. Nicholas, the angel-girl and the devil-boy.

St. Nicholas directed them toward the shoes and everything went black. When the lights came on again, the stage children were running out to the shoes, rubbing their eyes. The boy broke into tears when he found a piece of coal and a little black stick in his shoe. Andrew, the devil-boy stood up beside Tato and did a little jig. The little girl in the play, of course, found candy in her shoes. Angel-Olga, rose beside Tato, folded her hands in prayer and smiled broadly over to the little girl. The applause was long and hearty during the bows, even for the devil-boy, Andrew. St. Nicholas led all to a door in the back of the stage, and the curtains closed.

When the priest came out to make a speech, I tuned him out and unwrapped the roll of Necco wafers from my bag. Sucking on one, I puzzled once again about the differences of the toy giving, by American Santa Claus and our Saint Nicholas. How could they be the same person? When the priest finished, the curtain opened onto the choir for a last elaborate, joyous carol. The ladies began to sell some baked treats at the back. Tato told Mama that I should get a whole piece, because I had helped him with the costumes. She told him she didn't have enough money. He dug into his pocket and offered her a coin. She shrugged, and using a coin of her own, bought two pieces to divide for the four of us.

Back in school that Monday, I heard the children in my class whispering about what they were hoping to get from Santa Claus. I sighed. I really knew Santa Claus wouldn't come to our house, but maybe this year he might forget I was Ukrainian? The envious waves beat a little faster through me when the janitor set up a tree by Miss Egar's desk and when we hung the paper circles Miss Egar gave us to color. She hung the tinsel herself. I was mesmerized at how the tinsel moved and sparkled whenever anybody walked by.

During the final assembly, I enjoyed singing the now-familiar American carols. I felt a little calmer and just a little bit more American than Ukrainian. I decided I would ask Anna how the figures of the baby Jesus and Mary and Joseph that were up on the stage, were connected to Santa Claus or St. Nicholas.

Walking home, I began to talk in my head to Santa Claus. I told him that I really was one of the regular kids of the neighborhood, and if he could just forget that I was Ukrainian this year, everything would be fine, only he shouldn't tell Tato. I probably should have been on my knees with my hands folded. I hoped I'd remember when I got home.

The school holiday was long and lonely, except for the occasional time spent playing cards with Lidgy. When American Christmas Eve came, I was amazed to see Tato bringing home a small, lopsided tree from a tree lot on Cummins Highway. The salesman gave it to Tato for free after Tato helped him put the last few unsold trees on his truck. Mama put a big sheet under it to catch any loose needles. Anna and I made paper chains out of newspaper strips and the leftover white crepe paper strips. Anna told Tato he should have told her he was getting a tree so she could have bought some tinsel while the stores were open. Tato reminded us yet again that Ukrainians did not have trees or tinsel or presents. He only got a tree because he saw that Anna wanted one so much.

"In Ukraine," he said, "we put a big bundle of wheat in one corner to represent all our ancestors who had grown wheat on the family fields for hundreds, maybe thousands of years. These stalks came from those seeds that were first planted.

"When I was a child in Ukraine," he said, "I felt our ancestor's souls hovering around the bundle. I still hope that someday I will find some stalks of wheat to buy in Boston, if nothing else than a reminder of that sacred sheaf."

I got up early on American Christmas Day to see whether Santa Claus had received my request that he overlook my being Ukrainian, but of course, he didn't. Since neither Mama nor Anna had to go to work, Mama cleaned the house and Anna studied. Tato, before going down to the cellar, turned on the radio to some carols. I sat on the rocker and sang along.

When we got back to school from Christmas vacation after New Year's day, I had to swallow my tears when I heard of the dolls and puzzles and toy cars that Santa had brought. Miss Egar asked each of us to stand in front of the room and describe our favorite present. When my turn came, I said I got a book. I crossed my fingers and said the name of the book I got was Heidi. The lie was that Anna had given it to me last year.

When I woke on January seventh, Ukrainian Christmas at last, I ran to the tree, now almost without any green needles at all and saw a few packages wrapped in some reused red tissue. A small hope rose in me that maybe St. Nicholas had gotten more generous after all.

Mama came up the back stairs with Tato, looking tired after her long night's work. Instead of going to bed, she went into the living room and sat wearily. I looked to Tato for permission to take my stocking off the doorknob, where I had hung it before going to bed the night before. He said the usual,

"Hanging a stocking is not our custom." He frowned at Anna. "But Anna thinks you should have a little bit of your schoolmate's Christmas. I suppose we have to change some of our own customs now that we are in

America. But Stefchu, it is not the custom in Ukraine to exchange presents on the Holy Day of Christ's birth." Yes, yes, I knew.

I emptied the stocking on the floor, and found six candy kisses, eight new crayons, a hair bow, a pencil and from the toe, a fat orange. Mama frowned at Anna.

"You shouldn't be spending your pay for such things"

So, neither Santa Claus nor St. Nicholas had filled my stocking. Anna handed a thin package to Mama. Mama raised her eyebrows in surprise, and then unwrapped it, carefully folding the paper and ribbon. Inside the box was a square of cardboard with three small handkerchiefs held to it by a pin. Mama wiped away a tear. Tato's package had two large man-sized handkerchiefs. He smiled at Anna, shaking his head a little. Finally Anna gave me my package. The book inside was 'Alice in Wonderland. 'There wasn't any present for Anna. She didn't seem to expect any. She just said,

"Tato, I think we should have Christmas on December 25ᵗʰ next year just like everyone else in America does. It feels like Christmas then. Today it doesn't. Besides, Mama and I could have gone to church on American Christmas, because we have that day off like everyone else." Anna looked warily at Tato.

Tato frowned. "Our priest would never change the church calendar. We have never celebrated Christmas with the Polish and the Irish."

"It's not just the Polish and Irish," Anna protested, "It's the Italians, the English, everybody except us and the Russians!" Tato shook his head.

"I am not ashamed of being Ukrainian."

Mama said, "Stella, no book! Ve gonna eat, den you puttit dress for church." After breakfast, Anna went to her job. Mama went to her bed. If she didn't get some sleep, she would have trouble working through the night. Tato, on earlier Christmases also had gone to work, but this year, with no job for the day, he could go to church with me. On the streetcar, Tato spoke so softly, I could barely hear him over the screaming wheels.

"Another sad Christmas here in America." His head drooped. We walked from Park Street station, through a ferocious wind that slapped us with stinging bits of sleet.

Twice as many men in church stood in the right side pews, as women did in the left side. Tato said that women were finding jobs in this Depression sooner than the men, probably because they were paid lower wages. I sat beside Tato, because there was no choir in the loft. The singing of the few people in the pews was muted and joyless, though there was a more serious tussle with the tempo and key without the director. One of the good basses in the parish managed to drown out most of the arguments.

Downstairs after the service, the door to the kitchen was closed, though Chichko's half door was open, his beer and whisky on its narrow shelf. People stood talking in little clusters. I saw several men crying, blowing their noses into large handkerchiefs. Tato was talking with Mr. Kupchek, when he put his hands over his face. His shoulders shuddered, and he was crying too.

An hour or so before Mama had to go to work at five o'clock that afternoon, Tato, Mama and I stood around the dining room table for the traditional, meatless Christmas Eve dinner. We should have had the meal the night before, but Tato had had a plumbing job and couldn't come home until six, an hour after Mama had left for work. Anna wasn't home on either day, because as usual, she was between work and her law class. Mama and I sang the traditional Christmas hymn, Boh Predvichney, which always began the traditional, twelve-course, meatless, milkless Christmas Eve meal. Tato always claimed he couldn't sing. Mama cut two pieces of the honey cake she had made. Tato put a dab of honey on each piece and gave one to Mama and one to me as he spoke his wishes for us for the coming year. When he handed Mama her piece and brushed her cheek with his, tears welled up in his eyes, and he could only say, "I pray for work." His wish for me was that I continue my growth as a patriotic Ukrainian girl.

Mama served us some borsht and perohe and gave us each a little piece of pickled herring. She apologized for not making the usual jellied fish, or any of the other required dishes. It was lucky she had time to make four out of the twelve. She hoped the Apostles would forgive her for slighting their memory. She left the clearing of the table to Tato and me and went down the back stairs to catch her streetcar. When we were done, Tato sat in front of the radio and read a newspaper he found on the subway. I took my new book and sat down in the wide crook of the front stairs, where the light hung. I arranged my candy kisses, my crayons, my pencil, my hair bow and my orange on the step above, and began to read, falling joyously down the hole with Alice into her magic world.

I had asked Tato to write me a note for Miss Egar at breakfast about my absence. Instead, he sat me down and reminded me once again, in a whisper, so as not to wake Mama, about the two calendars. He said I needed to start to learn how to explain Ukrainian things to the teachers myself, so he wasn't going to write a note.

Standing in front of Miss Egar's twitching face, all I could remember to say was that we had to go to church because it was Ukrainian Christmas.

Her stern face got all red and her voice squeaked even higher than usual.

"Stephanie, this is not the first time I've caught you in a lie."

I told her I wasn't lying, but she was working her angry lips and didn't seem to hear me. She gave me a note to take to the principal's office. He shook his head disapprovingly as he read it and then wrote a note for me to take home. It said,

"Dear Mr. or Mrs. Chopek. Stephanie tells us that she was not in class yesterday, because it was Christmas. I believe you need to address her problem of lying. I would like a note from you as to the real reason she was absent yesterday. I would hope that you give her an appropriate punishment. Sincerely, Mr. Dunbar, principal."

Miss Egar told me to write fifty times, 'I will not tell lies anymore' and bring it back on Monday. "Penmanship will count."

Tato exploded when he read the note at supper. He asked me if I had told the principal what he had told me about the two calendars. Tears blurred my eyes. I told him that I had forgotten what he had said. He went over it all again, and asked me questions that I had to answer to show I was listening.

"This time, you tell them the whole story. What kind of teachers are they that don't know about the Julian calendar?" I went to my bed to cry.

The next morning, fortunately, was Saturday. Anna saw me writing 'I will not tell lies anymore' and gave me a stern lecture about how I should never tell lies, ever! Protesting that I hadn't lied (for once, I thought to myself), I told her what happened. She told my story to Mama, and then the two of them confronted Tato and told him he must write a note for me. Tato told Anna to write one herself, if she thought I couldn't explain it to the teacher. I cried that Miss Egar wouldn't believe me if the note was in my sister's handwriting. It had to be written by my father! I ran up to the attic to cry where I couldn't hear the ensuing three-way fracas.

Two pages of Tato's smallest handwriting waited beside my Li'l Orphan Annie cup on Monday morning. Miss Egar read it with the same red face and angry twitching lips that she had when I first stood in front of her. She said nothing, but pointed me to my seat. That afternoon, although I had tried extra hard not to be squirmy, I had to stay after school for a half hour. I was glad the entire Christmas season was finally over.

Books

January of 1933 marked a year since Tato had been laid off. He tended now to sit in conversation deep within himself. I saw his lips move occasionally and his eyes flare and tighten. When he did speak to me, his talk boiled with anger and despair and a deep sense of betrayal. If he had found a newspaper on a streetcar, he would read and reread the stories about tent cities and riots in various places. He listened intently to Roosevelt's fireside chats, his head moving back and forth in sorrow, unable to feel any of the hope Roosevelt was projecting. When commentators came on, he would yell his unanswerable questions at the little yellow dial.

He spent more time preparing his speeches for church events. On one of his rants in front of the Black Beauty stove, he told me that he wasn't as good as the people deserved. He needed to know so much more Ukrainian history, and so much more about its heroes and patriots. But at least he was trying. He saved every copy of the newspaper, Svoboda, and noted the historical and political articles up at the top of the first page so he could find them again. His most treasured resources were the few thin books he had acquired when he was active in the Chytalnia in Kozova. One was a short history of Ukraine, another a small selection of poetry from a variety of Ukrainian poets with little histories about them. He knew them all by heart.

Near the time of each of the most important poets' birthdays, he would give a few of the poems to some of us children to memorize for the memorial event. In his opening speech, he would present the few paragraphs of biography from his poetry book laced through, of course, with his own rhetorical embellishments. When he turned to stage right with a little nod, we children came out, forming a semi-circle in front of the stage curtain. One by one, each would recite his or her section of the much-practiced poem along with Tato's choreography of exaggerated gestures. Tato would follow our recitation with a passionate talk about why this poet was of such great importance to Ukraine as well as to each person sitting in the basement of the church.

I liked it best when the choir sang and the dancers danced. The songs I knew would dance on my tongue. When the curtains went up on the dancers, I felt the hard, ancient beat in my feet and could hardly keep them still while watching the male dancers do their high kicks and knee bends and the women dancers do their intricate, properly demur steps. Exhausted by the excitement of all that, I inevitably fell asleep when the speeches from the head of the church committee and the priest began and only woke for the food.

Sitting beside Anna on the streetcar coming home from the memorial to the poet, Shevchenko, I realized that I hardly saw her anymore. When she was home, she was usually at her desk surrounded by papers and books. If I approached her, she would shoo me away saying she had to study.

"What's Portia Law School anyhow?" I asked

"Well, I am trying to be a lawyer, so I have to go to a school to learn how. The only school that lets women in to study at night is Portia Law School. And there's only women there because no men want to go to law school with women."

"That's not fair!"

"No, it's not, but women aren't supposed to do what men do, I guess."

"What's a lawyer?"

"Well, say you do something really bad like steal something, maybe money from a bank or you hurt someone, and they catch you." I thought guiltily of the bookmark with the painted rose keeping my place in Alice in Wonderland and then about the blood that had come out of Patrick's nose when I hit him. "The police tell the judge that you did this bad thing, so then you need a lawyer to help you tell the judge your side of the story, so the judge can decide whether you should go to jail or not."

She looked at my worried face.

"It's hard to understand, I know, but lawyers do a lot of things to help people when they are in trouble. Anyway, a lawyer makes more money than a secretary like me does, which is what is important to me right now." I had a sudden warm feeling of connection with her. She was talking to me as though I weren't an insignificant baby. And if someone caught me with the bookmark, and I needed a lawyer, maybe she'd help me. Emboldened, I felt able to ask the question that was always simmering in my head.

"Why is Mama always mad at me?" She looked startled at the change of topic and wrinkled her nose.

"Well, for one thing, you could stop being such an itch and a pain."

"What do you mean?" I sat straighter and looked at her.

"Well, you just don't seem to realize that Mama is having a really hard time working two jobs, and trying to sleep, and trying to feed you and wash your clothes. You act like you're the Queen of Sheba or something. Like you can come and go as you please. Like you can just sit up in a tree and not answer Mama when she calls you! Of course she is mad at you! Look at you. When did you last wash your face or your neck or even your hands, except when Mama makes you? You go around all the time like something wild in the woods with all those boys. Of course, she is mad at you. Who wouldn't be?" She shook her head and glared at me. The friendly warmth evaporated. She had become my stern American mother again. Anna pressed on.

"Besides, she's afraid something will happen to you. It's been hard for her to come all the way across the big ocean from her small town in Ukraine to the big American city of Boston. Everything is scary for her over here, and you just make it much worse."

I slumped. "But it's so hard. Mama can't talk English, and she isn't like other people. I can't ask her about the bullies, or anything." Tears gathered in the corners of my eyes.

"Well, that's just the way it is. Just get used to it. You are too much of a crybaby. You have to learn to ignore things. It was even harder for me, you know. At least she understands some English now. " I wondered if Anna had ever had bullies say bad things to her or hit her with a rock, but I knew that I couldn't ask her now.

The bullies became more of a threat when Miss Egar began to let me go home right after school a few days a week. They had figured out the roundabout route Saul and I had been taking, so I tried to hide myself in the thickest bunches of kids going toward my house, but now and then they would just pluck me out, hold my arms behind me and give me a rap on the head. I saw that they didn't bother the Harmon Street girls, probably because their fathers were policemen, so I began to join the girls straight out of the big doors. Eleanor, with the long black hair, eventually noticed me behind them.

"Honestly Stella, you are just the worst tomboy! I've seen you fighting with those boys in the street. You really look stupid."

"My name is Stephanie." I said quietly.

"Oh, yes, I forgot you are getting all hoity-toity. Anyway, Sister told us just last week at our catechism class at St. Angelus, that we shouldn't be playing with boys at our age. You do know about 'occasion of sin' don't you?" I didn't, but it sounded bad. I wished I wasn't walking with them, but seeing the bullies sitting on some rocks behind some bushes, I pressed closer.

"You don't go to St. Angelus like we do, do you?" Theresa said

" I go to a Ukrainian church in Boston." I tilted my chin up, not at all eager to talk about my Ukrainian life.

"So, you're not a Catholic" Mary Catherine said, looking horrified. I thought it best not to go into the Catholic Church changeover to Orthodox part. I crossed my fingers.

"I am too a Catholic, my mother says so." They challenged me immediately,

"If you're Catholic why don't you go to St. Angelus?"

"Well, that's an Irish church and we're Ukrainian."

"You could still go there, if you were really a Catholic!"

"I go to a Ukrainian church." I repeated.

"So you can't be Catholic!"

I decided to try some other group next day, but the girls were waiting for me. They began to ask what I was learning in my First Holy Communion class. I told them I hadn't started any classes yet. They were horrified.

"You mean you haven't started to learn the 'The Penny Catechism' yet?"

They took turns asking me questions like, 'So, is God present on your altar?'

'Do you even know what the Holy Sacrament is?' 'I bet you don't know about Plenary Indulgences or Purgatory?' and 'Do you know the difference between a mortal sin and a venial sin?' I didn't know how to tell them that maybe the priest had used those words in a sermon, but they would have been in Ukrainian, and I wouldn't have understood such complicated words.

"You'd better take good care of yourself, because when you die, you're going straight to Hell," Mary Catherine said. "Yes, for sure." Theresa agreed, adding with a smirk, "Oh and don't forget to find yourself a Penny Catechism! It might save you."

199

On the Monday morning after they had made their First Holy Communion, they described their exciting day in every detail. Their dresses were wide and frilly. Their veils came down from sparkly crowns. The nuns made a special party at the church right after mass for the thirty children and each received a very special Holy Card from the hand of the priest himself. Later, at their different homes, each had a big supper with their many relatives. They described their presents in so much detail, I almost cried. At one house, an uncle had played his accordion all afternoon. Theresa's grandmother brought the little chocolate circles with the white dots on them, so she and her brother and sister went out back of their house and played mass.

"We made a moss altar, and I got my new, nun doll and my brother pretended to be the priest. He used the candy for hosts. I knew it wasn't Jesus, of course, but you know, I still got a shiver."

I was glad when we reached my house. Mary Catherine waved goodbye and said piously, "I'll pray for you, because I don't know anyone else who needs it more." When the last day of school arrived, I couldn't decide what made me happier: to be forever free of Miss Egar, or not having to walk with the girls for the summer anyway.

Bully Patrick and his brother spent summers at their grandfather's farm in Canton, and their two friends did something else, so once summer vacation began, I had no need to worry about confronting them. For a few days after a Saturday matinee at the Oriental, the gang would be in story mode, but the rest of the week, it was baseball. Of course, I was only a spectator. I liked rainy days better, because I spent them at Lidgy's house. He let me read his exciting Dick Tracy comics, and eventually taught me all the card games he knew, and of course, beat me every time.

The happiest times though were in the early mornings, before I went out to find the boys or Lidgy, and the evenings when I went to bed. It was then that I read my own three books, or the ones Anna brought for me from a library near her work. The day she told me the library had moved and she wouldn't get any more books, I was horrified.

I waited for Lidgy by his back steps on the day he usually went to the Blue Hill Avenue library. I knew Streychu let him go there by himself. When he came out the door, I begged him to take me with him. He wouldn't even answer me until I stamped my foot and threatened to tell Streyna he was being mean to me.

When we got to the library, I whispered to him to let me pick one book for myself. He could take four at a time, so wouldn't three fat ones be enough for him this week? He picked up his four books and ignored me. The next week, I argued with him the whole way. He told me to shut up and he'd see if I could get my own card. When he asked at the desk, the lady stared at me for a long while. She told him that while there wasn't an actual age limit for a card, I seemed to be too young. I told her I was going into third grade. She handed him an application with great reluctance.

I asked Mama to sign the application, and of course, she absolutely forbade me to go to the library with Lidgy. "I no vant you go cross Blue Hill Avenue!" That night, I followed Anna to her desk in the reception room. She looked tired, so I hoped she might not pay as much attention as usual. I put the application on the desk saying that it was OK with Mama if I went with Lidgy. "Did you ask Mama to sign it?" she asked. "Yes, but she was in a hurry and she said you could do it for her." She gave a quick look onto my innocently arranged face and didn't see my fingers crossed behind me. She filled it out and signed Mama's name. She usually signed for Mama for unimportant things, but I worried that she might mention this to Mama. I remembered that Mama was gone when Anna came home from school, and Mama was in bed when Anna was getting up, so by Saturday, Anna wouldn't remember to say anything. I didn't have to worry, maybe.

The next day, Lidgy didn't want to go to the library with me, so I went by myself. I had no trouble finding my way, and crossing with the light at Blue Hill Avenue wasn't the least bit scary. The librarian checked my application thoroughly, made out a card, and told me, in a serious voice, that the date she would stamp on the card in the books would tell me when the books had to be back in the library.

"Remember, they have to be back in TWO WEEKS, or else you have to pay a penny a day for each book." I just smiled. I knew I would never be late. Four books would never take me two weeks to read.

Once I began to look into the books on the shelves, I was excited by how many I had to choose from. I looked up to see a librarian walking over to me. "I'm Mrs. McGillvary. I think I can help you," she said and proceeded to run her finger slowly over the backs of the books. I tried to tell her I wanted to pick them out myself, but before I figured out how to say it, she had put four very thin books in my arms.

Indeed, I didn't need two weeks to finish those books. They were written for first graders and were quite dull. I decided I wouldn't wait for Lidgy. Another problem crossed through my head as I was walking home. If Mama ever saw me with an armful of books, she might guess that I was sneaking off to the library. I decided not to read in the house when she was home, even if she was sleeping, instead, I found a couple of trees in the woods that had reasonably comfortable nests of branches and read there until my skin was dented and red. I found a place behind some wood in the cellar to hide the books before I went upstairs. Since Tato had no interest in my relations with Mama and never inquired into the nuances of what Mama forbade me to do, I could bring my books up into the house after she went to work and read in total comfort.

I took other small precautions. I always went to the library when Mama was sleeping, but just in case she might have wakened, I took the path that started right at the blackberry patch beside the cellar door at the back of the house. The spray of thorny branches reached almost to the door and was so tall she couldn't see me, even if she was looking right down from her bedroom window. Having made all these decisions by myself, I felt quite grown-up.

First Holy Communion Class

One Sunday morning in July, the priest announced that children, seven or older, who hadn't yet taken First Holy Communion, should come to a beginning class on Friday afternoon in the church basement. Classes would continue until Labor Day. On the subway going home, Tato told me since Lidgy was going to the classes this year, I would be going too, even though it would be two more years before I was the right age.

"It will be better for you to go with Ladju now, than to go alone next summer."

I sighed. I wouldn't have minded waiting a couple of years. Mama began arguing with Tato about whether Lidgy could be trusted to take care of me. With Mama engrossed in the argument, I went to the front of the subway to feel the rush of cold air through the open grill, but almost immediately, she came to take me back.

"Good place to die if we hit another train," she said.

On our first trip to the church, Lidgy, full of his new responsibilities, made me sit quietly beside him. He made all the proper transfers between streetcars and subway, somberly and carefully. He made sure we took the right street to the church.

We quickly saw that the classes would be something to be endured. The priest spoke only in Ukrainian and mostly in churchy words we didn't know. Mama and Tato didn't talk much about God things. Tato might talk about people who looked religious, but didn't act like Christians, and I often heard both Mama and Tato asking God why he was punishing them, but that was all. Tato did teach me two prayers, which he didn't translate. Anna said they were the same as the 'Our Father' and the 'Hail Mary,' which the Catholic kids said. She said them once in English to me, and I only understood some of it. She did give me a thin book called, 'Bible Stories for Little Children,' a reward from her German Sister School days. I immediately read all the stories, though I had to read the many unfamiliar words more slowly. Some of the pictures were scary, but the stories didn't seem to relate to anything the priest was saying at our classes. I realized that I still wouldn't be able to answer the Irish girls' questions from their Penny Catechism.

I tried hard at first to concentrate on what the priest was saying to us, but within a short time I began thinking about last Saturday's movie with smart aleck, menacing Jimmie Cagney. Then the bug-eyed face of Paul Muni spooked me. He became the ogre in a story from the Grimm's Fairytales that I had talked the librarian into letting me take out. She told me those stories often scared little children. She was right, but I wouldn't admit it to her. A sudden burst of giggles from the toe poking under the table brought me back. The priest glared, and said in English, so we would be sure to understand, "For vat you doing dis? You Mama and Tato gonna be mad, you no gonna be shut up!"

On the second trip, Lidgy was more relaxed. We moved up and down the subway car, laughing at every lurch. When I landed in a lady's lap, she glared so hard at me, we ran to the front and held to the grill with claw-like fingers. I was thrilled to find a penny at my foot. I put it in my sock. I hoped that if I did die right here, something in me would leave my body and travel up through space, past the stars, past the moon and up, and up to the heaven the girls had told me about. But probably not because heaven seemed to belong to Eleanor, Mary Catherine and Theresa.

As we went out the church doors, Lidgy said he had a nickel and that the store where the Greek sold apricot 'shoe leather' was not far. He had a little swagger in his voice when he said he knew exactly how to get there.

"We turn at the broken hydrant, and then again when we see the wrestling poster with The Mongol Masher and Shirley Curls on it. It's on the left side."

It wasn't so easy, though. There were posters on every street corner. Lidgy guessed that the right corner was where a drunk was sleeping. I tried to hold Lidgy's hand, when we had to step out into the street to get around the man, but he wouldn't let me. Lidgy found the store after only a few backtracks and one encounter with a loud-talking drunk who seemed to want us to give him some money.

As we entered the dim room, a man came the counter looking annoyed. We heard some arguing in a strange language coming out of the back room. The display cases held no Necco wafers, Hershey bars, or licorice drops, like the store near the school did. Here, we saw, in the first section, two grey, sticky lumps, one with nuts, one without. Next to them were some black, gluey things that Lidgy said were figs. Then came a heap of sugary brown lumps. At last at the far end, we recognized the apricot shoe leather, stiff and orange, and rolled in a thick tube. Lidgy put his nickel on the counter, and I added the penny in my sock. The Greek unrolled a handspan of the shoe leather, sliced it with a long, razor-thin knife, rerolled it and put it on the counter. It was smaller than I had hoped for. I pointed to some mustard colored rolls and asked,

"What is that like?"

"Dat's anodder kind."

"Oh," I said. Outside the creaky door, Lidgy measured the edge of the apricot tube in thumbnail widths and laying the sheet on a concrete protrusion from the wall beside him, he sliced off a thin piece with his jackknife. I thought it was too short, but knew that I couldn't argue with him about measurements. I took the first tart bite. It yielded its sweetness grudgingly. When I tired of chewing, I rolled a piece around in my mouth to let it soften savoring the rich, fruity flavor. A fine drizzle started, so we began to run over the tricky cobblestones toward the subway.

Tato was at the Harmon Street stop with a large umbrella against the now heavy rain. Halfway down Harmon Street, the questioning began. When did you leave the church? How long did you wait for the subway? How long did you wait at Ashmont station? How long in Mattapan Square station? I let Lidgy do the talking, but I crossed my fingers in case it would help. He said that the priest had kept us longer than usual and he stretched the waiting times at the various stations to the limit.

"Besides, I don't really know, because there weren't any clocks around to tell time," he said a little too emphatically.

Tato sighed, looked at my innocent, crooked smile, and assessed Lidgy's pinkening cheeks. "It is almost 6:30. So, whatever you did, don't do it again. You shouldn't be adding to my worries like this."

That week, Lidgy got his father's old watch, because his father bought himself a new one. Lidgy decided that getting home at 6:15 wouldn't make Tato mad unless it was raining. Thereafter, he carefully timed little deviations for us on the way home: a stop off into the Public Gardens; a ride for several stations on a different line; a stop to go into a downtown toy store. The extra fare after a stop off was accomplished by ducking under the turnstile. I was more successful than Lidgy because he was taller, but then he always had an extra nickel for when he got caught, and I didn't.

At the last class, the priest told us to come back in two weeks. On that Saturday, we would go to our first confession. On Sunday, we would have our First Communion. On the way home, Lidgy and I slumped low in our seats. I asked him what he thought about God.

"Does he really sit up in heaven," I said, "and does he really know everything we are thinking, because that's what the girls are always telling me."

"I don't know," he answered. "I suppose the priest was telling us about that, but I couldn't understand him. Does your Tato say anything about God?'

"No, nothing much."

"Neither does mine. Hard to figure out how God could know what's in your mind every minute. And not just us, he's gotta watch every single person in the whole, wide world, and that must be gazillions of people."

"And how does he remember it all?" I asked

We sat uncomfortably in our own thoughts the rest of the way home.

The Indian Princess

The Thursday before school was to start, I joined the gang at the model-T.

"The leader of the cowboys is 'Tex'," Danny drawled. "He looks like Gary Cooper. The posse will be Cal and Bill and Sam. I'll be Tex, and you'll be Cal…. and you'll be…". Frank and Sully and Lidgy fell into line only after considerable arguing about how it was time for someone else besides Danny to be the leader of the cowboys. Andy took his usual part of a good Indian, a scout who helped the cowboys, because he owned a bow and arrow that his father had made. The arrow had a ping-pong ball on one end of a long, thin dowel. Turkey feathers were glued at the other end. The ball annoyed Andy, but he was afraid to rip it off. He told everyone to call him Hiawatha today. Danny said that Tommy was on his way, and he'd be the Indian Chief.

Then Danny pointed at me and said, "and you'll be the princess. You belong to the Chief." I stared at him, confused. "Me? An Indian Princess?" He pointed down to the model T. "You go over to the car and pretend it's the Indian Chief's teepee. I leaped joyously over the boulders that poked out of the water and pulled myself over the side.

I stood on the rotting flooring in front of the front passenger seat and turned to face the seat. When I closed my eyes, I could see the flapping sides of a teepee, just like the one in last week's Tom Mix serial at the Oriental. I opened my eyes and began to stir an imaginary pot on the cracked leather of the seat.

I listened to their yelping "Hiya!! Hiya!" As they made their way up the side of the Rockies. Then their calls curled back at me from behind the trees and bushes that hid the backyards of the two-deckers on Harmon Street. I heard them holler for Tommy. Then they were quiet. I stopped my stirring and turned my head to the right, straining for a sound of them. They burst out screaming from the bushes to my left. They sounded more like Indians than cowboys, but they weren't always fanatics about accuracy.

Danny caught my nearest arm and pulled me out of the car. Frankie grabbed my other. "Pretend you're afraid" Lidgy whispered from behind.

I began to wail theatrically. The boys pulled so hard and fast, I couldn't stay on the stones. My feet came down into the mucky, iridescent water. Instinctively, I curled my toes to hold my shoes on. Danny and Frankie pushed me up against a tree at the edge of the swamp and pulled my arms back around the tree. Andy pulled a rope from his pocket, and he and Sully did some arguing about how to tie my wrists together.

I decided that an Indian Princess would be proud and defiant when she was being captured by a pack of cowboys, so I stiffened my body and throwing back my head, yelled that the Chief was on his way to get them all. But inside myself was only exultation. They chose me to be an Indian Princess! A real Princess, and not just some nameless character minding the pretend horses or making whooping noises from the end of the line of the cowboys. I was finally an important part of their story. I looked over to Lidgy to see if he was proud of me. He was looking at Danny.

I put a little more drama into my wailing.

"You will remain here, until yo'ah Chief returns owah hosses." Danny drawled in his best Texas voice.

"Yeah, we're gonna go find him and he's gonna find out who's boss around here." Frankie said.

"Let's go boys!" Sully yelled. They swirled away twisting back to brandish their weapons at me: Frankie with a hacked up long, skinny piece of wood that he called his rifle, Andy with his ping-pong tipped arrow and bow and the rest with the toy guns they had gotten for Christmas. They gave a whoop and faded into a stand of scrub oak.

I stopped my wailing and rested contentedly against the tree trunk I closed my eyes and let my breathing settle in around my joy. After a while, I began to get a little restless. My head swiveled back and forth as I tried to guess how they would return. From the time Lidgy had become my protector, I had come to know every path through my magical block. Now six, almost seven, I didn't need him anymore to show me through the blackberry patch. I knew where the blueberry bushes hid in the middle of a scrub oak patch. I knew just about where each poison ivy clump hid out and where to look for frogs and snakes. If I'd been asked for daisies, buttercups, wild geraniums, asters, jack-in-the-pulpits or the elusive lady's slipper, I could have gone right to where each of them lived. I knew which trees had the best branches to nest into for a good morning of reading if the boys weren't around, and which were best for the pure pleasure of climbing to their tops.

I ignored the streetcar noise from Cummins Highway as I strained to hear any noises from the other three streets. I only heard a sputtering car. I heard Danny's mother calling his baby sister.

I began to sense that too much time had passed to accommodate the proposed story and a small unease began in me. I thought of how different this summer felt than the ones before. Last summer, I felt that I was part of the gang, even with all their tricks on me, but this summer, almost every day, the boys would ask me why I didn't go and play with the girls, as if I'd want to play with those Irish girls who only played with dolls. I had begun to understand that if it weren't for Lidgy being my cousin, I wouldn't be playing with the boys at all.

This summer, instead of just letting me make Indian noises or run behind them at the end of their line, Danny gave me more jobs to do. He'd tell me to go find a special ball he had left in his yard, or to get some water from Frank's outside faucet in the little canteen he carried. Other times he'd tell me to be a lookout for another gang who sometimes played enemies with us. When I got back with my report, I sometimes couldn't find them.

Even playing cards changed. One day when I got to the rock circle, they all looked up and I could see them squeezing giggles behind their straight lips. Danny said "We're playing a new game today. It's called Strip Poker. Guess you should go home, because it's only for big guys." Eddy made a funny noise in his nose, and then frowned into his cards. I had never heard of Strip Poker. I knew I could play the usual, easy version of poker, so I hunkered down and asked for the rules. Danny gave a quick and confusing review, which included taking off a piece of clothing every time you lost a hand. I won the first hand, but began to lose every one after that. Since I only had on a dress and panties, two shoes and two sox, it only took five plays to get me down to my panties. I couldn't look up at them, but I heard the soft, snickery catches in their throats. Suddenly I knew they had rigged this up to get a good laugh out of me. Furious at myself for the sob that suddenly came banging up through my throat, I decided that if this were what it took to be a real part of the gang, I would do it. "Deal" I said. I worked on getting Mae West onto my face, right up to the time I had to take off my panties and add the to the pile in the center of the circle. I squatted sidewards and squeezed myself with the longest arms I could make.

"Jeez, will you look at that." Danny said with disgust. "She ain't got no boobs at all. Looks just like a regular baby."

"Looks like any old boy without all his parts." Billy said.

"What a cheat." Eddy said and scooped up the cards.

"Listen, I heard of guys that don't have all their parts." Danny said.

"Like when they got 'em blown off, pxhh! With a bomb or something like that in the war. Jeez, I wonder how the hell they can pee?"

They turned away from me and began to share stories of a variety of anatomical disasters while the cards were dealt yet again. I reached out for my clothes, swiveled to put my back to them and tried to dress without standing up. When my dress was on, I snatched up my shoes and panties and fled down the path to the privacy of a blackberry picking spot where I was able to put them back on. I was crying too hard to pay attention to the painful rakes of the thorny stalks on my bare skin.

That last game of cards should have showed me they weren't really letting me be in their story. They hated me because I was a stupid, sissy-girl, and this was my punishment. As I began to sob, I began to struggle, and the rope pinched into my wrists.

I heard my mother yelling for me distantly from the back piazza "Stel----la! Stel----la! Verr you are! You commit home, right now. I gottit to go to vork. You commit home."

Now, however, unable to move, my anger flared up to a white heat. The boys were probably watching her from somewhere on Harmon St, and I could just see them laughing their heads off at her. It was all her fault that no one liked me. Lidgy's mother never yelled for him, so they didn't even know that she talked just like my mother.

The whine and hum of the mosquitoes grew. The dreaded mosquito time had arrived. I felt the pierce and sting on every part of my skin. I shouted, "Danny, Sully, Frank, Lidgy, Andy, Eddy…" even as I knew that no one would come.

Then I tried "Tah…….to! Tah…….to!" I always called him 'my Dad' when I was with the boys, so they wouldn't razz me for using the Ukrainian word, 'Tato' but my brain was working on some other level now. I remembered that he had a wallpaper job today, so he'd be working late. Besides, he might have gotten off the trolley one stop earlier for some of Streychu's home brew. If he did that, he wouldn't be walking down Harmon Street at all. And certainly, Lidgy, by now safe in his house from all the mosquitoes, wouldn't be telling my father that I was tied to a tree in the swamp.

As the itching intensified, I pulled more frantically against the rope. As I did this, I noticed that if I pulled one arm away from the other, the loop tightened on that wrist, making a looser loop on the other wrist. After a few tries, I slid one wrist out, and I was free. Did they make those loops as another test of my stupidity? At least now I knew. I really was just a dumb girl, just as dumb as they thought I was.

I raced down the path to my house and up the back stairs into the kitchen. The clock said 5:30. I went out onto the back piazza and threw myself onto the cot, rubbing myself into the bedclothes like a dog on a pile of stink. The rubbing brought on an unbearable burning. I ran to the bathroom, pulling my dress over my head as I went. I filled the tub with cold water and sat shivering in it. Tears came again when I thought of how happy I'd been lately thinking that Lidgy and I were bosom-buddies, how happy I'd been when Danny told me I'd be the Indian Princess. Why did everything have to change? Did I do something to make Lidgy mad? But then, maybe Lidgy had hated me from the beginning. He had only played with me and talked to me, because he had been forced to take care of me. The boys had hated me too, but they didn't want to make things hard for Lidgy. Boys always stuck together. They probably wanted to get rid of me for a long time now, and tying me up in the swamp was the only way they could get rid of me once and for all.

Suddenly, the 'Nevers' began to shake through me. 'Never' play stories in the woods again. 'Never' go to the Saturday movies with the boys again. 'Never' watch them play ball again. 'Never' play cards or marbles with them again. 'Never' play with Lidgy again. 'Never sleep over at Lidgy's house.' Never! Never! Never!

When I heard Tato slowly climbing up from the cellar where he left his wallpapering box, I could tell he was tired. I dressed quickly and ran into the kitchen to light the gas under the borsht Mama had left for supper. It wasn't until I put the pot on the hot pad on the table that he looked at my face.

"What happened to you? Didn't you know that the mosquitoes were biting you? You are old enough now to know better. Go look at your face." I went to the bathroom, and holding onto the sink, I jumped to the level of the mirror and caught a brief look at my distorted face. I almost started to tell him what had happened, but as I looked into his sad eyes, I knew I couldn't. He was sad enough already. He said no more, just stared out at the birch trees across Harmon Street.

If it had been an ordinary summer night, I would rinse out the dishes and go outside to join the street games. But tonight I hesitated. I went to the front piazza and hugged the wall so I could see down Greenfield Road, but not be seen from below.

The streetlights had just come on, though the darkness was only tentative. A variety of kids were ambling up Greenfield. The gang was already sitting on the curb under the light, Lidgy right in the middle of them. Mary Catherine, Eleanor and Theresa, stood on the corner watching the approach of the boys from more distant streets. How could I go down there tonight? What would I say to Lidgy? To the boys?

I tossed my head and put a snarly look on my lips, like one of the rustlers just before Tom Mix caught him last week at the movies. No, they would just laugh. Maybe a know-it-all smirky look likes Bette Davis? No, I needed a really threatening look. I made big Paul Muni eyes, but lost it immediately. Lidgy would know it was a fake face.

I went down the front steps and looked through the glass center panel of the front door. I watched and waited, trying not to scratch at my bites. The light under the streetlamp had begun to make a golden cone down to the pavement. Danny had an arm up against the street lamp and was pressing his face into it so he couldn't see while he was counting to a hundred. Before he yelled, "Ready or not here I come." I had opened the door, and with my faced arranged in an impervious Joan Crawford, I raced down the street to find a place to hide.

Shoes for Third Grade

The next morning, a Saturday, when Mama woke after only a few hours of sleep to go to the bathroom, she yelled into the kitchen that we were going down to Mattapan Square after lunch for some school shoes. I felt an abrupt panic. My books were due at the library today and the library didn't open until one. If I went down to Mattapan Square for shoes after lunch, then back home to get my library books and then to the library, I would never make it to the Oriental for the two-o'clock double feature. Anger pounded through me. I looked down to my feet. My sock-covered toes poked like white balloons out of each sneaker. I really did need some new shoes, but I couldn't go today!

I climbed the sour cherry tree in the grassy corner of Greenfield and Harmon. It had a reasonably comfortable cradle of branches, and the leaves had gotten thick enough so Mama couldn't see me when she leaned out from the kitchen window. I slid the beloved bookmark from my library book and once again admired the delicacy of the ink drawn flower with the windblown yellow petals. I supposed that if I really wanted to get right with God before confession, I should throw it away. Or maybe give it to Ksenya, admit I stole it, and ask her to put it back into some book at the Beacon Hill House. I could almost, but not quite, see myself doing that.

The tree felt sticky whenever I readjusted myself, but fortunately, it was only my sweat, not sap. I stopped reading when I saw Mama leaning out of the kitchen window with her teacup. The iceman had just squeezed his little horn on the side of the truck where he sat holding the reins of his horses. Mama turned the card in the window so that the size of the ice block that fitted into our icebox showed right side up. The iceman scraped away the insulating straw, grabbed one of the huge cubes with his tongs and heaved it onto his leather covered back. Mama opened the door for him so he could bring it upstairs.

The iceman and his horses had barely moved around the corner, when I heard the ragman shouting. "Eya recks! Eya recks!" Anna had told me that he was saying, "I have rags! I have rags!"

Actually, he had everything but rags. His wagon was full of pots, pans, dishes, knives and forks, pitchers, pictures, and little pieces of carpet. When he had some room, he'd buy things from people if they weren't too used up. Mama ran down with a breadboard that Tato had found in someone's trash and had sanded for a long time. She haggled in Polish and Yiddish for a short while, before she took his coins. The Irish ladies stayed on their porches and shook their heads when the ragman called to them.

Next to trundle up was Andreas, the green-grocer, who sang out "Fruits, fruits, a rooty-toot toots!" and then a long three beat chant, "Potatoes! Tomatoes! And Onions!" He threw a rope around the fire hydrant to hold the horse when Mama came running out. Since he was Greek, and the words he sang were the only ones he knew in English, he and Mama haggled with their fingers, popping out a certain number for the price, and pointing to the marks on his scale from time to time.

Mama picked over the potatoes and chose fourteen, two for every day of the week. She first chose large ones, but when she checked the coins in her apron pocket, she chose smaller ones. "My own potatoes will be ready soon," she told him in Ukrainian. He tried to tempt her with tomatoes and beans, but she had been harvesting hers already, so she just shook her head. The ladies along the street who came out to buy from Andreas did not do any haggling. Other vendors came and went, some pulling small carts themselves. They offered a variety of languages and goods. They aimed their sing-song up to our kitchen windows where Mama sat, stopping so could see their offerings. Mostly, she just shook her head.

I preferred watching Mama haggle from the cherry tree than go with her to the shops along Blue Hill Avenue. She took me to translate whatever few American words didn't come readily to her tongue. With the Italians, she was aloof, unmoved by their effusive arm swinging, or their merry-eyed, flattering speech. With the Greeks and Syrians, she walked through the displays shaking her head and made herself look like she was at the point of leaving. 'Whaddaya want,' 'I vant rice, but I go down da strit.' 'So, I give two pennies off a pound' 'Nu, down da strit I get big nice rice four pennies offa pound.' 'You tink I'm made from money lady? So, hell's wid it, three cents!'

At the Jewish Kosher butcher shop, she rejected piece after piece of meat, until finally, the butcher said he was showing her the very best one. Then the price haggling dance began. She insulted the meat, he insulted her judgment, she offered a lower price, and he countered with a higher. She left with the meat and a glower. When I looked back, the butcher would be smiling at our backs, and when I looked up at Mama she'd be smiling too. "I can get my price from him every time. He's a real fool." When the wife was behind the counter, Mama took whatever she offered, since she had learned that the lady refused to play the game.

The haggling at the Five and Dime embarrassed me the most. She'd try to haggle for a kitchen ladle with some poor kid of a clerk. If she saw a pair of gloves with a thread hanging off the thumb, she'd give that a try. I would move away and ignore her calls to translate. I changed myself into Shirley Temple, leaned on a counter, and pretended I just happened to be in the store watching this crazy woman like every one else.

Mr. Tsapar always came last on Saturdays, driving by just before lunchtime. After his black truck stopped at Lidgy's house, he turned into Harmon St. to park at our back door. Though he didn't beep or sing out, Mama came right down. He pointed out the crates with the biggest, fattest chickens, but Mama knew how many coins were left in her apron pocket and inevitably pointed at the smaller ones.

Mr. Tsapar, a tall, dignified, white haired man, dispatched the chicken with a swift whack of his cleaver on a wooden block tied tightly over a back fender of the truck. He handed the chicken to Mama who held it aimed so that the gushing blood wouldn't get on her apron. Once, the chicken got away from her and I gasped to see it run down Harmon St. without its head, leaving a trail of blood behind. Mama walked after it calmly, picking it up where it finally fell. She never haggled with Mr.Tsapar. Maybe it was because he was Ukrainian.

Finally done with the vendors, Mama put some hardboiled eggs and a few cut-up tomatoes on the tiny piazza table along with a loaf of bread, some butter and mayonnaise. I was glad to see it was only 11:30. It would help if we went early. I went to my cot at the far end to eat, hoping she wouldn't see the mosquito bites on my face. Everyone's face glistened a little in the heat.

Mama picked up the dishes and without looking at me said,

"Go wash your face and change your dress! We are going for some shoes."

Tato slipped me my movie nickel as I scurried off. I wondered if Mama knew that he did this every Saturday. I decided she probably did, but didn't want to fight with him about it. He always gave Mama any money he earned with his odd jobs, so she could divide it into her envelopes, he held back one nickel for me and a few for the beer he bought after the Sunday service down in the church basement. When he didn't work, he didn't have the nickel, so he just shook his head sadly. He still had his beer at church though, because Streychu would always buy him one.

When I opened the closet I shared with Anna in 'her' room, I saw that the one dress I owned had become three. The two new ones were faded a little and some of the hems were torn, but they were not like Anna's hated, heavy brown and navy dresses from long ago. These were probably from Varvakha, whose daughter, Olga, was a little older than me. I chose the red and navy plaid with a wide bib collar. It was only a little bit too big. I tried to tuck my toe balloons back into the sneakers, with no success.

Mama walked rapidly ahead of me, her strong stocky figure moving arrow straight down the middle of Harmon Street. Running to catch up, I saw Danny on his second story front porch. Frankie, in his side yard, stared over at us, too. I kept my eyes down on my white balloon toes and held them to a slower, more careless gait. Mama, just then, turned around and hollered, "You comit faster, you go too slow." I saw both Danny and Frank throwing their heads back to laugh.

I had told her over and over that in English you say 'come' not 'comit,' 'want' not 'vanit,' 'do' not 'doovit.' Tato didn't speak that way, but he was one of only a few at the church who spoke really good English. Most of the men and women sounded a lot like Mama. Wouldn't it be just as easy to say the words right? But no matter how often I told Mama, she never seemed to change.

Murray's was a small clothing store with a section for shoes in the back. Mr. Murray, a red-faced, red-haired beefy man, did the selling of almost everything except for the things in the woman's section. His wife, small and dressed in black, moved restlessly through the stacked underwear and hanging dresses patting things into place or refolding them. I had never been in the shoe department, because someone always gave Mama her daughter's outgrown clothes and shoes. I wondered why no shoes this year.

Mama marched to the back wall and pointed me to a bench. Mr. Murray followed.

"She gottit have shoes for school on Tuesday. Look vat she do to dem shoes."

"Well, yes, children do grow." He knelt in front of me and removed my torn sneakers. I saw Mama's startled face when she saw all my mosquito bites, then noticed that my sox were damp and dirty. She glared at me, while speaking to Mr. Murray.

"Ve vannit shoes from ledder,"

"Leather shoes" I said to Mr. Murray.

"Make plenty big, she growit too much. Her feet bigger my friends' girls even they older, oddervise I take dey shoes." He came back with several boxes.

"How much each?" she asked.

She chose the cheapest. Mr. Murray put the shoe on me and pushed with his thumb to show her there was a lot of room in the toe. She shook her head and said, "Bigger." I felt tears of embarrassment burn in my eyes and wished I still had my canvas shoes on, because I would have run out of there.

He brought another size and tugged on the shoelaces until the holes met in the middle. He put three fingers down on the toe box, and then slid my heel up and down in the shoe. "These are too big."

"No," Mama said. She cocked her head at me. "You valkit now."

I got up and walked. My heels rose up with each step. I almost tripped.

"Gut" she said, turning to face Mr. Murray. "You can makit cheaper?"

"No" he said pointing, "The price is on the box."

"I no can payit so much."

I hung my head and studied my fingers. Mr. Murray looked away and was silent for a minute. Then he said softly, "I wish I could, but I can't. I am barely staying in business as it is."

Mama looked at me and I translated the first part into Ukrainian, "Ya be lyubev, ale ne mozhu," but couldn't think of how to say 'barely staying in business as it is.'

I untied the leather shoes and put the canvas shoes back on. Mama shook her head a few more times. She stood up and started to walk out, but then returned and opened the envelope and gave him all that was in it. I never knew if she had given him the right amount, or if he gave her the shoes for whatever she had, because at that point, I walked out to the street and leaned against a lamppost.

I stood by the curb when she stopped at the fish man's tiny store. Mama put the newspaper-wrapped mackerel into the bag with the shoes and grabbed my hand to cross Blue Hill Avenue, this time not at any light, but in the middle of a block. She glared left and right, willing the drivers to make way for her. She let me go once we had crossed.

I stayed close behind Mama on the way home. If I could only have gone straight up Blue Hill Avenue to the library after getting the shoes, I could have saved so much time. Now I was sure I'd be late for the movies. If I walked fast enough, maybe I'd only miss the previews. But I'd really be mad if I missed the Tom Mix serial, because last week he had been tied to a tree, just like I had been in the swamp, and the Indians had piled brush around his feet and you could see one of them coming very close with a flaming torch. But then, they would probably start the next episode with the man with the torch much farther away, so Tom Mix's horse could get loose and have time to trample him down. Then Tom Mix would somehow be able to get his hands untied and the horse would somehow be right there, and away he'd go. I figured I was lucky the boys had decided not to start a fire at my feet.

When Mama went upstairs, I ducked into the cellar door to get my books. Moving quickly, I entered the deep overhang of the blackberry bushes and raced down the path around the swamp, coming out on Cummins Highway, hot and sweaty. The library had never seemed so far away.

I hoped that at least Mrs. McGillvary wouldn't be there, but she was putting books on a shelf. I plunked the books up on the counter and just in time remembered to pull out my bookmark. I held it in my hand with my library card as I went to the children's section. "Well, what can I help you with this week?" Mrs. McGillvary said, moving toward me. I wanted to say, 'I don't have time, please, I don't need any help!' but said instead,

"I just want some fatter books. The ones last week were too skinny and I had to read them a lot of times."

She frowned, "But what kind of a story do you like?"

"It doesn't matter. I just like fatter books and not the ones for really little kids."

"There are books that are better for girls…"

"I don't care. I like them all." I was fidgeting from one foot to the other.

The bookmark was stuck to the card, so they came out together from my hand.

"What kind of a name is 'Chopek' dear?"

"Ukrainian." I answered, my heart beginning to pound as I wondered how to pluck the bookmark from her hand.

"Are your parents immigrants?"

"Yes, I guess." I answered, suddenly ashamed.

"Oh… Well…you seem so young…" She studied me again, frowning, and then brightening said, "What an unusual bookmark! It is hand painted, I believe."

I said nothing, but I felt my face get hot. I shouldn't have had it in the hand with my card.

"Where did you get this, my dear?"

I swallowed and crossed my fingers, "It's my sister's. She goes to Portia Law School and it's hers."

"Well, yes," she said slowly, looking very confused, "of course. Then let's get some new books for you." She traced her finger slowly down the spines. She opened a book, closed it and handed it to me. She went further down the shelves taking a book out, returning it, choosing another. I could feel tears behind my lids, and angrily dug a fist in to stop them. I remembered to say 'Thank you," ran to check them out, putting the bookmark safely into one of them.

All the way home I pondered angrily on why she was picking on me all the time. She didn't choose books for every child that came in to the library. She never once chose any for Lidgy when I had gone with him. But somehow she seemed to think I needed help and I didn't, I really didn't.

When I got back home, I began to feel like I was in an old familiar dream, the one where I was trying to get somewhere and my feet seemed to be in something sticky and I could barely lift them. When I got to the blackberry patch, ready to duck into the cellar door, I could see Mama in her garden, just a few feet away at the back of the house, chopping at some weeds with her hoe. She faced right at me, so even with only the slit of space I'd have to cross, she'd see me. I waited, every muscle tensing with the strain. Finally she finished the row and moved out of sight.

I pulled open the cellar door, stashed the books, retrieved my nickel from Tato's tool drawer where I had hidden it under a little box of nails, and slid it down into one of my sox. I felt it settle uncomfortably under my instep, but it would have to stay there, because I never knew when the bullies might find me. They'd stolen my nickel before.

I took a quick look and flung myself out of the cellar door into the blackberry patch. Why was everything so hard all the time, so hard!

When I got back on Cummins Highway and headed down to the Square, I suddenly felt overheated and exhausted. I wanted to stop and sit on a low wall to catch my breath, but I realized there were no other kids heading down to the Square. I was definitely going to be late. Sure enough, there was no line at the ticket booth either. I reached up with my nickel and took my ticket and ran through the velvet-curtained door. The first feature had begun. I'd never know how Tom Mix got loose! My body didn't begin to relax until I had found a seat and Buster Keaton's somber, bug-eyed face was making me laugh.

Finally, the second feature began, and I was back again in the serene dream world of yearning, love and sorrow. I walked home with the glide of Norma Shearer, feeling her lips making words from my mouth. As I turned onto Harmon Street, Tyrone Power took over my body, which was yearning to kiss Norma. Then I felt myself to be both of them at the same time, centered in their kiss, surrounded by their passion.

The jolt came when I passed the boys, lumped on Freddy's porch stairs. Danny shouted over, "So how's the Indian Princess?" The rest were writhing with laughter. I'd have to remember to walk a block further on Cummins Highway and come around the long way next Saturday. I looked straight ahead.

Mama was bustling between the kitchen and the piazza. "Ver you been? I callit you and callit you!!" Tato, coming out of the kitchen, just as I reached the top step, put a hand on my shoulder and gently moved with me to the piazza.

Mama had lightly buttered the boiled potatoes and made them fragrant with fresh dill from her garden. She did the same with the boiled beets but put a few drops of vinegar on them. She had cut the mackerel into four small pieces. Tato waited for Mama to sit down, before he spoke.

"Today, I got a letter from Ivashkiv. You remember the man who spoke at our rally against Polish atrocities? He told me about how many Ukrainians are starving in the Russian part of Ukraine. Not just a few Ukrainians, oh God, no! Millions! He seems to know more than what was printed in the Svoboda last week. The New York Committee is asking each city for money so they can take some actions. I think we should have a big rally in November in some big place. We would advertise this time in English papers, and get all the Ukrainians in Boston for once to come together to tell Boston what is happening to our poor Ukrainians. We should get a better collection of money that way."

Mama's voice was high and sharp,

"Another rally! On top of all the concerts and plays you are already planning! You know you do most of the work, while the rest of them are fighting each other. And how much money do you think people can give? You know what I say about squeezing beets!"

I suddenly thought how much smarter Mama sounded when she spoke Ukrainian than when she spoke her usual stupid slapdash mixture of Ukrainian and English. I turned to hear what Tato would reply, but he seemed to be looking at something down on Harmon Street. When Mama said no more, he got up and went down to the cellar.

Third Grade, First Communion, and a Piano

The day after Labor Day, when I woke on the piazza, I carefully peeled the damp sheet from the tender, sunburned skin that always came after our trek to Carson Beach. Lidgy had stayed well clear of me throughout the day, which I understood was how it would now be. The heat of · yesterday had survived the night undiminished.

Ready to tiptoe through the kitchen, I saw Mama at the kitchen table. She had put out the milk and cereal and had even filled my Little Orphan Annie cup with cold Ovaltine. Since second grade, a piece of buttered bread to eat on the way to school was faster and quieter. If I got up a little later, I skipped eating altogether. I must have looked surprised at I sat to the feast.

"I slept last night," she said by way of explanation.

As I ate, she told me how she hated one of her teachers, Professor Derdiedas. "That wasn't his real name," she said smiling. "He taught us German, so that's why we called him that, you know: Der, Die, Das." I knew no German and almost asked her what was so funny about his name, but just watched her smile instead. She went on.

"He always chewed on his bottom lip, and if you didn't answer right, he would make a fist. He was quick to take the boys into the closet with his switch. Poor Tato went quite often. He didn't do that to the girls. I hope you have a nice teacher this year. I didn't like Miz Egarr. Now go get dressed."

I chose the pale yellow dress with tiny red and orange flowers. The red bow at the round white collar made it just perfect. I took a peek at my panties to see if they needed changing, but decided they could go another day. The shoes were nice, but too big. I knew I couldn't run in them.

Back in the kitchen, Mama made me a few curls on the top and front hair with the heated iron. She tied a red ribbon on a hank of my top hair. She didn't pull like she had on Sunday morning. I said "Goodbye" and she smiled at me again. I smiled back.

Mary Catherine, Eleanor and Theresa were waiting at the back stairs.

"I guess you won't be playing with the Harmon Street boys anymore." Eleanor said, "We heard what happened. I bet you thought Danny was just thrilled to have you hanging around all last summer! You never should've been playing with boys."

I caught one of the long toes of my new shoes on the ground and struggled to stay upright. Just ahead of us, Lidgy was tussling with Andy, and the other boys were trying to stomp on each other's feet. I didn't want to catch their eyes, so I just watched my feet lift and slide in and out of my shoes the rest of the way to school.

Checking the assignment sheet on the front door, I smiled to see I was to have Miss Frazier. The boys told me once that she was the best third grade teacher. The other teacher was cranky. So, they were wrong about doing a hex. This time, I hadn't done a hex, and I had gotten the best teacher anyway!

Indeed, Miss Frazier was sweet and calm and absolutely nothing like Miss Egar. When she spoke, she smiled and looked kindly into our eyes. She kept the boys' attention by giving out one little job after another, praising each of them lavishly for their great talents at the task.

When I got to my own corner, a group of girls from my class were jump roping. They motioned me to join them. They had two long ropes for Double Dutch. Later, a girl named Alice and I skipped rope facing each other. She knew the most rhymes. She said her mother taught her. The boys passed by, and I put on as happy a face as I could. I hoped they saw me, because I wanted them to know I didn't need them anymore.

The Harmon Street girls waited for me at my back stairs, as always. I hated their talk about God and Jesus and Mary, or the dolls they played with, or their big family parties. I thought it too risky to tell the girls that the next Sunday was to be my First Holy Communion.

On the morning of the review class and first confession, Lidgy walked ahead of me, and in the streetcar, sat between two people. I resolved not to cry in public. This was the way it was going to be. At the church, the priest spoke in Ukrainian. When he told us to think about the bad things we did, I could understand every word.

"When you go in with me for confession, you have to tell me what you did bad. I'm sure you know what is bad! Bad is when you hurt someone, maybe not always from hitting, but hurt them maybe with lies or mean words. Think hard now," he said sighing.

I couldn't really put my bad things into words very easily. I felt like I had done something bad when Mama told me how hard it was for her when I was born and that I wasn't a boy like Tato wanted. I felt like I had done something bad when Anna had had to take care of me when I was a baby, but I didn't know exactly what kind of sins they were, except that everyone in our house was hurt.

I knew about lying, of course. But did my lying count when I crossed my fingers behind me? I never really hurt anyone when I lied, did I? I only lied so someone wouldn't be mad at me, or so I wouldn't be yelled at. But, maybe I forgot to cross my fingers sometimes.

Stealing? Yes, the bookmark. Did I hurt the Beacon Hill boy who owned it? He probably never even noticed it. Liking a pretty picture was a sissy thing. I was sure I loved it more than he ever would. Was that a sin? But then, I did take some pennies from Anna's purse once. I felt a little relief that I could at least confess to that.

But I definitely wasn't sorry about the blood on Patrick's nose. He deserved it. He hurt me first. I looked at the others around me. They all looked confused. The priest shrugged.

"Nu, starting with you," he pointed to the first one on the bench, "come to me in back of the altar and you will tell me all your sins."

For the first time, I felt a sense of fear. If I didn't pass this test, I wouldn't get to wear the plain, but nicely white, georgette dress Mama had borrowed from Varvakha. Mama had carefully washed and pressed it and had even borrowed a veil. That had excited me more than the dress. If I failed, everyone at home would hate me. When it was my turn, I stopped at the door of the little room feeling funny in my stomach. He waved me in and pointed for me to kneel at his feet. He put a piece of cloth over my head.

"Well, tell me your sins," he said in Ukrainian.

I stared at the floor, my brain whipping back and forth between Ukrainian and English trying to think how to say bookmark.

"So," he said, before I got any words out. "Did you maybe take a few coins from your Mama's drawer?"

Relieved, I said, "Yes" though I had stolen from Anna. I thought again about mentioning the bookmark, but he was going on.

"And maybe did you say something not so nice to your father."

"Yes," I replied, glad to comply. I had my hands folded in front of me so I couldn't cross my fingers behind my back. I blinked my eyes. I had just told two real lies!

"All right then, you are forgiven." he said in Ukrainian. You say two Otche Nashes and five Bohorodetse Dyivos." That would be no problem, I knew those prayers. He said a prayer over me, made the Sign of the Cross, and I was dismissed. I hoped my other sins, especially the lies I just told, could just slide into the others and be forgiven or forgotten. I joined the others who were still kneeling. Outside at last, I ran after Lidgy, light with happiness. Lidgy looked sour. I wondered how his confession went, but I didn't dare ask.

Mama instructed me how to receive Communion. I was to open my mouth wide when the priest offered me the little spoon with the bread and wine in it, and I must not close my mouth until he turned the spoon in the space over my tongue and removed the spoon!

The next day, my hair was curled on both sides of my head as well as the back.

Mama carefully pulled on the gauzy, white, long sleeved dress. She stretched the cap over my head, and pulled a little of the curled hair out of either side of the cap, patting it into place. I loved the way the sheer veil came down from the bottom edge of the lace cap, down over my shoulders ending at the hemline of my dress. Varvakha had provided long white silk stockings as well. The white, Mary Janes someone else had given Mama were so tight, I could barely walk, but I said nothing because they looked just exactly right with the white stockings.

People smiled at me in the streetcar. I smiled back. I spent the streetcar ride examining the mass book Tato had given me at breakfast. I fingered the outline of the two angels staring at a chalice above an arrangement of rosy flowers and worked the gold clasp. I marveled at the solid gold color of the page edges when the book was closed. Tato had set the white ribbon, caught at the top of the binding, right at the beginning of the service. The words were written in the Old Slavonic of the church service, but sometimes when I stood by Tato instead of going up to the choir loft, I had read along in his prayer book, and it was close enough to the regular Ukrainian, so I could follow it.

The seven First Holy Communicants went down the aisle behind the priest marching in step with the choir's joyous opening hymn. We three girls filed into the left front pew, and the four boys took the right.

I had my little book opened before the priest began. The words I had been listening to and singing all my life came right off the page, through my eyes and onto my tongue. I sat, elated, glowing with the approval of the congregation. At communion, I remembered not to close my mouth, though the sting of the wine startled me.

We had our pictures taken on the basement stage by a man in the parish who had a photograph shop. Mama and Tato smiled at me whenever they caught my eye during lunch. My godmother, Tato's cousin-Marena, gave me a long box. I unwrapped it with a huge excitement. Inside, its eyes closed, was a doll, half my height, with shiny Shirley Temple curls. I lifted it out of the box. Its eyes popped open and stared at me.

"You be careful, now," Mama said. "This is a very special doll. Shirley Temple, you know. A very special present from your godmother. We will put it on the chair in the parlor when we get home, and you can look at it any time you want."

I was a little embarrassed to be holding it in my lap on the streetcar, and was happy to put it into one of the black chairs in the living room. I quickly learned that I shouldn't ever hold it when Mama was in the house, because she would take it right out of my hands and put it back into the chair. I tried to think of how to play with it whenever I was alone in the house, but I couldn't imagine how. I became content to let it be Mama's treasured living room decoration.

On Monday, the Irish girls were at the bottom of the back stairs. I almost told them about my First Holy Communion, the doll and my prayer book, but I knew it was safer to keep my two worlds apart.

The next Saturday, a long enclosed wagon, pulled by two horses, arrived at our front door and the driver and Tato and Streychu began to wrestle a huge padded object up to our living room. I was sure it would get stuck in the front stairwell, but it didn't. Mama told me later, that when Tato bought the design of the house, he made sure that the downstairs front door, the bend in the middle of the stairs and the French doors at the top of the stairs would be wide enough for a casket, so we could have a proper wake for whoever in the family died first.

When the object had been set in place in the living room, Tato peeled away the padding to reveal a piano. A piano for me? I had never really wanted one. I had plunked a few notes on Stella Daviskiba's piano when Tato went up to visit her father, but when Stella told me how hard it was to learn, I lost interest. Apparently, someone at church told Tato of an apartment that had to be emptied. If Tato helped, he could have the piano for free, but he had to pay for the cost of moving it to our house.

Mama told me that every Saturday morning, a Mrs. Graham would come to give me lessons. She had students stretched throughout Mattapan, including Stella Daviskiba. My lesson would start at eleven and end a half hour later, and would cost thirty cents. Music books would be extra, but Stella's mother said she'd lend us Stella's old books.

"I don't have thirty-cents in my envelopes for lessons," Mama said, "but Anna told me she can give me an extra thirty cents for her room and food, because she got a raise from $10 to $14 a week! Something President Roosevelt did. I didn't get anything extra for my jobs, so I don't know, but for now, you can have the lessons." She wagged a finger at me. "I won't be able to know whether you are doing her lessons right, but if the teacher tells me anything bad about you, you will have no more lessons."

Mrs. Graham was small, thin and red haired under a small, off-center hat. She never gave praise, nor did she give any blame. She focused on how my defective passages should be practiced. She listed the problem measures in my notebook, crossing out the ones I had conquered and putting a new checkmark on the ones still needing work. She was neither friendly nor unfriendly.

I never had the terrors friends told me about when they had their recitals, because Mrs. Graham never offered any. She was my teacher until I finished high school and never changed her teaching techniques. I sometimes wondered if she would recognize me if I met her on the street. But on the whole, to be exposed to neither praise nor blame worked just fine for me. It freed me to concentrate on the complexities of learning how to transform the lines and black dots on a page to a new and exciting way to tell a story.

Front Page Story- Nov. 13, 1933

The fateful day of the 'Rally to protest the Russian Starvation of Ukrainians,' began in a rush of breakfast, followed by a quick distribution of costume pieces by Mama to Tato and Anna. Since I had no costume, Mama set out my only skirt and blouse, adding a borrowed apron and sash from church. Overcoats covered us from the ogling streetcar crowd. At the church, at a prearranged earlier-than-usual hour, the priest did a rapid spoken version of the Holy Service, without any singing by the choir or deacon.

Those carrying Ukrainian and American flags went out to the street first. There was a brief struggle as they lowered the tops to fit through the door and people had to dodge the moving bottom ends. Then the banners reading Glorious Ukraine, or We Protest the Starving of Millions of Ukrainian went out. The banners were well lettered, but they were in Ukrainian, so any non-Ukrainian standing on the curbs would not be able to read them. I saw Anna talking angrily to Tato. The choir, the priest and heads of various committees went next followed by the costumed parishioners.

The meeting place was the Tremont and Boylston St. corner of the Public Gardens. It was sunny, but the breezes had sharp edges. Much to Tato's surprise, the various groups had come early. There was much chatter about the several big ads for the Rally in the American papers. At the appointed time, each group stepped into the street smartly behind their Ukrainian and American flags and organizational banners. Our choir sang as we marched, another group had a little combo of accordion, sax and clarinet, while another had a few military style drums. The groups left spaces between each other but they weren't big enough to lessen the discord. The choir director was visibly annoyed when he made the last cut with his hand at the end of a song, because the people at the back of our group were still singing the last phrase. But, there could be no mistaking the pride and fervor of their singing.

At the Auditorium which had a wide balcony above the floor, various of the young, costumed men and women who were not in the choir on stage, spread themselves around to every door to show people to their seats.

Carefully avoiding Mama's searching eyes ahead of me, I ran to the top of a wide, two-story, staircase to stand by Taras, who was the usher at the big door to the balcony seats. Taras rumpled my hair and told me that my job was to smile at everyone.

"You are the official welcoming committee, OK?"

We stared down at the main floor, which was just about full. Mixed in with the horde of people coming up the stairs, I saw four uniformed policemen and four men dressed in black. They separated and stood in the doorways to the balconies. Looking down, I could see policemen and men in black in every door downstairs. My smile disappeared. Taras took my hand when he saw a policeman approach us. The policeman said,

"You look at the people in the left side of the balcony. If you see anyone shouting, tell me. I'm watching the right side."

Everyone stood for 'My Country 'Tis of Thee,' which was often sung instead of 'Oh Say can you See" in those days. Tato introduced all the dignitaries on the stage then gave a longer introduction for the first speaker. He stopped as a man began to yell from his row close to the stage. People scooted out of their seats so the policeman could move in, his billy club poised. He grabbed the heckler by the collar and pulled him up and over the seats, and bumped him into the aisle. Another policemen locked an arm, and the two of them dragged the fellow off. Then more heckling rose from all around the hall and balcony. Tato tried to continued with the introduction.

Taras held me with one hand and waved the other toward someone on the left side of the balcony. The policemen raced down the aisle and came back with a slight woman. She pulled herself loose and began to run down the wide stairs. The policeman followed and threw her down onto the sharp edges of the stairs. She screamed in pain. My body began to shake with fear. Taras left me against the wall and ran to a pair of policemen to tell them of another heckler.

Down on the stage, the speaker, who had given his speech in English, was applauded, and Tato introduced the next man. But, as the policemen attacked more and more hecklers, the noise in the auditorium drowned out the words from the stage. The speaker stopped then started again, uncertain whether to continue speaking over the noise. I stood, wide-eyed; stunned by the way the policemen struck the hecklers with their billy clubs. I watched blood fly off the hecklers faces and puddle in their hair. I covered my ears against the screaming of obscene words, the screaming of pain.

The volume on the speaker was turned up just as someone was saying, "…At least five million men, women and children starved when soldiers took their bread away. Probably another five million when they came and took their animals and any food in sight…." I heard a thin shout. "Long live Stalin!"

I sat down with my back against the wall, and squeezed myself with my arms. I could hear sirens outside, and realized that the noise inside the auditorium was subsiding. One last policeman stood at the edge of the balcony scanning the auditorium below. I saw Mama standing at the end of an aisle, searching every corner of the auditorium for me. When her eyes swept up to the balcony, I waved, jumping up and down. She saw me, shook her fist in my direction and waved for me to come down where she was. I got to her side just as everyone stood for the Ukrainian National Anthem,

"Ukraine has yet not died, neither her glory, nor her will. Some time again, good fortune will smile down upon our young brothers. Our enemies will die like the dew before the sun, and all our brothers will prosper in our land. Soul and body we will give for our freedom, and we'll show that we are brothers in Kozak glory."

I felt my breathing slow down. I looked around and saw men and women weeping into their handkerchiefs. Tears came to mine as well, and after that I could never hear our Anthem without crying too.

The next evening, Tato spread a raggedy newspaper he had found on a streetcar over the dining room table.

Imagine, my very own father's picture in the newspaper! I hoped some of my schoolmates would see it. Then I saw the headline:

FISTS FLY IN ROUTING REDS

Turning the page for the rest of the story, I saw the second picture of several police violently subduing a man. I had seen that happening!

19 ARRESTS FOR ATTEMPTS TO BREAK UP UKRAINIAN MEETING IN PROTEST TO SOVIET RECOGNITION

While fists flew, and army of 60 police and plain clothesmen, assisted by men in Cossack costume wearing curved sabres, and beautiful girls in beautiful costumes of Ukrainian peasantry, crushed an attempt by Communist sympathizers to break up a protest rally at the Municipal Auditorium on (page torn), South End.

ROUTING REDS

Arrests for Attempts to Break Up Ukrainian Meeting in Protest to Soviet Recognition

EAR NATIVE COSTUMES IN UKRAINIAN PARADE

I noticed the picture of three costumed parish women beside Tato, on the right, wearing his caracurl Kozak cap.

Seen as an aftermath of several letters in which the Rev. Joseph Zhelekhivsky, pastor of the Ukrainian Orthodox Church, Arlington Street, South End, was threatened with death, the heckling was matched with prompt and rough handling by the big force of policemen. Before the end of the afternoon 19 were arrested and many more evicted.

Ushers at the meeting dressed as Cossacks and the girls as peasants with headdresses of flowers, strings of gaily colored beads and flower embroidered shirts, pointed out the Communists to the detectives and policemen who rushed them out of the hall and downstairs to the waiting patrols.

Priest defies Reds

Women screamed, children cried and some of the Communists yelled and swung their fists to resist attempts by the police to eject them peaceably. Several were bleeding from cuts to the face and several carried swollen eyes and noses as a result of the blows.

When the noise of the combat had subsided somewhat, Father Zhelekhivsky added a somewhat dramatic touch to the meeting by announcing from a platform draped with American and Ukrainian colors that the Communists could not frighten him into silence and that he was prepared to continue his fight against Moscow despite three letters threatening to bomb his home and his church. Police guarded him after the meeting.

William F. Sullivan of Roxbury, who promoted the meeting and the parade that preceded it, said that he admired the Ukrainians (rest of paragraph torn off, unreadable) ....newspaperman, who told how the Communists had barred American correspondents from the Ukrainian districts in order to prevent news of the famine from leaking out.

The Communists, however, yelled in derision at his description of conditions and as quickly as they yelled, they were pointed out by the ushers and then ejected, not without a considerable show of resistance.

Despite the fact that 19 were arrested and many others evicted from the hall the heckling was continued throughout the course of the meeting. The meeting was preceded by a parade of the Ukrainian societies through the center of the city.

Tato came from the kitchen and put his arm on my shoulder. He read the names and said that two people were listed as in their twenties, ten in their thirties, four in their forties, and one was listed as sixty-three. Six names were English, while the rest seemed to be from Eastern Europe countries. He looked down into my eyes.

"It was a great day, and yet it was a very sad day. I'm sorry you had to see such bad things, to see that we have real enemies here in the United States. I suppose we were able to teach a few Americans something about the starvation Stalin gave Ukraine, but we need to teach more of them. We'll have to work hard to keep the patriotic strength we are feeling today. Can we do it? I don't know. I just don't know."

My Ukrainian World- My American World

In my Ukrainian world, the excitement of the Rally gradually subsided. The priest was not threatened again. The newspapers never mentioned the communist hecklers again, nor the ten million dead of starvation either. Tato met with several of the Ukrainian factions to encourage more political activity and was saddened when the inter-organizational committee quarreled and disbanded. The relationships of the church board members began to deteriorate into backbiting and spats. Tato withdrew somewhat from the running of the church. He spent more time writing speeches.

In my American world, in January, the government announced that Prohibition was over. The men chattered loudly and happily in the church basement. The women murmured and raised their eyebrows. Chichko, standing by his moonshine and beer, said nothing at all.

At home, Mama began to scare me. One morning, I came back for a school book I had forgotten, and I heard Mama shrieking over and over from the bathroom, "I gonna kill myself!" I pounded on the door. After a brief silence, she said in a calm voice, "Just go away, I'm all right." Tato was alarmed when I told him that night and tears sprung to his eyes. He looked at my frightened face with his frightened eyes and took my hands in his. "Don't worry about this, I'm sure she doesn't mean it. It is just so hard right now." I was not reassured. I heard more such shrieks over the months, though mostly, she only called on God, screaming, "Bozhe, Bozhe!"

In my adult life, she told me the hysterics came because she was going through her 'changie-life,' by which I guessed she meant menopause.

The rest of us retreated from one another. Tato lived in the cellar, except when he had a rare job somewhere. He came up for meals and was mostly silent. Anna was gone every weekday and night. Weekends, she studied in the little reception room at her desk, emerging only to eat quickly. I disappeared into my rich and satisfying world of books, piano, afternoon dancing and Saturday movies.

My American world had become easier. Though I still grieved for my life in the woods with the boys, I found a new joy, jump roping with the girls on the corner. At recess, they let me join their wall-ball bouncing, jump roping with rhymes, Dodge Ball, and Jacks on the little apron of cement close to the back wall of the school. No one talked religion. Each had already invited me to her house after school. I didn't return the invitations, because I didn't know how Mama might react. After the religious wars with the Irish girls and the trauma over the direction for the Sign of the Cross to make a hex, the one thing I never talked to my new friends was my Ukrainian world.

My biggest happiness was having Miss Frazier as my third grade teacher. She was a bit plump with a tight, graying, black bun at her neck and a quick smile. She kept us calm and interested in her lessons. When she saw some boy gazing out the window, she'd invite him to the chalkboard to do some easy sum or multiplication. Then she'd smile so happily, he'd think he had done something really special.

She didn't keep to a strict routine. She might surprise us with an unexpected spelling competition with animal cracker rewards, or hand out unlined paper and crayons and tell us to draw a picture of a tree or a bird. Of course, feeling so comfortable in her class, I reverted back to my frantic hand waving whenever I had a question, or she wanted an answer to something, like an arithmetic word problem. I was sure that my waving hand didn't bother her like it had Miss Egar and Miss Jordan.

Miss Frazier kept the students after class as a reward. Sometimes, she'd choose four or five boys to move some desks around, or she'd ask a girl or two to clean her board and slap the dusty erasers out the window. Sometimes she asked only one of us to stay to help her get supplies from the supply room. Everyone hoped to be asked to stay alone.

One day, she asked me to stay and tape some pictures of the Santa Maria, Nina, and Pinta around the walls. I was thrilled to see I was only one there. After I had finished and was standing in front of her desk to see if she wanted anything else, she smiled,

"I've been wondering where your parents came from."

"Ukraine," I said proudly.

"Oh, and just where is that?" she asked.

" I don't know exactly, but I know Poland has the half where we came from, and the other half of Ukraine is under the Russians."

"Oh," she said. "Doesn't that make you Polish?"

"No, my father says we are 100% Ukrainian and 100% American."

She wrinkled her nose every so slightly and laughed.

"I've never heard of that country," she said. "Do you speak the language?"

"Yes, I do. I can show you!"

I prepared to recite the third section of Shevchenko's poem, 'When I die, then Bury Me' which was 'Yak ymry, to pokhovayte,' in Ukrainian.

I set my feet with my toes pointed outward and placed by hands over my heart, like Tato had told us to do onstage. I began.

> "Pokhovayte ta vstavayte,
> Kaydane porvite
> I mene v semyi veleki
> Vcemyi volyni, novie
> Ne zabuyte pomyanyte
> Nezlem tekhem slovom."

I was pleased that my hands remembered when to dramatically lift and cross over my head and when to pull them apart as though breaking the chains around them. When I finished, I lowered my head sadly, put both hands back on my heart and then waited three beats in silence, as Tato had instructed, before I looked up into her eyes. Miss Frazier was silent a moment. She looked as though she were holding back a laugh. Her eyes blinked rapidly. She said hesitantly,

"Yes, hmm."

Her eyes made a few more blinks. "Well, dear, let's you and I sharpen some pencils." As I handed her the pencils, she talked about going to a ballet and asked me if I had ever seen any. I told her I had seen some in a movie that had made the boys laugh, but I liked the circle of netting they wore. She said it was called a 'tutu.'

"I dance a lot though." I said, still worrying about her odd smile after my poem.

"Oh, you do? Where do you dance?"

"In front of my radio. I make up stories about fairies and elves and witches and soldiers. I dance sort of like Ginger Rogers, but maybe not quite."

"Well, I'm sure it must be very nice. I hope someday you can go and see a real ballet in a concert hall, though. It is much more beautiful than a Ginger Rogers dance."

Walking home, I was oblivious to all around me. My brain could only go back and forth on whether Miss Frazier liked me. I wished I hadn't recited the poem, or said anything about Ginger Rogers. I didn't want to see Mama just then, so I climbed up into a tree to watch for her departure to work. Suddenly, I saw the bullies leap out of the bushes where they had been hiding and catch poor Saul. He had made the mistake of taking the usual way home. They knocked him down to the ground. Just then, Mama opened the window and gave her usual garbled shout for me, and the boys mimicked her as they gave Saul a last punch. Mama saw them and yelled,

"You rotten boys you stoppit det. Stoppit or I gonna tell the polyees." How she was going to do that, I couldn't imagine. We had no phone.

They ran off, yelling, "Just wait until we catch STEL-LA!"

Mama slammed down the window and soon was pumping herself toward the streetcar line.

Perhaps I had seen too many Charlie Chaplin and Laurel and Hardy movies, or maybe I just remembered how the boys used to pretend to be drunk in front of the bully-boys, but one day, I started a silent routine in front of some second graders. I went strutting in front of them. Looking up into the sky, I tripped over an invisible obstacle and let my body go splat onto the ground. It was easy enough with my enormous shoes. They laughed. Eager for the approval that their laughter implied, I became a haughty aristocrat, holding an invisible monocle to my eye, before I did another big fall. On another day, I added a wheeling drunk to my routine. The laughter was my joy.

Of course, Mary Catherine, Eleanor and Theresa had to deflate me a bit. At recess, huddled together, pretending not to notice me, Theresa said, "No wonder Stella's flopping on the ground. Her shoes are so big she can't help it." Eleanor said a little more loudly," I've never seen such big shoes. I bet when it rains she has to go to the girls' room to empty them." They had to wrap their arms around themselves to control their laughing.

I stood up to move away. Mary Catherine stood too and said, "Just make yourself scarce, kid, we've decided you are a very conceited brat, so bye-bye." The other two stood and walked to another place along the wall.

I had no idea what conceited meant, but it couldn't be good when followed by brat. I craved the well-used dictionary on Anna's desk. Part of me was glad I would never have to walk with them again, but I didn't like that kind of laughing at me. At the end of the day, Miss Frazier, probably noticing my troubled face, asked me to stay and get some colored paper and two boxes of white chalk from the supply closet down the hall. When I got back, she asked me if something had happened. She said she thought I came back from recess looking sad.

I burst out crying.

"Nobody likes me. The boys I used to play with don't like me anymore, because I'm a sissy-girl, the bully-boys make fun of me and the way my mother talks and they are always telling me to go back where I came from, even though I told them I was born right here in Boston, and sometimes I have to go a long way around to go home so they won't push me down to the ground, and now the girls called me a conceited brat. I don't know what conceited means, but I know it must be bad. The little kids like me though."

"Oh, dear," she said sighing. "Do sit here by me and don't cry. You see, boys in elementary school just don't like girls, any girls, but they will change, believe me they will. They will! Some boys start liking girls in sixth grade, some later, but sooner or later they all will start liking girls. So you see it's not you they don't like." I didn't believe her.

"I think you are wise to avoid the bullies. Standing up to them just makes them worse. Best to avoid trouble. Maybe if you got home faster, your mother wouldn't have to call you. But as to what the girls called you, conceited. That means that you think too much of yourself, that you are perhaps too proud of being smart. I think they see you waving your hand in class because you know all the answers and nobody likes that.

"Now as to what to do about it. You know, you are a smart girl, no doubt about that. Remember that all-day test we took last month. Your test numbers showed that you really are a very, very smart girl, so you don't need to ever worry about that. What you have to concentrate on is trying not to show everyone you are smart. The boys don't like it and neither do the girls. You do want them to like you, don't you?

"Yes," I murmured.

"So, you need to stop trying to be the first to answer the questions or problems. You might try waiting until I call on you, after I've given others a chance to answer. Try to learn to do everything a little more quietly. I know you can do it. I'll try to help you. I'll be watching you, and when I have you after school next week, we'll talk about how well you are doing."

Walking home, I couldn't bear to think that now, along with everyone else; Miss Frazier thought I was a show off. But, gradually, helped by a special look from Miss Frazier, I did learn to hold my hand down. I learned to wait to be asked, though I knew it wouldn't change what the goody-Catholic girls thought of me. I would just hope my jump-roping friends would stay friends with me. I would only act silly in front of the little kids if no one else was around. That was too much fun to give up altogether.

Leaving Miss Frazier's class on the last day of school, I felt a great sadness. I brought her a rose from Mama's garden that morning and lingered after everyone had left. I tried to say goodbye but could only look down at my feet. She broke the silence and told me she had enjoyed having me in her class, and that she was sure I would do well in fourth grade. She stood, took the rose and shook my hand, then walked me to the door.

On the first Sunday of summer vacation, Tato announced that in addition to Ukrainian classes on Saturday at Oakland Hall, there would be dancing classes for children between the ages of seven and twelve. Olga would teach the class at her home in Mattapan.

Mama fussed about me crossing Cummins Highway by myself to get to the Saturday Ukrainian lessons at Oakland Hall. I almost told her I had been crossing both Cummins Highway and Blue Hill Avenue regularly on my way to the library, but realized that might be unwise. She went to Lidgy's house to talk to him about taking me. When she came back, she yelled at me that boys in America were a little too free. I took it to mean that Lidgy refused. Tato told her he would take me, so she quieted down.

The teacher, a woman who didn't go to our church, pointed the twenty or so children to the seats in front of a moveable blackboard. Lidgy sat in the back looking bored and angry.

The slow exposition of the Cyrillic alphabet, which both he and I had known for a long time now, was boring. The copying of these letters onto endless sheets of paper was painful. Saturday after Saturday, I sat listlessly, wishing I could join in the whispering and laughing of the kids in the back rows.

The teacher who insisted we call her Panyi Lesya, which meant Madame Lesya, became more and more frazzled trying to quash the elusive waves of whispering with her own, too quiet voice. When she was writing on the board, she was constantly distracted by the spitballs that hit her back. She tried to vary the routine with having us draw the Ukrainian flag with blue and yellow crayons. She tried to explain that the golden yellow color on the bottom stripe represented the wheat fields of Ukraine, and the blue stripe, the sky above, but the noise level had become too high. The children knew she had no idea how to control them. Boys left their chairs to poke at each other. The girls watched and giggled at the boys. One Saturday, she left the room in tears and didn't return.

After a few weeks without classes, a Mr. Antonovich took over. Lidgy didn't return to classes. I guessed that Streychu didn't care whether Lidgy went or not. He had none of Tato's fierce patriotism. Mr. Antonovich had a heavy smell of alcohol when he arrived, and when he left the room to go to the bathroom, he would return with an even heavier smell. Whenever anyone whispered or talked, he'd take them to a spot on the wall and turned them to face it. At one point half the class was standing widely separated along the long walls. Before long, the room remained quiet.

He did no more alphabet repetition. Instead he did only 'dictatzia..' He would read through a simple text, and we were to write it down. One sound-one letter was easy enough, though I later learned there were a few spelling conventions, which of course he never bothered to mention. He never corrected any of the papers, but he did weave around the room to see that we were writing something down. Not long afterwards, he had the oldest girl there, Irena, who read Ukrainian easily, take over the reading. Mr. Antonovich sat with his head propped on his stacked fists and closed his eyes.

I begged Tato to let me stop going, but Tato said that even with a bad teacher, a good student could find something to learn. He told me to bring my papers home, and he would correct them. This was not what I wanted to hear.

The prospective dance class excited me. Perhaps, finally, I would learn how to dance the stage dances. While I could imitate most of the individual steps, I couldn't remember the sequence. On the first Friday that Olga was to give lessons, I ran the six blocks to her house imagining that I would be dancing on the stage by the end of the summer. About fifteen children of different ages squeezed into her small living room.

"All right," she shouted, "Make a line! Stand straight, straighter. Pull your head up! Make your neck long! Pull in your chin! Feet side by side! Stand taller!" She walked among us, poking the small of the back, pushing up a chin. She'd call for hands-on-hips, and then jerked the crooked elbows either backwards or forwards. "Taller! Now walk around in a circle! Look up! Look up! Never, never look at your feet!" And then still louder and more urgently, "Smile, you must smile! Doesn't anyone know how to smile?"

And so it began. Never with any music, she might teach or review one step and the appropriate arm and hand position during a lesson. Her harangue to stand tall, smile and never look down kept time with her rhythmical clap and became our music. At the end of the summer, she promised we would begin again next summer, but we had to continue to practice the few steps we had learned, so we could start where we left off.

Any chance of doing a whole dance had become barely a wisp of a dream.

But, the best classes during that summer unexpectedly took place on Chocha's piazza. Sitting beside me on the streetcar, on the way home from church one Sunday, she told me to come up to her house on Monday evening around seven and she would show me how to do Ukrainian embroidery.

As I walked up to her house the next evening, I could not quite believe that I had understood what she had said. But there, on a table, was some cloth and hanks of red and black threads. She began by showing me how to baste an open, starched grid of thick, linen threads onto a piece of soft, white cloth. She called the stiff grid - kanva.

"This kanva keeps your count of stitches. Watch how I make a cross stich, an X, by putting the needle in and out of four connected spaces. Now you do it." I hunched over my task.

"Now, if you need to do, say, four X's in a row, this is how you do it." I carefully copied her example.

"Now, watch how I always make the first line of the cross stitch go from the bottom left hole up to the top right hole, and then I cross under to the top left hole, then over to the bottom right. That way, every cross stitch crosses exactly the same way."

That maneuver took the rest of the evening to learn.

The next week, there was a rose pattern on a paper with grid lines.

"Let's try just a little patch of the pattern. Most importantly, you must count the stitches very, very carefully. The first line goes like this: two blanks, one black cross, three blanks, one red cross. Second line: four black stitches, one blank, one red, one black one red." I miscounted one the empty spaces, then made two reds where is should have been one, and of course crossed some the wrong way. She showed me how to take the stitches out, and admonished me to count more carefully. The next time I came over, she started me on the real rose pattern, one slow row at a time. As the weeks passed, my stitches began to increase a little faster than the ripping.

When the red rose and the black stem and leaves finally emerged, Chocha told me there were now no errors, the pattern was done, and it was time to pull out the kanva. Grasping one of the starched threads with a pair of tweezers and tugging firmly, she pulled the lowest horizontal thread from under the crosses, then the next and the next. When I learned how much of a pull was necessary, I finished all the horizontal threads and finally the vertical threads. Left on the cloth was a geometrical, cross-stitched, red rose with black leaves. I could not believe I had made such a beautiful thing.

My Worlds Collide

On the first day of school that fall, I peeked into the third grade room as I went by to my fourth grade room ready with a wave for Miss Frazier, but she was surrounded by the children of her new class and didn't look over at me. The lady standing in the doorway of the fourth grade room was a small, unsmiling, blond lady, the dreaded Miss O'Donnell. I remembered what the boys had said about how she shook children. Neither Tato nor Mama had ever done that to me. Feeling more than a little scared, I put my head down and slithered in.

Once we were all seated, she picked a small boy to hold the big flag, a girl with thick glasses to read something from a paper, and a timid-looking boy to say the Pledge of Allegiance.

"This will be our opening service every morning." She said sternly. "Stand quietly and at attention."

She pointed at the small boy. He lifted the flag out of the holder, teetering a little with the weight of it before he got the end planted at his feet. The Pledge of Allegiance boy started without putting his hand on his heart. Miss O'Donnell stopped him, picked up his hand and fixed it into his chest. A few hands in the room lifted quickly and stealthily to their hearts. Miss O'Donnell nodded to the girl. She lifted the paper close to her eyes. She read, 'The Lord is my Shepherd, I shall not want…." After stopping several times for big words, her lips began to tremble. At the last word, she ran to her seat. Miss O'Donnell scowled and hummed a note. The children hummed back a variety of notes and Miss O'Donnell began 'My Country 'tis of Thee,' "For those who do not know the 23rd Psalm, I have copies on my desk. You will memorize it in two weeks." And so the first day of far too many, began.

I was jealous the boys would be having Manual Training. The girls had to have Domestic Arts. I wanted to learn how to use the tools myself in Tato's cellar, but girls were limited to learning how to push a needle through cloth. As it turned out, my eight-year old fingers never did as well as most of the other girls who had nine-year old fingers.

Though I eventually learned the techniques of basting stitches, backstitches and buttonhole stitches, the results at the end of the year were still uneven lengths and wobbly lines. My work was consistently judged to be of B quality. Conduct and History also came in as B's. I despaired when Chocha saw my card and said I was never going to be as smart as Anna. She said she thought she had taught me to stich evenly.

For the rest of the year, we worked on pink gingham bags with a drawstring top. When I brought it home finally, Mama gave every seam a careful look, and I was reminded of her story of Anyelka, scraping with her fingernail at the shirts Mama had made for Tato before their wedding. She shrugged and made no comment about the bag, and I was left to believe the worst.

My fingers also continued to misbehave during our penmanship classes. We had learned cursive letters in second and third grade. Now it was time to learn the Palmer Method so that we could write beautiful cursive. Miss O'Donnell told us to grasp the pencil in our first three fingers and to curl the other two underneath.

"Now," she said, imagine that your fingers have turned to cement from your fingernails all the way beyond your wrist. Your fingers can't move, your wrist can't move. Only your arm moves. Now, we will practice circles and straight lines. Remember move only your arm, never your fingers or wrist."

It sounded simple enough, but my fingers refused to turn into cement. Throughout the year, two of the boys and I had to take seats directly in front of her, so she could rap our moving wrists with her pencil. Having her hover over me, made it impossible for my arm to perform the push-pull. It took until the year's end before I was able to make letters this new way. Unfortunately, the more I used my arm instead of my fingers, the less readable were the words.

New for fourth grade was Miss O'Donnell's daily Geography Class. Every morning we had to repeat the names of the continents as she tapped them on a pull-down map. When she was satisfied we knew the names, she pulled down another map.

"This is Europe. This is where our ancestors came from." She spoke for a while about what 'ancestors' were.

"Now, this is Ireland." A rare, tiny smile curved her lips. "This is where my own ancestors came from. They came to America because the potatoes over there had a disease. Without potatoes to eat, they got very hungry and many died. Lots of other Irish families came too. That all happened about eighty years ago."

"Now, I want each of you to tell me, if you can, where your ancestors came from and maybe when they came to America."

Patrick stepped up quickly, and looking smug, tapped the Irish ball that the rabbitty country beside it seemed to be reaching for. His grandparents had come over, but he didn't know when. A Brady, an O'Neill, a Flaherty and two Sullivans came up to say the same thing. They suddenly seemed a little bit more important.

Miss O'Donnell pointed to something that looked like a boot for Alice Busconi, and a funny shape at the top of the map for Annie Anderson. John Hesse was the first to say he didn't know where his family was from.

"Be sure you ask your parents tonight. Ask where they came from and when and maybe something interesting about your family."

Saul, the son of Mr. Feltstein, the hardware store owner in Mattapan Square, who had helped Tato so much, also said he didn't know.

"Well, it is just amazing that your parents have never told you. You probably were just not listening, Saul. You be sure to come prepared tomorrow."

When my turn came, I stood confidently and spoke proudly.

"I'm from Ukraine. My mother and father came from Ukraine with my sister, just before the war started. I was born here. My ancestors were Kozaks and they rode big white horses." Miss O'Donnell's eyes pinched together. She tilted her head. I don't know why I said that about the Kozaks. Tato had once told me laughing, that we might have had Kozaks as our ancestors. They had ridden once or twice through Kozova, though several centuries ago. I hadn't really understood about centuries.

The class nickered softly. I lifted my chin a little. My feet felt cold and one temple felt warm. I had been stupid again. I crossed my fingers behind my back, though I had always believed Tato's Kozak remark. Miss O'Donnell glanced at the map and turned her narrowed eyes back at me.

"And just where might this country be? Do come up and show me."

She knew I couldn't. I went up to the map and swept my eyes from left to right and up and down. I saw the words 'Poland' and 'Russia'. Tato had certainly talked about them a lot, but he had made it clear that they had been our conquerors.

I shook my head, lowered my chin and said, "I don't know where it is."
Miss O'Donnell's lips almost made a smile.

"Well then. You make absolutely sure to ask your parents about where it
is, and whether you got the word, Ukrainian, wrong. Be prepared to tell
the class tomorrow just where on this map you came from. And you
might ask your parents about the white horses again. Now, please
Blanche, your turn."

She flushed out another Italian, a possible German, a Swede and finally
Rose, a new girl, who shyly said she was from Albania.

Alice Knightly stood last, and speaking quietly, said, "We're English. My
father said most of my ancestors came over a few boats after the
Mayflower."

"Oh," said Miss O'Donnell, stretching her lips into a smile. "At last, a real
American!"

I went straight home after school. Tato was preoccupied when he came
home.

I guessed that he would tell me I should know by now where Ukraine
was, so I didn't ask. I asked Anna in the morning while she was dressing.

"Did Tato ever make you show where Ukraine is on a map at school?"

"Oh yes, and it was never there," she said. "But, I'd look for Poland, and
then the city, Lemberg, and point to that. We lived only about a hundred
miles from there. Lemberg is the Polish name for the city. The Ukrainian
name is Lviv, and it won't be on any map. Also, you can usually find the
Black Sea. Ukraine is just above it, but of course you never see the word
Ukraine."

Miss O'Donnell pulled down the Europe map first thing next morning.

"Saul, did you ask your father where you came from?" Saul stood.

"Yes, I did."

"You know that because you are Jewish, that even if you come from a
country like Germany or Austria, you are still only Jewish, not German or
Austrian."

Saul stared at her, looking confused.

"But anyway, please tell us what country you came from."

"My father says one of my great grandfathers on my mother's side came
with my great grandmother to Boston from Germany before the Civil

War. My grandfather from my father's side came from Russia before the World War, and my grandmother was from France."

Miss O'Donnell was not pleased with his answer. She stared at him a long time.

She turned slowly and pointed to Russia, Germany, and France. She turned to me.

"Stephanie. Did you find out if there is a country called… what was it you called it?"

"Oo-kray-IN-a," I said, trying to sound knowledgeable "But my father said that Americans call it YOU-kraine."

"Well then, show us where it is, this mysterious country of yours that is not even on the City of Boston School System maps."

I went up and looked for Poland, and then for Lemberg and the Black Sea.

"So you still can't find it?" she said angrily.

I suddenly saw the dot for Lemberg. I pointed to it, and said:

"He said we come from near here."

"So, you are Polish after all. I thought so."

"My father says I am not Polish." I said.

"I'm afraid you simply do not understand. You are to show us where this country is or tell us that you are mistaken, tomorrow!" Anger tinged her voice.

She turned to John Hesse.

"Now John. I presume you asked your father and can show us your country?"

John stood, his face reddening under his mop of curly hair, "My father said it's none of your business."

That night, after Tato and I had finished our potatoes and peas, I asked him, "Are you sure there is a place called Ookraiyina?"

"How can you ask that? Of course there is!"

"Well, when Miss O'Donnell asked me to find it on the map, it wasn't there!"

He said something under his breath. He took a piece of paper and pencil. Scowling, he made a rough sketch of Europe: Norway and Sweden jutting out at the top, Spain protruding at the lower corner, the Italian boot, and the Black Sea. He made a big circle and a smaller one.

"Now this is Russia, this is Poland." He made another circle over the bottom parts of the two countries. "And this is Ookraiyina, " he said writing the name in Cyrillic letters.

"Now, where we come from is in the Polish part" pointing to the western part of the circle "The rest of our country is in the Russian part."

I frowned. But where was this on Miss O'Donnell's map?

"Now I want you to go and tell the teacher that there really is a country called Ookraiyina. Well no, you better called it the English way, Ukraine. Tell her that it has been conquered by Poland and Russia, but we hope, only temporarily. Show her how it fits over southern Poland and Russia."

I knew that would take more courage than I had, even if I understood his map.

"How do you spell Ukraine in English?" I asked hoping to change the subject.

Sighing, he took the pencil and carefully wrote in English capital letters- UKRAINE.

The next morning, I decided to just tell Miss O'Donnell that I was mistaken. We were Polish after all. Didn't Mama tell me that Tato's mother, Anyelka, was Polish? What difference did it make anyway? In spite of my decision, I trembled with guilt the whole morning. Tato would call me a traitor of the worst kind if he found out.

When Miss O'Donnell started the Geography Class, instead of calling me up to the map, she talked about the boot, Italy, and how Columbus had come from there and crossed the ocean to discover America. She never even once looked in my direction, and by now, I never raised my hand for anything. She was probably tired of the whole thing. I certainly was.

Still feeling like a traitor, I couldn't look at Tato when we ate supper together that night. He asked if I had shown the teacher where Ukraine was, I crossed my fingers behind me, and nodded.

The winter was long and cold that year. Tato often went down to the cellar to add some coal, muttering that the coal we had wouldn't last until spring. After supper and a half hour with the radio, he'd go to some friend's house. I was glad I was now old enough to be left behind. I never minded being alone as long as I had books to read.

Mama's hysterical outbursts from behind the bathroom door continued. When I heard her scream out a long outburst of words I couldn't make out, followed by the sound of her fists pounding the walls. I ran to my bed and pulled the perena over my head. I told Anna about Mama's screaming. She said Mama was just tired from so much work. Then I told Tato. He immediately blamed the letter she had gotten yesterday from her sister. "Listen to this!" he said opening the letter up.

'I sit to the table, with what paper I'm able. I greet you my darlings with tears and with kisses.

My tears have not ceased since you left us for America so many years ago. I try always to bring you good news so that I do not make you suffer more in that strange land, but today I cannot hold back. Today our beloved mother lies in bed burning with fever. I wash her body every hour with the leaves she gave me for fever. There should be whiskey in it, but I have no money for it. She is like a dried leaf in her bed. Have you anything to say to her before she dies? She is waiting for your words. You know she loved you best of all the rest. I am ashamed that I cannot care for her, as I should because my daughter is sick. I run back and forth between the two houses as best I can. Good bye, I thank you for your kisses and prayers that brought us a bag of dried beans.'

Tato sighed. "The dried beans means she got the dollar Mama put in the letter. I tell Mama not put money in the mail, because most of the time it is stolen."

I stared at Tato. I wanted to tell him what she said as she sat sobbing at the table, with the letter in her hand yesterday, when I got home from school, but the words didn't come.

"I don kerr," she had yelled at me. "I gonna safe some money, gonna gerra ticket, gonna go on det sheffa cross det ocean. I no kerr I drown. No gonna stay here, no gonna listen vat Tato says. No gonna die in dis strangie-place. Gonna see my Mama. She no gonna die viddout me. And you" she said with her wild eyes on mine, "you gonna come vid me and help me like I helped my Mama." I turned to Tato and pleaded, "You won't let her make me go back to Kozova with her, will you?"

"Kholyera!" he shouted out. I made myself smaller. "Believe me, I will never let her take you there. If I had a dollar for every letter Mama's sister has written about their Mama dying, I would be a rich man." He struck his fist slowly on the table every few words. "How can Katerina do this to her own sister? My brother, Michael, writes to me and says that Mama's Mama is a fine and a healthy eighty years of age. She still collects flowers and herbs and gives them to sick people. Mama's sister has no mercy. All she wants is for Mama to keep sending her money. She doesn't understand that we don't have anything to send! Mama can't take this on top of every thing else. But, no, believe me, Mama isn't going to go back."

The Bad American Child

The long awaited last day of fourth grade arrived. Miss O'Donnell would soon be only a bad memory. With fifteen minutes left on the clock, the school secretary appeared at our door and pointed Miss O'Donnell toward the principal's office. Miss O'Donnell chose mousy Louise to sit in front of the room, presumably to keep order.

"No one, and I mean no one, shall leave their seat, Do You Understand!" Miss O'Donnell said before closing the door behind her. Within seconds, the room erupted with chatter and laughter, though no one left their seat. Louise, at Miss O'Donnell's desk, looked terrified. Patrick, my nemesis of the bully gang who sat next to me, pulled my sweater from the back of my chair and flung it toward the door. Terrified to leave my seat and more terrified that Miss O'Donnell would punish me for my sweater being on the floor, I made a swift move to pick it up and return to my chair. Of course, at that moment, Miss O'Donnell opened the door and stood squarely in front of me. Her palm struck my cheek, jerking my head violently to the side.

"I wasn't doing anything!" I gasped.

"Sit down, or you'll really be sorry." She hissed. The bell rang, and she told us not to move. She glared at me. I dropped my eyes to the desk. We sat in silence for another long fifteen minutes before Miss O'Donnell dismissed us with "Good riddance to a terrible class. I just hope you behave better for your next teacher."

Rose and Alice walked home with me. They said Miss O'Donnell had been really unfair and wasn't it great school was over. Alice began chanting an old jump roping verse. No more learning, no more books, no more teacher's cross-eyed looks! When Mary Catherine and Eleanor and Theresa passed us, they pointed at me and howled with laughter. Rose and Alice left me at the corner of Greenfield Road, where they turned down toward their homes. I ducked into a back path so Mama wouldn't see me. I needed to cry, so I headed toward the Rockies. I had forgotten that the path skirted the back yard to Mary Catherine's house. As I came around a blackberry bush, I found myself facing the three girls sitting on her back stairs.

My body tensed. I turned to go back. They stood and held me with their eyes.

"You know, Stephanie" Mary Catherine began. "It is really so sad about you. You have no clue about how stupid and conceited you are. No one likes you, you know." The three of them were smirking with the laughter about to erupt onto their faces.

I have never been able to remember leaning over, picking up the bottle that was somehow by my foot and heaving it at Mary Catherine. My first memory was seeing the bottle hit the side of her head and her crying out. The second was hearing the bottle smash on the ground. At that sound, I turned and ran around to the front of her house, then down Harmon Street, up to the piazza and my cot. I pulled the blanket tightly over my body and head and lay motionless.

I heard Mama call for me, before she headed up Harmon to go to work. I didn't move. A little later, hearing male voices down on the back steps, I pulled back the blanket and went to where I could look down on them. A man, in a police uniform was talking at Tato with a very severe, lecturing tone. I heard him say he was Mary Catherine's father and something rather lengthy about a bottle. I began to shake. The policeman left. I heard Tato telling me to come down. When I got to him, he grabbed me, put one of his legs on a stair and upended me across his knee. His hand came down on my behind four or five times. Shocked by this very first spanking he had ever given me, I screamed against the shock. When he stood me up in front of him, his face was red.

"I can not believe that my very own daughter threw a bottle at another child. I have never felt so much disappointment in my life. I thought you were a kinder child, a smarter, more sensible child. And now I have to face a policeman about this! You are just lucky the bottle didn't break against her head. Imagine how she could have been hurt! Did you give it a single thought before you threw it?" He didn't wait for an answer.

"Now, you should stay by yourself for a while and think. Think hard about what you have done. How badly you might have hurt that girl. No matter what she might have done to provoke you, you had no right to throw a bottle at her. So just think about it. I don't think I want to see you for a while."

When Mama was eating breakfast the next morning, Saturday, I heard her telling Anna what Tato told her about me. She started to cry. Anna muttered something angrily. I wrapped my head with the blanket so I wouldn't hear any more. Neither called me into the kitchen for breakfast.

When I heard Mama go downstairs to kibbitz with the vendors, I crept toward Anna's bedroom. Anna was getting into her girdle and stockings, slip and dress. Avoiding her eyes, I peered into the closet to find something to wear. Anna put her hand on my shoulder and spun me to face her.

"Oh, for heaven's sake. Look at your arms! You go wash yourself and use a washcloth and soap. And don't forget that filthy neck. You are always so dirty. And your fingernails are black! " She stuffed some books, notebooks, and a pad into the briefcase Streychu had given her as a child. I guessed she was probably going to her school.

"So go and wash yourself. Are you deaf?" She turned and left. I wondered if she was too mad at me to be my lawyer in case I was arrested.

I dressed quickly and went back out on the piazza to contemplate the day. To just sleep in the cot all day tempted me, but, of course, someone would find me. I knew I had to stay away from the house and everyone in it. I just had to decide what to do in the space of time before the library opened. After the library, I could lose myself in the movies at the Oriental. But surely, Tato wouldn't give me a nickel today. I knew I couldn't ask Anna for one after what Mama had told her, and I knew I could never have asked Mama for a nickel whether I had been bad or good.

Overwhelmed by the longing to disappear into a long, double-feature afternoon at the movies, I reached under my cot and pulled out my box. I found only a penny in it. When Anna finally went down Harmon Street to get the streetcar, I went to her bedroom and opened an old pocketbook. In the bottom of one corner, I found another penny. I went to the kitchen window to see that Mama was still with the ragman. When he snapped his whip at his horse, Mama turned to pick out one of Mr. Tsapar's chickens. I went to her bedroom and found a nickel and a penny in Tato's pants pockets. I took the penny and put back the nickel. There was one more place I could look. I listened for Tato's steps coming out of the cellar and then the slam of the back door. I raced down to the cellar and began frantically looking into his nail boxes. One of the boxes, I had discovered long ago, did not have nails in it, but I forgot which one.

Just as I heard Mama and Tato coming back into the house, I opened the box with Tato's small collection of coins for buying himself a beer down in Mattapan Square every now and then. I took two of the pennies and put the lid back on the box. I slid the guilt of stealing the money into the guilt of the throwing of the bottle and dropped it with the five pennies into my sock. Since I was headed straight for Hell or jail anyway, what difference did the stolen four cents make?

I took a back route to the Rockies. I avoided the path that went by Mary Catherine's house. The gang was never in the woods anymore. I climbed to the top of the Rockies, found my usual flat stone to sit on and realized that my guilt would not stay down in my sock. When the sobs gave way eventually to a gentler crying, I wiped my nose with my fingers and dried my hands on the hem of my dress. I didn't know what I could do to set anything right again.

I looked up to see that the sun was just past overhead, so I began the trek to the library. I deposited my books on the table and turned to leave.

Miss McGillvary walked quickly to my side.

"Is everything all right? You aren't getting any books today?"

"No, I'm not. My sister brought me some Campfire Girl books from her friend at law school, and I want to read them first."

"Oh," she said. "I had four books ready for you today."

"Well," I thought sullenly, "I don't really want the books you chose. I would like once, just once, to choose some myself." But, of course these words didn't come out. What was really going to happen after I got home from the movies was that I would probably never go to the library or the movies again. Nothing was ever going to be the same again. I would probably be punished forever. I just had to be ready for it somehow.

"I'll be back when I'm done with the Campfire Girls," I finally muttered, feeling an unwelcome addition to my already overwhelming guilt. I was sure I'd never be back.

As I had hoped, the movie drained my head of its imponderables. Walking home, I became the heroine so completely, I might not have answered to my name. Reality struck when Mama called me to supper. Anticipating a barrage of words, I was surprised when Mama and Tato and Anna talked around me at supper. No one mentioned any bottles or stolen pennies. I ate Mama's mackerel and the mashed potatoes quickly and retreated to my cot to find out if the Saturday night tub routine would happen. Mama scrubbed me harder than usual and only muttered, "You vas alvays vild Hamerican kid. I knew sometink vould heppen like dis."

Sunday morning, down in the church basement, Chocha came up to me and whispered down in my ear. "Whatever was in your head when you threw that bottle? I am so ashamed of you. I saw it in the paper yesterday. Now, everyone, everyone will know. You should be very, very ashamed of yourself."

My first thought was that Miss Frazier would see the newspaper and hate me forever. My head reeled. What if Kuzh saw it and never danced the polka with me again? But then, if it had been in the paper, Anna would have shown it to me with some lecture or other. Maybe Chocha made it up to make me feel worse. How would I ever know?

The summer days shuffled along slowly. I left the house early and moved uncomfortably from one familiar tree crotch to another. My body seemed to have outgrown them during the winter. I managed to get lost in the adventures of the Campfire Girls, which involved camping and hiking, always in beautiful places. The girls were close friends, closer than I had ever been with anybody. When I finished the series, I thought to go to the library again, but what if old Mrs. McGillvary had seen me in the paper? I decided to read Heidi and Alice in Wonderland again instead. When the bookmarker I had taken from the Beacon Hill house fell out of the pages of Heidi, I felt a sudden pang of fear. I ran up into the attic and slid it into a thin space next to the dormer window.

I could not figure out how to avoid lunch with Mama, but she didn't mention the bottle incident. Now, her stories stressed how good she, herself, had always been. She usually ended with how Anna had been such a good Ukrainian little girl.

The Ukrainian classes, the dance classes and the piano lessons went on, each with its own way of moving my guilt to one side for a while, as did going to the Oakland Hall dances on Saturday nights. Apparently, neither Olga, the dance teacher, nor Mrs. Graham, my piano teacher, nor even Kuzh had read the news article about me, or else they had chosen to ignore it. Maybe Chocha did make up the newspaper story. Actually, Kuzh chose me to dance with him more often that summer, and because he had taught me so well, other men dancers began to choose me as well. My radio dancing usually brought forgetfulness, but disappointingly, not always. When certain kinds of sorrowful music filled the room with my guilt, I could not move any part of my body.

Mama and Tato seemed to quarrel more loudly than usual whenever they were together that summer. Mama often began by hissing at Tato that he was drinking too much at the church picnics and downstairs in the basement at the dances. Instead of going quietly down to the cellar, he would yell back at her that he hated to be out of work. He hated to take the drinks that were always offered to him, but he couldn't help it. He was just grateful that there were some that cared enough about him to treat him to a beer or two, because lately the church committees were always fighting about something, and he was feeling like a rooster in a flock of geese.

Mama and Anna quarreled too. Mama had gone back to reminding Anna that it was time for her to be married, which was difficult for Anna to answer logically.

By the end of summer, I almost believed my punishment, such as it was, was over. Lidgy, about to go to seventh grade in the distant William Barton Rogers Junior High School in the fall, seemed to have forgotten that our house was never to be entered. He began coming over after supper with his new game, 'Monopoly' so that Anna, the almost-lawyer, would explain rents and mortgages and the complicated rules. She did, but then Lidgy told her that he couldn't believe that you really needed to know so much to play. He said he was going to drop some of the rules, and Anna said he shouldn't. Neither of them paid any attention to me when I picked up a token to join in the game.

We alternated the Monopoly game with putting together the jigsaw puzzles Anna had begun to buy on her way home. The latest Boston fad, they were sold cheaply, so Anna sometimes had to stand in a long line. The challenge of matching colors and finding the shapes that fit together was endlessly absorbing. I thought I was faster than Lidgy and told him so. Lidgy told me to shut up. I began to forget to be sad.

When the dreaded first day of fifth grade arrived, I watched for the three girls to pass my house before I went down the stairs. I avoided looking at anyone walking near me. Surely everyone knew about what I had done to Mary Catherine. I read the list posted on the school door quickly and ran to Miss Smith's fifth grade room. At recess, which I had been dreading all morning long, none of the girls I had played with last year made any mention of the bottle incident, so my body began to relax a little. Mary Catherine and her friends came nowhere near me.

Miss Smith, a bland, pale woman, taught us in a soft, dull voice. I was content at last to be unnoticed, so I never lifted my hand during question times. Now and then, Miss Smith would stop me as I was leaving at the end of the day and looking through her little row of books, she'd give me 'A Book of Poems for Children,' or 'Stories of the American Revolution.' I didn't find it odd that she never spoke to me when she was giving me a book, or when I returned it.

Section V

1935-1936

Nobodies and Somebodies

Stephanie M. Sydoriak

Anna Graduates

One cold, sleety afternoon, I heard a man's voice in the dining room. I hid behind the kitchen door, which was opened to a thin slit. The voice came from a strange man sitting at the dining room table. Tato was explaining how he lost his Walworth Pipe Company job in 1932, and how he hadn't been able to find a job since then. He told him about Mama's two night jobs and how hard it was for her, so he wanted to know about Roosevelt's work project, the WPA. The man stood and walked through the living room and then disappeared into the tiny reception room with Anna's desk. He looked into the bedrooms and nodded over to Mama and I sitting stiffly at the kitchen table. Tato walked anxiously behind him.

When the man was done, they sat down on the stiff black chairs in the living room. The man began to ask Tato question after question. Their voices were too soft for me to hear from the kitchen. Then I heard Tato escort him down the front stairs.

"Kholyera!" he said when he came back into the kitchen. "He says I have a radio, and Anna has some law books on her desk, and even with our big mortgage and Mama working two jobs, I am too rich to work in the WPA. I'll bet that if I were Irish it would be a different story. Kholyera!"

I cringed with fear, as always, when he cried out that word. I didn't know until I looked it up in a Ukrainian dictionary as an adult that this frightening word only meant 'Cholera'. I laughed that I had been so frightened when he said it.

"Why didn't you take the radio up to the attic before he came?" Mama asked, going into her bedroom to get dressed for work.

"How could I know to do that?" he asked, his voice rising dangerously.

"I don't know, but I know that I cannot work two jobs like this forever!" she screamed back. "I would prefer the grave to this. I CAN NOT DO THIS ANYMORE!" She stomped loudly down the back steps.

Throughout that school year, Anna sat with her law books later and later into the night, until the last of the finals, in late spring, had been passed. At the graduation ceremony, everyone applauded loudly when she got her diploma with the announced designation of Magna Cum Laude. A professor praised her winning paper on Constitutional Law. I hadn't realized how short she was until I saw her lining up for a picture with the other graduating women. When everyone began to leave the courtyard for some punch and cookies, Tato leaned to embrace her, and unable to speak, looked deeply into her eyes and embraced her again. Mama smiled as she looked on, but did not offer an embrace of her own.

Without the cost of the law school, Anna told Mama she could give her a little more money for her envelopes, which made Mama cry. Not much was made of her graduation at the church, beyond a few claps on her back and a few handshakes. She was a girl, after all, as a few men made sure to tell Tato.

In the subway going home from church, the week after Anna's triumphant graduation, I heard her and Mimi plan to go to a movie that afternoon. Anna told Mama she needed a little bit of a celebration, a little time off. She would start tomorrow to study for the Massachusetts Bar Exam.

A few Sunday afternoons later, she decided that another afternoon off wouldn't hurt either. She told me she had been collecting the things that we'd need to make some real Ukrainian Easter Eggs.

"I went to Halya's house one day after choir rehearsal and saw her beautiful eggs. She learned how to make eggs from her mother. She gave me the address of Surma, the Ukrainian store in New York, so I ordered what we need to make them. First, though, let's cover the table with newspapers."

I opened the direction sheet and saw many patterns. Mama leaned over and looked at them.

"Yes, I remember learning what the designs mean. I know there are designs to show love. Others remind us of the world around us. Yes, look. There's the sun, stars, the moon, and there's a horse, goosefeet, a spider, ram's horns, and wheat stalks. The priest told my cousin that the designs go back before Christ himself was born."

I couldn't believe Anna meant that I was going to be doing these eggs even after she had put out two candles, two pens and two lumps of wax. I watched, fascinated, as she heated the double-layer pen point in the candle flame, then pressed the back of it into a lump of beeswax and waited for the wax to melt up between the two layers. Her hand shook a little when she started to draw on the egg with the melted wax flowing off the point. She told me to try and I found it very difficult to heat the pen just exactly right so the wax neither flowed too heavily or not at all. She told me this was only practice. We would make a real egg the next Sunday night.

On Sunday night, Anna boiled some red, orange and yellow crepe paper in three pots. Halya had told her the crepe paper would make just as good a dye as Surma's expensive German dyes. Mama hovered over the operation lest Anna spill anything. Looking at the pamphlet of patterns Anna had laid out, I could not imagine how such straight lines could be drawn on the ever-changing curvature of an egg. Mama shook her head at our drunken lines, as we knew she would. I asked her if she made eggs in Kozova.

"Some people did, but not very many. To make such fancy eggs, you had to learn from a master. But I was happy to dye my eggs some pretty color and be done with it."

The look on her face told us she didn't think we'd be accomplishing much by ourselves, but over the weeks, Anna's lines became straighter. Mine never did, but I learned not to care as much.

The crepe paper dyes were strong on some eggs and blotchy on others. I couldn't help being sad when I finally finished an egg only to find out that one of the dyes didn't take. Anna tried washing the eggs with soap, giving them a final rinse in vinegar like Halya said, before we started. That helped the splotching a little. Several years later, when Anna bought some German dyes from Surma's, we found that Halya's advice about the crepe paper had not been correct.

Of course, a couple more disasters happened. When I held the finished egg up against the flame a little too closely during the process of melting off the solidified wax patterns, I made a scorch mark, which didn't wipe off with the melted wax. Mama almost closed our operations down when the rag I was using caught fire from the candle. After that, Anna melted the wax off my eggs and said I could do it when I was older. My final test of character came when an egg slipped out of my fingers as I was adding it to the finished ones in a bowl. I could only sob at the mess.

The directions from Surma said that you should make a hole at the top and bottom of the egg and blow until all of the raw egg came out. Anna said she was afraid she'd break the egg, so she didn't do it. Later that year, one of my eggs oozed a horribly stinky smell out of an almost invisible crack. I was very sad to throw it away.

Anna's eggs made a nice bowlful for the center of the dining room table, even with the blotchy dyes. Mine had wavering lines of differing thicknesses that took strange trajectories, and there were spots from dropped blobs of wax, so I kept them in a box up in the attic. Now and then I took them out to search for the rare places where I had actually made a bit of a straight line or a nice round flower. I wondered if I would ever make a whole egg as nice as Anna did.

Anna, like a true daughter of Tato, began to have egg-making lessons at our house for her church friends. She did wait until her studying for the bar exam was over, though.

Afraid to Hope

One Friday evening at supper, Tato looked around the table at us, and tilting his head to one side as if puzzled by something, said,

"Today, when I was fixing the sink at that lady's place on Commonwealth Avenue, she told me that she recommended me for a job as janitor to the principal of a private school called the Chestnut Hill School. She said I should go to the school on Monday morning and talk to the principal. I talked with Mr. Feltstein on my way home. He said he heard of that school. It's for very rich, American-only children. Their families come from the very first people who came to Cape Cod from England hundreds of years ago. Just imagine!" Mama searched his face for a moment then stood to get some butter.

"If they are so high-class, why would they hire you?"

"Probably the pay is low."

"Nu." Mama said with a shrug.

Tato, hunched over breakfast on Monday morning, muttered into his coffee cup.

"Who am I? A fifty-year old immigrant without two nickels to rub together. No real education. What can I say about myself to this principal? Why I am wasting my time going there?" He stood and walked heavily down the stairs.

At lunch with Mama, just as she was telling how Tato became a stenographer at the courthouse in Kozova, Tato came noisily up the stairs.

"Marena!" he bellowed, "Marena! The principal wants me to be the janitor."

"You got the job?" she asked, surprised.

"Yes, yes, I did!"

"How much is the pay?" she asked.

"Well, not so much. A dollar less than Anna makes. Thirteen dollars a week. Fifty-two dollars a month. She said they might give me more after the trial period. But maybe you could stop working one of your jobs!" Mama looked up in alarm. "It would be easier on you, Marena, to have only one job."

Mama shook her head.

"Well, at least I finally have a job," Tato exulted. "I start tomorrow. School has finished for the children. I have to be there at eight in the morning and can leave at five, at least in the summer. Winter days I might have to get there sooner to heat the building. The principal, I am supposed to call her 'Madam,' told me she and the teachers would be finishing up at the end of this week." He sat across from Mama.

"She told me that tomorrow the janitor, Mr. O'Leary, would show me the cellar. She spoke in a nasty way about the old janitor. She said she, not Mr. O'Leary, would tell me what needed to be done. But, you know, Marena, I can hardly wait to start. I haven't worked in so long!" He stared off to a corner of the kitchen, and then sighing said,

"You know, there is something that bothers me. Madam and the teachers called me 'Chopek,' not 'Mr. Chopek,' and I am wondering why. No matter where I have worked around the city, everyone called me Mr. Chopek. I think that calling me 'Chopek' is to remind me that I am just a janitor, and I must remember my place in their society."

"I just hope you hold your pride and your tongue when you are there. What does it matter what they call you?" Mama said wearily.

That night at supper, Tato described the new principal and his interview to Anna.

"This little lady looked as though she is made of sticks. When she looked me in the eye, I felt I began to shrink. She told me, 'You are not exactly what we had in mind. I wanted someone with experience; therefore, I can only hire you on a trial basis. At Christmas I will decide whether to keep you.' I didn't want to tell Mama this. Better she should feel good for now. But it is insulting to be told I might not be able to do a janitor's job!" He hesitated, "Oh, I think she will be a difficult lady, no matter how hard I work. And who knows what the teachers will be like? They are all women, you know."

Tato left early and eagerly the next morning. Around six in the evening, I heard him come up the stairs. He sat heavily at the kitchen table, his eyes focused on the middle of the table. Anna, already home from work, stopped stirring Mama's cabbage soup. I stopped putting out the bowls.

He sat in a dramatic silence, and then shaking his head, he stood and began to pace in front of the stove.

"What have I done? What have I stumbled into?" Horror and panic distorted Tato's voice. "Right away, Mr. O'Leary takes me down the stairs to the cellar. It was too dark to see where I was going! Most of the sockets had burned out bulbs! Boxes and barrels and things stuffed between. Cobwebs everywhere! I kept asking him about the furnace which was surrounded by valves and pipes with joints wrapped in rags and tied with wire, but he only pointed to a thermometer and said, 'That will be your purgatory and hell.'"

Anna poured the soup into bowls and she and I ate. Tato continued to pace.

"I tried to get him to tell me where the tools were, where the brooms were, but his head was all wrapped up with the principal. Finally, when he took a breath, I asked him again if he could explain how the furnace and boiler worked. He kicked the old, black sides and said, 'O lad, it's a damned, damned thing!' Then suddenly, he went like a squirming worm through all the piles of things with me running behind him, and we were up in the kitchen. I don't know how I will find anything there when I am alone.

"After I ate my lunch with Mr. O'Leary in the kitchen, he left for good saying, 'My parting wish is that the whole place burns down with her in it, and that she rots in hell.' The razor-blade lady came in just then and said, 'Follow me!' She began to show me through the rooms on the first floor. 'First, you must start with painting. That is the most important. Here on the first floor we have kindergarten, intermediate, first and second grades. Intermediate is for children not quite ready for first grade. And there are classrooms upstairs. Oh, and the children's furniture will need painting too.' By then we were at the assembly hall, which is right next to the front door. 'This room needs no painting, but you must oil the wood paneling and of course you must oil all the floors before September.' "What is this woman thinking? I ask you!"

He moved his palms and fingers slowly down his cheeks. "But that wasn't all. The big kitchen and the dining room full of tables and chairs have to be kept swept and mopped during school. She made it sound like I was a very lucky man because she would get regular window washmen for all the upper windows. All I had to do was the first floor. Then she brings me to one side of the school. The field looked about as big as my father's wheat field in Kozova. She says the grass needs to be mowed at least once a month. Then she shows me the other side. Another big grass field the same size as the other one. It is flat only where the swings and seesaws are. The rest goes straight up a hill to the many big trees around the edges. And all I saw was a small mower, just like mine here at home! There aren't enough hours in a day to get all of this done this summer!

"But then, she takes me up onto a deck between the play yard and the building. 'And, oh yes,' she says, 'the deck needs to be oiled every other week in the spring and fall.' She stares at me with evil eyes, and I am afraid to ask her where to start, but then, she says, 'Paint the classrooms first. Oiling the floors can be done after school starts.'

"Right then, one of the teachers came running out of the kitchen, yelling that water was pouring onto everything. I told Madam that I knew plumbing, and she told me I would have to pay a real plumber to undo any mistakes I make. So, I fixed the pipes, but it took me almost the rest of the afternoon because I had to spend so much time looking for tools in the cellar. The rest of the time I spent trying to get the grass mower in the cellar to work. Old grass bunches kept the wheels from turning, and I couldn't find anything to sharpen the blades or to oil the wheels. When I brought it out to the yard, she was on her way home. She said, 'I forgot to tell you, you must make a jungle gym for the children before September.' So Anna, Stephanie, what is a jungle gym?" We stared back dumbly. Neither Anna nor I ever had any playground things at our schools.

The next Sunday we drove out to the school in Vuychu's car so we could see it all for ourselves. Tato had looked at a map down at Mr. Feltstein's store during the week, so he was prepared to argue the route. I sat between Vuychu and Chocha on the front seat bench, and Anna sat between Mama and Tato in the rear. As expected, the arguing between Tato and Vuychu escalated with every turn. But Tato noted that even with a few of Vuychu's extra zigs and zags, the trip was shorter than taking the streetcar into Boston to get the bus out to Chestnut Hill. But, he'd never be able to afford a car. He knew that.

While Tato fussed with the keys, everyone stood quietly in front of the building admiring the pattern of dark wood beams crossing the creamy plaster below the bell tower. Blooming rhododendrons made a thick border with a large house higher up the hill on the left side of the school. I veered off to the right side of the school and gazed at the swings and seesaws and sand piles. It wasn't fair!

Following Tato through the sun-lit rooms, we spoke softly. Photos of various classes were hung thickly on both sides of the wide staircase to the second floor. At the secretary's office door, there was an extra-large, brownish photo of the school with students and teachers standing stiffly in straight rows. 1887 was written in one corner with lovely flourishes.

We followed Tato into the secretary's office. Soft chairs and a table with a silver tea service stood to one side of the room. A desk and files were on the other. A cut-glass vase on a windowsill spread rainbows to every corner. Mama turned to me and said, "Don't touch anything!" just as my hand was moving toward some china cups.

Tato unlocked the door to the principal's office. Anna said it looked like a museum room. This time it was Tato who told us not to touch anything. We walked on the soft carpet, our arms clasped behind us, to get a closer look at the many objects on the display shelves. I saw a stuffed owl, dishes covered with exotic sea shells, a corn necklace, a tiny loom holding four inches of an intricate pattern, browning photographs of ancient, columned buildings, a little sculpture of a head and another of a body without head or legs. Tato moved us all out gently before we had seen even half of the things.

"I'll show you the older children's classrooms, now." Tato said.

I wanted to stay in the sixth grade room, but Mama nudged me out. "You stay with me," she hissed. Tato led us up a smaller, steeper staircase to a group of little rooms under the eaves with bookshelves built into every wall. Little round tables and stools were scattered throughout. Each floor-to-ceiling window had a soft, padded, flowery, chintz window-seat. I sat on one and looked out into the top of a pine tree. Quarreling squirrels and a jaybird flitted along the limbs. Mama's hand grasped my arm. "Don't go so near the window," she said, her voice tight. "Please, don't, don't. Let's get out of here, this is a terrible room, so high, it scares me." She shook my arm. I don't want you ever to go in these rooms!" She shook me again. Chocha shook her head.

When Mama got ahead of us, Tato whispered that he'd bring me back to the school as often as I wanted in the summer. "You'll be able to help me in a lot of ways." I rode home in a trance of joy and didn't hear Tato and Vuychu arguing about how to get home.

A few days later Anna showed Tato a piece of paper and said,

"I asked if anyone in the office knew what a jungle gym was, and one man who has a child in private school sketched one out for me. "

Tato studied the drawing. "Oh, I can make this easily. It is just pipes put together in a big cube, so children can climb in many directions. I just need the right size of pipes. I will ask Madam how big she wants it. You were clever to think of asking in your office, Anna. How ever would I have found out what a jungle gym is?"

On Saturday, walking home from an Oakland Hall dance, Mama told Tato that their friend, Olena, had a job putting together the injection needles that doctors use. The factory was on River Street, about five blocks from our house. Olena's boss asked her if she knew any women he could hire, because the Army wanted more needles.

"And she says I should come with her on Monday. Oh, just think! If I got the job, I could work in the day, and maybe, just maybe, sleep again like a normal person."

Mama did get the job and immediately quit both her nighttime jobs. The two jobs had meant twelve hours away from home, while the needle job took less than nine. She said she would earn only three dollars less than the two night jobs put together.

"I'm afraid to be happy just yet though," she said to me at lunch. "I don't trust Tato to keep the school job, because he has a temper if he's pushed hard enough and that Madam pushes. She sounds just like Anyelka herself. Oh, she was such a witch! Yes, I will be surprised if he doesn't lose this job pretty quickly. And who knows how Anna will do. Anna still has to pass the bar exam, and maybe she won't pass. Maybe it will be too hard for her, she's a girl, you know, and then maybe they will just pass the men. There must be a reason why there are almost no women lawyers." She shrugged.

"It is hard to do the same thing over and over at the needle factory, but it's better than working at night. But I know that jobs can come and go. This Depression isn't over yet. But right now, with the extra money, I can maybe buy a little piece of beef for Sunday dinner, instead of always having a chicken, and maybe if Anna gets a lawyer job, maybe we can even start to pay back some principal of the mortgage. But oh no," she shuddered, "I need to shut up. I am afraid to even think about such things."

She put out some milk. "Tato says he wants to take you with him to the school this summer, only you have to promise me not to go up to those high windows." Her face showed she knew I would go up there.

"I won't go up unless Tato's with me," I said, looking down at my glass. There had been no time to cross my fingers.

That summer, I was at the school almost every day. I was afraid, like Mama, to be too happy. I had a constant nagging feeling that something was about to happen to spoil my adventure. I might break something or leave a mark somewhere. Worst of all, Tato might suddenly decide to give me a punishment for throwing that bottle at Mary Catherine. Ever since I did that, he had been different. He had turned so quiet. Was he was trying to find the right punishment for me, or was it something else?

I found a strange contentment in working with him, being needed by him. Now, I was doing more important things than cutting crepe paper for angel wings. I had the difficult job of dripping oil in just the right amount onto deck boards in front of his wide, cloth covered broom. I had to use all my strength to hold the ends of the heavy pipes and synchronize my twisting with his as he was putting the jungle gym together. I had to calculate just how much paint to take up on the brush so none would drip off on the way to the wall. The reward for me was eating lunch with Tato in the soft shade of a tree and listening to his ramblings, usually a little less angry than they had become recently.

"You know, Stefchu, one of the teachers told me that the building was made to look like the old buildings in England, where these people came from. You know their families are the ones who fought against England so they could make America. They put together the wonderful constitution that held the country together with sensible laws. They made a good country. I will always thank them for letting us in and letting us be Americans, but we will never belong with them. Maybe your children's children.

He thought a moment. "And where does Elias Chopek belong? When it comes right down to it, I haven't become friends with even lower class American people. Maybe Mr. Feltstein. I have my citizenship papers, but am I a real American, or just a patriotic Ukrainian who happens to live among Americans? I don't know. I really don't know." When we finished lunch, he stood and glared at the school.

"And now to figure out what to do next. Each day I come here, I don't know where to start. She expects me to do the work of five men! For myself, the most important thing is to clean the basement so I finally can put the tools all in one place so I can find them quickly."

We stood then. He told me I could go play and he'd call me if he needed me. He turned to the school, and I ran down to the incredible, wide-spreading, horizontal branches of the beech trees. I walked out until my weight began to bend the tips. Then I climbed one of the pine trees whose tops I had seen from the library windows. I was glad Mama wasn't there.

Over the weeks, I wandered through every one of the first floor rooms admiring all the marvels on the walls, on the shelves and in the drawers. Where my schoolrooms were identical and unadorned, each of these differed from the others. Pink prevailed in one, blue in another, and yet another was a kaleidoscope of colors. All had flowered curtains and pastel tables and chairs. I spent hours in those early grade rooms playing with the beads, puzzles, games, crayons, yarn, and paints.

The fourth, fifth and sixth grade rooms on the second floor had a different interest. I opened one of each stack of books to compare theirs with mine and found my fourth grade geography book in their third grade. The arithmetic problems we had in fifth grade were in their fourth grade books. I studied the fifth grade group photo on the staircase wall. The names under the pictures were not the usual Billy and Alice of my school. I whispered their names: Sterling, Spalding, Dorothea, Morgan, Patience, Elihu, Louisa, Prudence, Elliott and Charity, and tried to memorize each name with its face. After a few weeks, I could cover the names with my hand, and say the right name for each face. In the sixth grade room, where they would be in the fall, I assigned them desks and played teacher. "You, Sterling, won't you erase the board for me, please? And you, Prudence, I'd like you to review the spelling words I am putting on the board."

The afternoons always ended with a long sit up in the forbidden library rooms. I felt no Mama-guilt in curling up in a window seat and looking into the tops of the trees, or far down onto the fields. I waggled my thumb and fingers at my nose toward Mrs. McGillvary, wherever she might be, as I chose my own books, 'thank you m'am!' I could go from a brightly illustrated book of fairy tales, to a fat book of Civil War stories for boys, happy that she couldn't wrinkle up her nose at me. I would read until I heard Tato calling up to me that it was time to go home. I stood then, and smiling, said, "I'm leaving now, children. Do be good until I return tomorrow."

Anna takes the Bar Exam

Tato finished the painting of the first floor rooms by Labor Day and had begun on the second floor. The crisscross pipe construction of the jungle gym stood large near the swings. But, in spite of much effort in the cellar, only the corner where he had assembled the resurrected tools looked orderly under the bright, newly replaced bulbs.

I was sorry to lose my sweet, summer days at the school. I could only follow the sixth grade students on an occasional Saturday visit. Once I knew I had Mr. Ambrose, the only male teacher in the school, I was eager for my own sixth grade. Unlike Miss Smith, he pushed us to think in new ways. I began to acquire a readable handwriting since he didn't insist we had to turn our fingers into cement. The only B's on my report card continued to be in the Domestic Arts, though my stitching began to look straighter to me. I felt myself to be on the verge of growing up into a real person.

I had a happy mix of friends that made a large enough group to discourage the bullies. We went to the movies together, and I would ask one or another up to my house since Mama wasn't home until five from the needle factory. I was asked to their homes. Lorraine had a grandmother living at her house who kissed her when she came in. I usually came away feeling jealous. Thinking about it, I was sure I didn't want Anyelka kissing me and not sure that Mama's saintly mother would want to kiss this wild child.

Because Mama was home from the needle factory by five these days, I no longer flung myself around the living room to Wagner's or Beethoven's musical commands. I sat to my homework or practiced the piano. Streychu, having bought a new radio, gave us his old, portable one. Tato put it on the kitchen table, and soon Mama was addicted to a serial called Stella Dallas. I sat at the table while she made supper. We learned that Stella Dallas was a poor, tormented mother with an inordinate love for her child, which made for much drama and distress.

Events moved slowly on these serials, with a predictable pattern of days for a dramatic incident and days for discussion by various characters, followed by a Friday afternoon disaster, which was sure to get you back at the radio on Monday. I never knew how much Mama really understood, but she never asked me for any explanations either. Sometimes, during a commercial, she would turn to me and say, "Trobbers, trobbers, always dey got trobbers." But at least, she seemed to momentarily forget her own troubles while listening to theirs.

Anna's long-awaited Bar Exam took place just before Christmas at a boy's high school. Law School graduates came from their prestigious schools in Boston and Cambridge. Before the exam, the proctor told them that only a third of them would pass, and if a choice came between a man and a woman, the man would be admitted rather than the woman, because he was the family's source of income.

When Anna came home the night of the exam, she looked both annoyed and worried.

"It sure didn't start right. When I sat at my assigned desk, my chin was just above the desk. Apparently they had been made for boys taller than my four foot ten inches. I tried to explain to the proctor that I could not sit all day like that and write an exam paper. I asked him if I could change my seat. I thought that the ones in front were smaller. He said sternly, 'No, the seats can't be changed. Look for something to sit on.'

"I looked and I told him I couldn't find anything. By that time he looked at me as if to say, 'Get lost, what are you doing around here anyway?' Then he looked on the shelf behind him and gave me the thickest book. It was a Bible. I was shocked. It seemed irreverent to sit on the Bible, but I had no choice. I said a prayer, and began, inspired from above and below, I guess." She laughed. "It turned out to be too small and uncomfortable." She sighed. The lines in her forehead deepened, " I don't know how I'm going to last until I find out how I did. I think I did well, but then maybe I really didn't."

She began to study the case assigned to them for the Orals. She had me come and sit at her desk, pacing in front of me as she pleaded the case. She said it helped her to have a live person to look at. I understood nothing of what she said, but found the timbre of her new, decisive voice fascinating. The morning of the Orals, she wrapped and rewrapped her long hair until the bun was smooth, tight and prim. She hoped that the high heels would add a little height, and the hat would make her look older.

When she came home that night, she looked drawn and shaken. After she'd sat a while at the kitchen table she put her head on her hand and said,

"What a horrible day I've had! I don't know where I am. Could be the top, could be the bottom. There were five examiners sitting on the bench. They looked down at me for a long time. I began to feel all jittery and wondered if I was supposed to say something first. Finally, the Chairman of the Board began questioning me. 'And where did you graduate from?' I thought that was a stupid question. He had the information in the file in front of him. 'Portia Law,' I said. Then, very condescendingly, I thought, he asked, 'And how did you graduate from Portia Law?' 'Magna Cum Laude,' I said, 'And how many girls graduated Magna Cum Laude?' 'Six,' I answered.

"And then, in his high class, Boston accent, he said, 'What business have you, a young lady coming from the wheat fields of Europe, knowing so much about English common law, whereas our boys have such difficulty learning it?' I couldn't believe my ears. I have no foreign accent. I've lived here all my life except the first year. Then I wondered whether he wanted a dissertation on Constitutional Law. Remember, I won a prize at Portia for my paper on Constitutional Law, so I knew I could do it, but what did he really want? Then I decided that the question didn't deserve an answer. I swallowed, looked up and said I was brought up in America. I was only a year old when I came here."

" 'Thank you very much, Miss Chopek,' they all said and then began talking to each other. I guessed that I was done, but how could I be? I had been in there only five minutes! No one had asked me a single question on the case I had spent so long preparing. Everyone else taking the Orals was in there at least a half hour. So, now I'm sure I haven't passed. I don't really know yet if I got a good score on the Bar Exam, and I don't know long it will take to find out about this fiasco."

In later years, when she repeated the story, I said that maybe the Chairman was actually complimenting her, though in a patronizing way. She was unconvinced. "If you had heard his voice, you would know it wasn't a compliment."

About six weeks after the Orals, Anna received a call at work from her Bar Review teacher. "You have passed! And I know you won't believe this, but a Harvard man didn't write the highest score of the written exam! You had the highest score! You were first on the list!"

Anna waited until Tato was home to tell us the unbelievable news. As soon as Tato finished his supper, he ran down Greenfield Road to tell Streychu and Streyna and share a beer, then ran up to Blake Street to tell Chocha and Vuychu and share another. On Sunday, he told all the men down in the church basement, especially those who had chided him for sending a girl to Law School. One of his best friends said what he had said when she graduated, "You know, you spent all this money sending her to school, but how much difference will it really make? Who will hire her? She's a girl after all." Tato spent the next fifteen minutes arguing with him. "He could have just congratulated me!" he said angrily on the streetcar going home.

On Monday, of course, Tato told all the teachers at the school. They were the most impressed of all.

Anna, buoyed by her success and armed with her Bar Exam rating, started her job search by going to law firms in the near vicinity of her office after work. They looked at her first place rating, then said simply. "We are truly sorry, but we do not hire women lawyers in this firm." She traced a wider circle through the city, but even at the less well-known law firms, she got the same response.

One evening, she came home with an especially angry face.

"Would you believe it? I was called into the President's office today! I was never in his office before, though I've had some dealings with his son, who is Treasurer of the company. I was worried I'd done something awful, but he shook my hand, and said,

"'Well, young lady, my dear friend, the Chairman of the Board of Bar Examiners, told me that a Ukrainian girl, who worked for my company, had received the highest score on the Bar Exam.'" Anna flung out her arms, "That friend was the same chairman that had been so high-falutin' to me during the Orals!" She sat heavily.

"Then the President said with a really fake smile, 'Congratulations to you, young lady. I was so impressed, I decided to find a place in my legal department for you.' I thought, well finally! Then he asked, 'and how much are you now earning?' 'Fourteen dollars a week, but I've been doing secretarial work.' I said. He thought for a minute and said, 'Well, from now on, young lady, your salary will be eighteen dollars a week!' I thanked him and left, but I thought about it all day. I asked around, and I found out that this was really insulting. Starting salaries for men lawyers are fifty dollars a week. I am going back tomorrow to protest!"

Tato and Mama told her to think about it a little longer

One day about a week later, she came home frowning angrily.

"I finally was allowed in to see to the son, the Treasurer. I thought he was a reasonable man. I told him his father had offered me a job in the legal department at eighteen dollars a week. I told him this was much below the men lawyers. He defended his father's rules about the women's salaries, but then he said he could raise my salary to twenty-five dollars a week. Still, only half of what the men make! I thanked him and left. I know I have no other places to try, so I have to take it." She snorted, "I thought I'd have trouble because I was an immigrant child, but now it's because I'm a female."

By late spring, she had acquired two secretaries and a male assistant and her pay increased by a few dollars, so for a little while, she began to feel better.

Learning to Endure

Once the school year started, Tato came to supper every day with some revelation about this high-class society at the school. Mama served her food, paying him scant attention. Anna went to listen to the radio after she ate. I hoped Tato noticed that I was still his most reliable listening ear. One night, after both Mama and Anna had left, he leaned back in his chair and fixed his eyes on mine.

"Madam had a gathering of the older children in the Assembly Hall today. I did some sweeping by the open doors, so I could hear her clearly. She was shaking her finger at them and telling them that they were members of the highest class in New England, America really, so they must become worthy of such an honor. They must learn to be kind to those beneath them. Hah! I thought. Dear Madam tells them to be kind and she herself could not be more unkind to those under her. And wouldn't it be kind for the children to call me Mr. Chopek once in a while. So, you see, they are taught to think of themselves as better than the rest of us.

"When she was done with the assembly, she came out the front door looking for me. By then I was arranging all the useless things from the cellar so they would be by the curb for the trash men tomorrow.

"'What do you think you are doing?' she screamed. ' The junkman will buy all this. Put all these things back by the cellar door and I will call the junkman to come tomorrow morning. These are valuable things.' Nu, can you imagine, Stefchu? This rich, high class, better-than-anybody school selling their junk to the junkman?

"So I had to move all that stuff, bundles of old newspapers, piles of odd metal pieces, empty cans of paint and oil. Can you believe it! I had found a box of burned out light bulbs and a box of empty spools. I am afraid I am getting a hernia."

I was already waiting for the second installment of the trash episode, when Tato came upstairs the next evening. I had to wait until some household problems got solved between Tato and Mama before he could sit down and go on with the story.

"So, this morning, the junkman comes. He tells me he will give me a dollar for the heaps of paper, and two dollars for all the metal things. He said the burned out light bulbs and the spools were worthless, as if I didn't know that. He told me to throw the spools into the furnace. I called the Madam down to talk to the junkman herself. She argued with him about everything, and finally got four dollars out of him. Imagine! She told me to put the burned-out light bulbs and the empty spools back in the cellar, because maybe a different junkman will take them! 'You see,' she said, 'you would have thrown it all away. Those four dollars will pay for some chalk or pencils for the teachers. Let this be a lesson. I will give you the phone number for the junkman, so before you throw anything away, you can call him. I also want you to look through all the teacher's wastebaskets while you empty them to see if they threw away something worth while."

Before Halloween, Tato went to a doctor and found out he had an ulcer and the beginnings of a hernia. He told the doctor about the stress of working for this unreasonable principal and the doctor told him to find another job.

The Sunday after the doctor's appointment, Mama and Anna went straight home from church. Tato and I got on a bus to the school. We passed masses of red, orange, gold and yellow trees streaming leaves pushed out by the wind.

"Look, Tato, look how the leaves are making piles everywhere!" I said.

"Yes, and there will be piles waiting for me to rake at the school. Maybe you could help me." He sighed. "You know the doctor told me to look for another job, and I have been thinking hard about that. But just where is this job waiting for me?

"The Madam is a regular devil, but then there are the teachers. They are all women, and I never thought I could work only with women. I thought 'How do I talk to these women?' But, little by little, I realize that although it is different talking to men, it is not so bad to interact with them. They seem to laugh a lot, and they do say meaningful things. I think I have become friends with a few of them, especially Miss Bartlett, who gave us that delicious maple syrup her parents made last spring in Vermont.

"And the children. I knew, of course, that I loved my own daughters, and my brother's and sister's children, but to find that I love all these children surprises me. Well, I don't love every single one of them. A few are pretty nasty. But though Madame has told them they are superior, I am still like a father to them.

"Well, except in one way. I told you that the children call me Chopek, except that some of the children think my name is Joe Peck, and then they call me Peck. I laugh and then I'm angry." We got off the bus and turned up Hammond St. to walk to the school. We stopped to look at the fields stretching to either side of the school. The stands of trees above the playground were brilliant with new fire.

"But look, Stefchu, look at the beauty of all this. Doesn't this matter too? How can I possibly let the Madam force me away from all this."

When we finished raking and piling, Tato said he'd call me if he needed me.

I raced up to the sixth grade room. The desks were full now. I put a scrap of paper on top of the desk with the name I found inside. I was surprised to see some of the desks full of crumpled papers, open books and dirty handkerchiefs. Apparently they didn't have a desk check on Fridays like we did.

'Joe Peck' supervising the flag-raising with the children

I began to dream of one day being in the school with all of them. I would recognize them from their pictures on the wall, and I would say, 'Hi, Patience! Hi, Morgan!' They would be really surprised that I knew them. But of course, when I went to make that horrible egg, I didn't even dare look up at them, much less say, 'Hi.'

Once winter was close, Tato had to study the furnace. He had worked with factory furnaces before starting the Pipe Factory job, so, drawing on his memory of what the various valves and gauges controlled and measured, he began to understand the beast.

Once he had fired it up, he saw that it wasn't going to be easy to maintain the seventy-two degrees the Madam demanded.

" That old boiler can't handle the job. I tell her that, but she tells me I am just too lazy to shovel in enough coal. Now, she is going around looking at each thermometer and complaining almost every day. It gets nasty sometimes. So I watched her route to the thermometers and now I sneak around a corner ahead of her. I breathe hard on the thermometers and push the mercury up to maybe seventy-six. When she shows up, I pretend I am looking at what it says. When she gets to the thermometer, it usually reads close to seventy-two. Once I breathed it up too high, and she told me to cut back on the coal, or the bills would be too high! When she's done, she forgets about them, and if a teacher comes in to say her room was too cold, Madam says it is her imagination or maybe she is sick."

When Tato said that one the young teachers asked him about a boy who kept telling lies, Mama listened skeptically. "A teacher is asking you?" she asked. She lifted her eyebrows even higher to hear that another had invited him into the teachers' lounge for tea.

"And you know," he said, "A Miss Upton came down to my cellar to see me. She is very young for a teacher. She began to cry when she talked about Madam, and how nothing she did was right. She thinks she should leave. I had to think very hard about what to say to her.

"'So', I said, 'I work under this witch-lady too. I have an ulcer and a hernia, and now I can only eat the softest foods. Don't let yourself get an ulcer too. Remember why you wanted to be a teacher and teach! Forget that old-maid principal. She isn't going to fire you. She is mostly noise, at least I hope so. Listen with one ear, but give your attention to the children.' She cried a little more, and then left. I don't know if I said the right thing to that poor, young girl. I don't even know where my words came from." Mama shook her head and clamped her lower lip under her teeth.

The parents were another mystery to him. He had a new story every night from watching them come for their children

"These are people unlike any I know. You should see how big their cars are! Mostly, it is maids or butlers who pick up the children, but now and then the parents come to talk with Madam or to watch the children's events in the Assembly room. The mothers hardly ever speak to me. Many are taller than me, and they have faces that look a little like horses. They don't seem to care at all what kind of clothes they wear and they walk with wide steps.

"The men are always dressed up though. Many of them walk with canes, even though they are young. I suppose it makes them feel more important. Now and then, one of the fathers stop and slaps me on my back and says 'Fine job you're doing on this old stack of wood they call a school! Hope Madam isn't giving you too hard a time, old chap!' But, to be fair, one trustee did ask me about the boiler. I said we need a new one. The trustee said they didn't have enough money because of the Depression. Another asked me what I thought about Roosevelt. I had to think about my answer, because I didn't want him to think I was stupid. Of course, he probably didn't care what I think. He just wanted to be seen talking to the poor janitor.

"But, one man seems to really listen. He's a very tall, skinny man. He lives up on the hill. One day he shook my hand and said he was Susie's father, Mr. Saltonstall. I saw that name in the paper once, so I asked him if he was the Leverett Saltonstall who was in the Massachusetts Congress. He laughed and said yes, he was Speaker of the House. When I told him I was a Ukrainian immigrant, he began to ask me questions, and he seemed really interested. Now we often talk. I can't believe he is such an important man."

Over the years that his daughter was in the school, Mr. Saltonstall and Tato continued to converse. Later when Mr. Saltonstall became first the Governor of Massachusetts and then a United States Senator, Tato felt a great deal of pride in having educated him on Ukraine. He thought it would help him as a Senator.

When he talked about the children, his eyes would be soft and full of concern for their hard little lives.

"I often help the little children with their boots and raincoats. Of course the Madam saw me. She told me the children must do this themselves, and besides I have not been hired to talk to the children or help them. So, now when it rains or snows, I stand inside the cellar door, which is around a corner. The children know that if they put their foot in, I will take their overshoe off. So far Madam hasn't noticed. I also make sure she isn't around when I talk to them.

"There is one little girl, Deborah, who told me she has not seen her mother or father for a year! They are touring the world and she is alone in the house with just a Nanny. Can you imagine that! How hard it must be for little Deborah to have only a Nanny and not her own mother and father to talk to. I told her she could talk to me.

"And then there is Douglas. He comes to school hungry because the cook sleeps late. Apparently the mother sleeps late as well, and the father takes his breakfast near his office in Boston. This should not happen to a child. I go into the kitchen and get a piece of bread and spread it with a little jam, but I have to be careful the other children don't see. I leave the bread and jam inside the kitchen door, and he eats it up fast, poor child."

I couldn't help saying, "But Tato, nobody ever made my breakfast. I go to school lots of times without eating." He looked at me, annoyed.

"Now you know that's altogether different. We maybe didn't have a lot of food in the pantry, but there was always something for you to eat. All you had to do was take it."

At Christmas, he was comfortable enough to suggest to the teacher in charge of the Christmas program that he could talk about Ukrainian Christmas customs and what they meant. She said that would be wonderful and could he make a manger? Tato said, Of course, and could she perhaps get some straw or maybe even a sheaf of wheat?

Well before Christmas, Tato began writing about how he celebrated Christmas as a boy in Kozova. His final copy was ten, hand-written pages. On the Saturday before the event, he took me to the school to help him make the manger. I held boards and handed him nails. He handed me little bundles of straw to smooth into the manger. "Miss Talbot couldn't find any wheat, but at least we will have straw for our table." He said. When he was satisfied with the manger, he told me to sit in the back and listen to his talk. He especially wanted to know if he was talking loud enough. Hardly referring to the pages he held in one hand, he went right into the best of his story-telling modes, his voice and eyes and gestures, as always, adding layers of meanings to his words. I was mesmerized by the flow of his story that I had only heard in bits and pieces over the years.

Tato was in a fury when he came in the kitchen door the night of his talk. He threw a box and a card onto the table and flung out his trembling arms.

"Do you know what the Madam said to me when the Assembly was all over?" He didn't wait for any of us to answer. "Well, it wasn't right away. First, she came out in front of the students and teachers and parents and said..." He tuned up to a high, chirpy, female voice. "'Thank you so much, dear Chopek, for sharing your customs with us." His voice descended into an angry roar. "But then, she told me to come to her office. I went up and she had the nerve to say to me, 'Chopek, the trustees thought about giving you a Christmas bonus, but they decided not to offend you with a money gift.' She handed me this card. He stopped, unable to continue. See, it says, 'Thank you for your good efforts.'

"They didn't want to offend me?" His voice rose as he repeated it. "They didn't want to offend me?" His cheeks and nose turned a frightening red.

Anna and Mama didn't know what to say to calm him. Anna asked him how his talk to the children went, and he said, sullenly, "Fine." Mama could only say that supper was ready. Tato went to the table and opened the box of decorated cookies. He said it was from the cook.

"At least someone thought to give me something we can eat."

Mama exclaimed loudly that they were so nice we would each have one for dessert tonight. If we had one apiece every night, they would last for four days!

Tato muttered that there was no way he could continue to work at the school.

The next day, Saturday, Mama and I went with him to the school to help him clean up. Mama swept. Tato and I dismantled the manger and swept the straw into a bag. It would be tucked under our Christmas Eve tablecloth to remind us that Christ was born in a manger. Tato filled the furnace with coal and set it to burn low, so he wouldn't have to come in for a day or so. Tato and I joined Mama, who had just finishing cleaning the kitchen stove, at the wide, kitchen window. We watched the snow falling in thin swirls over the field and the hillside above.

Tato said, "I think and I think about whether to work here. The teachers, the children and some of the parents respect me, but I am treated like mud beneath the feet of Madam and the trustees. I earn next to nothing, and they don't want to offend me with money. Have they any idea how hard it is to live on my miserable pay?"

Mama laughed, "Well, this is America for you. You are a somebody and a nobody all at the same time. I think you are pretty lucky to have this job. Many people at the church still have no work or maybe they are with the WPA. We're too rich for that, remember?" She turned to get our coats. "Poor people like us cannot afford to say what we think. We must swallow and swallow, then swallow some more."

Steps forward, Steps back

When the serious January cold set in, Tato knew that his thermometer breathing was not going to raise the mercury up to seventy-two degrees. Madam threatened to fire him at every thermometer confrontation. One Thursday morning, he folded down my piazza cot, lashed his pillow around it and shoved it into a large cloth bag. He told Mama he was staying at the school overnight because of the furnace. He came home on Friday night looking sleepy. He told Mama he missed her good supper.

"I was comfortable enough. I spread those small children's nap blankets under me, and spread some more on top of me. I put the cot near the furnace and set the alarm for every two hours. After school, I banked the fire, and then around midnight, I began to shovel in more coal. When Madame was checking the thermometers in the morning, they were at seventy degrees, easy to breathe up to seventy-two. I might have to do that the rest of the winter, but I'm afraid the coal will run out before Madam expects."

Eventually Madam figured out that he was sleeping in the cellar. She queried him relentlessly about how much extra coal he might be using. He argued that he couldn't get to seventy-two degrees without using more coal. The furnace was not big enough for such a large building, it was not insulated enough, and the radiators needed some work by professionals. Madam just shook her head and strode off. He expected to be fired every day, and every day he thought and rethought what he would say when that happened. Now, he was home only on weekends. His ulcer flared up. He asked people at the church and at the Saturday night dances to tell him if they knew of any jobs, but no one did. He relaxed a little when she hadn't fired him by the end of the severe cold.

Just before American Easter, (we had had Easter according to our church calendar a few weeks earlier) one of the teachers asked Tato to talk about Easter customs in Ukraine at the Assembly before Easter vacation started. Tato agreed and told her that he would bring his daughter, Stephanie, to do a dance and demonstrate how to make a Ukrainian egg. My poor dance and egg making performance was bad enough, but I felt a greater sorrow because I knew so many of them by name, and none of them knew me.

When Easter vacation was over, I didn't tell any of my friends my Chestnut Hill saga. None of them would have believed that any one at such a school would have wanted to watch me do anything like that anyway.

Tato must have still been somewhat worried because, over the Easter vacation, he made one last round of the factories in Boston. He found no mobs like in the early days of the Depression, but no jobs either. Mama dug up and planted her vegetable garden afternoons after Stella Dallas, and before she started making dinner. Neither spoke much, but some days their unspoken anger seemed to stretch out the walls.

Finally, it was the Friday before the last week of school. When Anna came up the stairs from work and passed through the kitchen, Mama told Anna and me in an angry tone to stay out of way while she was cooking. She often said this, but this time I noticed that she was folding a piece of blue paper into the table drawer. Her sister usually wrote asking for money on that color of paper. Anna went to her room. When she came back, she too was scowling. Tato's feet made an unusually loud noise on the way up the stairs. Why were they so extra angry tonight?

I decided not to say anything at dinner about the talk Mr. Ambrose had had with me after school. He asked me first why I had chosen to take the Commercial Course track, instead of the College Course next year in junior high. I tried to explain.

"My family can't afford college, and I don't really know if I want to go to college. My sister worked as a stenographer to pay her way through law school, so I'll have to do that too." Mr. Ambrose chewed at his lip for a minute.

"I would like you to talk to your parents, or they can come to see me. I think you should take the College Course. I don't like that students have to make such a decision at this age, but that's how it is. I believe taking the Commercial Course would be a waste of time for you. You need the challenge of the College Courses." I suppose I looked startled. I had never expected such words from him.

"Your IQ number shows that you are a smart girl, and you do all your homework. I think, in time, you can achieve real success. If you keep up the good work, I have no doubt that you will get a scholarship at one of the many colleges in the Boston area."

I did not have any real idea of what college was really like, except that it was very hard work. And what were IQ's and scholarships? I wished he would explain it a little. Why should I go? Was college like Law School? I knew I didn't want to go to Law School like Anna did, but couldn't have told anyone why. But at that moment, I was so overwhelmed that he thought that I, a girl, was smart and should go to college, I suddenly wanted to go more than anything else.

I checked faces around the supper table. If I told them now that I wanted to go to college, the answer was sure to be a resounding 'No.' I watched them a little longer to be sure. Tato was scowling, Anna was scolding me loudly for forgetting the butter knife, and Mama's eyes were red when she brought in the fragrant pot of chicken soup. Tato ladled some soup into his bowl, and then looking up, he began shaking the spoon at us.

"Well, Madam took me to her office today, just as I had been afraid she would all winter long. The school treasurer told her how much the extra coal cost this winter. She looked like a dog about to attack me. I told her I only used as much coal as I needed to get the thermometers up to seventy-two, which is what she wanted. Oh, we went round and round. Finally, she said that I would be on trial for one more year. She was against the increase of three dollars a month in salary that the trustees had decided to give me next fall, but I would have to work three dollars a month harder. I told her I had made inquiries about Public School janitors, and they made almost twice as much as I was. She just laughed in my face.

"So what choice do I have? No one at church knows of any jobs out there. No jobs at the factories. But, can my ulcer and I live through one more year with that razor-blade lady?"

Mama glared at him. "You let that Madam make you suffer. You could make a stone face if you tried." Anna said, "It wouldn't hurt to keep looking for another job." Tato lifted his hands.

"I thought I was so far ahead of other men in Kozova and here at the church, but as an American, I don't have enough education to feed my family. Even if I wanted to improve myself, it's too late. It will always be like this for me." He buried his face in his hands. Anna pointed a finger into her chest,

"Well, I have an education and that hasn't stopped the company from humiliating me. I cannot believe that I, a lawyer, have to stand in line and punch a time clock every morning, noon and night. The men lawyers in the company, my male assistant, none of them have to do this, but I do, because it is a rule of the company that all women have to punch the clock. Every day I feel like making a complaint."

Mama glared at her. "What if they fired you? You didn't have such an easy time getting this much of a job. You should just punch the time clock. Why should you take it so seriously? It's such a little thing!" Anna glared at her, "It's not a little thing to me," she sighed. "How am I ever going to get anywhere like this? I've worked so hard, and I just know I'm never going to make it as a real lawyer. Men always act like women are dumb and worth nothing, and I know I'm not dumb."

Mama looked from Anna to Tato back to Anna.

"So, you, Hilko, you have teachers and children to talk to, work that takes clever hands and good planning, and you, Hanya, you are doing a lawyer's work. I don't know just what you do, but I don't think any bum off the street could do it. But me, I sit there every day doing the same things over and over. My fingers do it themselves. Any one in the world could do what I do. I, too, would like to know if this is all I am good for?"

I looked up into their frustrated, angry faces and decided to wait until Sunday night supper to tell them about my talk with Mr. Ambrose. Maybe they would all be feeling better. I needed time, anyway, to think about how to tell them what he said.

But the mood in the house remained heavy. At suppertime, on Sunday I could not see a positive answer to Mr. Ambrose's request in their sullen faces, so resigning myself to rejection, I waited until everyone was almost finished devouring Mama's tender, fragrant roast chicken and stuffing. Turning to Tato, who was my best bet, I sighed deeply and started my prepared speech.

"Mr. Ambrose told me that he thought I shouldn't be in the Commercial Course. He said that I was smart and should be in the College Course. He said he was sure I could get a scholarship when I finished High School."

Mama and Anna responded before I could say anymore. Their words crossed back and forth over each other, and sometimes they were talking at the same time: Mr. Ambrose was dreaming. Don't forget you are a girl. You can't plan on getting a scholarship. You must study secretarial so you find a job like I did. You have to save money first. Maybe no college would even take you.

Tato, quiet through their exchange, finally interrupted and asked me to repeat exactly what Mr. Ambrose said.

He looked around the table at each of us for a moment, and then said slowly, "I think her teacher is right." The three-way, rapid-fire argument that ensued was painful to listen to and I wanted to go hide somewhere. Tato finally put up both hands, saying, "Stop, stop. Now look. If she doesn't get a scholarship when she graduates High School, I'm sure we will be able to feed her for one more year, and maybe help her pay for a year at a nighttime Secretarial School. She can always work in a store or restaurant during the day. But if she takes the Commercial Course now, she wouldn't even be able to get into a college. My teachers at Chestnut Hill have often talked to me about their colleges, and the more I hear about them, the more I believe that she should have a chance to go, even if she is a girl. Mr. Ambrose is the teacher. Shouldn't he know if she could get a scholarship? "

The next morning, I gave Mr. Ambrose Tato's note, which said that he should change me from the Commercial Course to the College Course. Smiling broadly, Mr. Ambrose shook my hand and said, "There, you are on a better path now."

The serenity of being on a good path lasted less than a block. Questions with no answers blew through my head. How would it really be at the Junior High School, far away in Hyde Park? Was it as big as Lorraine said it was? Would I get lost? Would the bullies find me? Would I be in classes with my Chittick School jump-roping friends? Would anyone there like me? Would the teachers be like Miss Egar or Miss Frazier? Would anyone walk the mile and a half to the school with me? Would it all be too hard for me? And what if I wasn't as smart as Mr. Ambrose said?

To be Somebody in America, at Last

On Monday night, Anna came home looking as angry as I had ever seen her.

She stared at the red borscht in her bowl as though it were something evil.

"I can't believe what happened to me today! " She looked up, tears sparkling in her eyes. " I've been working for over a week on a report, a really complicated report. We had just had a big, big bond loss. My boss asked me to research it and put everything together in a report. I finished it and gave it to my boss late in the afternoon, yesterday. Today, when he came back from the big meeting with the President and lawyers from the various bonding companies, I could hear him bragging to everyone in the office about how the President had congratulated him for the excellent report. I didn't hear him once mention to anyone that it was me who prepared the report. And worst of all, he didn't even come by my desk to thank me for all my hard work on it!" Her tears overflowed "This is the last straw for me. I am going to start looking for another position." Mama and Tato looked frightened as she ran to her room.

On Thursday night, Tato was late. Mama was muttering that the fish would be overcooked, when he came running up the stairs. His face was round with a wide smile. He held up a box of chocolates. "Look what we have for dessert!"

Mama disappeared into the dining room with the fish, and yelled back, "Come in here and eat! Now!"

Tato's smile widened even more as he followed her into the dining room.

"You won't believe what happened to me today. I know you won't. Even I don't believe it." He put his hand on his heart. "I thought I knew all about America, and yet I never expected this from these young American women."

"So, it's only a box of chocolates. Sit down now," Mama interrupted. "The food will get cold. You can tell us later."

"No," he said. "You have to hear it now." He filled his plate as he spoke.

"Madam left the school right after lunch, so I didn't have to worry about her all afternoon. I was going to the teacher's lounge to tell them I was ready to lock up. Then I saw the kindergarten teacher, Miss Long, waving at me from the teacher's room. When I went in the door, the teachers, all of them, stood up and yelled 'Surprise!' A decorated cake was on the table. It said 'Thank You, Chopek.'

"I couldn't understand what was happening. Then Miss Bartlett said the teachers wanted to thank me for all the help I had given them this year. One of them told how she sent a little boy to me, because he was always starting fights, and it had really helped. Another one said her class really enjoyed my story about my schooldays in Kozova. Another thanked me for bringing Stephanie to dance and make the egg." I sat up. Was she talking about me?

"There was a lot more that they said. I was shaking my head, because all these things were nothing much at all. Finally, Miss Long cut the cake, and Miss Turner poured the tea into the fancy cups. The cake and tea were very delicious. Then they gave me the box of chocolates, all wrapped up in this paper." He pulled out a carefully folded, shiny gold packet, and put it on the table. "I passed the box around, and then they asked me to talk. I didn't know what to say, so I thanked them for this big surprise, and told them about how Madam was only going to keep me on trial for the next year. I told them how little my pay is for a school janitor, so I had finally decided to quit, but then that maybe after this party, I had to think about it some more. They all clapped. 'Please stay, Chopek,' they all said." He blinked his eyes rapidly and his voice trembled.

"And you know, all the way home on the bus and streetcar, I was thinking over and over about how these good American ladies are thanking me, ME, this low-class, uneducated foreigner for how I have helped them with the children." He shook his head slowly. "How can I quit the school now?"

Anna sighed. "That must have been nice to be appreciated like that." She turned to him and spoke emphatically, "This is why I 'm so glad you came to America. What would have happened to you there? To Mama? To me? I would never have been a lawyer over there."

Mama wrinkled her nose. "America is such a funny place. Anna is a special lawyer person, with all those high marks and honors from her school, but still her boss treats her like a nobody. And you," she stared into Tato's eyes, "You have always been somebody special at the church, smarter than the rest. And now, somehow, you are somebody very special to the teachers, even while you are a nobody to the principal. But at least you can be proud of yourselves in front of some of the people in this country. But me…" Tears welled up in her eyes. "Do you even know how long since I have been proud of myself in front of anybody. Not since I was a dressmaker in Kozova! In America, I have been a nobody to everybody from the day I got off the boat. People, even you, think I'm stupid because I can't talk in American so good. And I have had to work so hard here, but how? Cleaning floors, cooking in restaurants and now putting needles together. Sometimes I think I can't make another one without screaming." Tato looked at her, his face full of surprise at the intensity of her words.

"Oh," Tato said, looking suddenly embarrassed. Tato stood and walked to the kitchen for some water. He came back chewing his lips.

"Marena, I forgot to tell you something in my excitement about my tea party." He looked liked he'd been caught in a lie. " You see," he said, speaking quickly, "the assistant cook told me she found another job that pays her better. I thought about telling Madam about you, but…" From his reddening face, I guessed he hadn't been going to tell Mama about this at all, maybe because he didn't think she could do such a job, or maybe he was ashamed of her uncertain English. "But, I thought I would ask you first, ask you what you would think. Do you think …would you…would it be too hard for you to learn to help cook American food for maybe a hundred people? And… and… well, you would have to get along with Madam, and that might be the hardest thing to learn. What do you think? Would you want to try it? I worry that you have only worked with Ukrainians."

Mama looked at Tato as though considering whether to be insulted. Then she lifted her head and said, "Of course I can do it. And Madam will not get the better of me, like she does with you." Tato's eyes made some quick blinks, but he didn't respond. Mama went on. "I will need to know how much pay I'll get, but maybe it won't matter if it's low, because last month when the new tenants, the Murphy's, moved in downstairs, I told them a higher rent than I had been thinking of asking. I raised it a lot, because Mr. Murphy told me he has a job with the city, and his wife is a schoolteacher. They should be able to pay more. They didn't even argue about it." Tato's face said that Mama should have talked to him first. He sighed, "Then I will talk to Madam tomorrow."

On Friday night, Mama looked at Tato expectantly as he came up the stairs, then busied herself setting out the latkes, sour cream and green peas from her garden.

She motioned us all to sit down. "Eat now while it's hot." she commanded. Tato picked up a forkful of peas, then set them down. He looked at Mama's face carefully before speaking, "I talked to the Madam today, and she told me that she would take you on trial in September. At Christmas, she will decide whether to keep you. You will get a beginner's pay, ten dollars a week, and only for days you work, not when the children have vacation days." He hesitated. "You wouldn't have a job in the summer. What do you think? Could we manage?"

Mama shrugged. A little smile began in her eyes and then curved her mouth. "I will manage my envelopes somehow. I always have. I know the manager likes my fast fingers. He'll take me when there is a school vacation. And you know, maybe it will be good that we will be together working at the school. I have been lonesome for you for a long time now."

Tato spread the sour cream carefully over his latkes. "I talked with old Mrs. Swenson, she's the main cook, you know, after lunch today. I told her you maybe would be the assistant cook and how you worked in restaurants before. She told me she's old and has been getting sick a lot lately. She's thinking of quitting maybe by Christmas. She thought that if you were good enough, maybe Madam would give you her job. " He paused. His face didn't look as though it believed his words. "But you see, the main cook plans the menus and makes out a grocery list for Madam. She has to figure the right amounts of everything for a hundred people, and you have never done that. The job might be too hard for you."

"Hah," she almost shouted. "Too hard? No, no, no. I know all the quick ways in the restaurants, after all, and I know how to figure out how to go from cooking for ten in a cookbook, to cooking for a hundred. We did use recipes on paper when I worked for Nickolai, and I have been good with numbers since my father gave me his accounts. And as for how the food will taste, well a little garlic and even the fussy Madam will enjoy my cooking." She smiled with her whole face. " So now maybe I will be a real American chef. Maybe I will finally be a somebody here in America like the both of you." She nodded first to Tato, then to Anna, looking deeply into their somber faces. Her eyes just skimmed over mine.

"Well, I know everything isn't good at your work just now, but maybe it is my turn to have something that is important. She waved a forkful of the latke, "I am no fool, you know. I know that I will never be able to go back to Ukraine, back to my family. We are here, for better or worse, so it is time for me to be a real American somebody now."

Anna and I couldn't help but smile back into Mama's new proud face. Tato put a hand over the pain of his ulcer. Hs face reflected a sharp uncertainty. Sighing, he scooped a spoonful of sour cream to put on her latkes.

Mama nodded a little 'thank you', and then said, "Maybe we should all go to the movies tonight. It's the night they give the free dishes, and I would like to have some." Tato and Anna's faces registered surprise. Mama had never before made such a suggestion. They looked at each other, "Yes, let's go."

The dishes were being offered at the Mattapan Theater, not my grand, Buddha-filled Oriental. The ceiling here was low and the walls were unadorned. The low, nondescript building abutted Mattapan Station where trolleys and buses came in from many routes. The walls shook when one would go by, and the noise blanketed the dialogue. The movies shown were old, unlike the first run movies at the Oriental, but the draw of the dishes kept the seats filled.

Mama saw the poster for the evening's double feature and smiled happily. "I like-it dat Macaroni, he plays good." I corrected her, "Mickey Rooney, Mama." "Yes, Micaroni. And look-it! Mae Vest. Dis gonna be good movies tonight."

She laughed through the double feature, as did Tato and Anna. I didn't know if I was laughing because the movies were funny, or because the family was laughing together. On the way out, Mama carefully chose two dishes and two bowls to take home. "I like-it da callahs." she said, tracing the soft red and yellow petals and the green leaves on the pale orange dishes. "Maybe someday I gonna have a whole set."

Epilogue

Tato

Tato worked until the late forties at the school, developing close friendships with several teachers, often speaking at assemblies about life in Ukraine, and always enjoying the children. Tato recounted with a sour pride his cleverness at defusing Madam's demands over the years, but she won in the end. Sometime in the early fifties, Chestnut Hill combined their administration with Beaver Country Day School, a larger but just as prestigious school several miles away. Madam called Tato into her office and informed him with a wide, triumphant smile that one of the janitors at Beaver Country Day would be replacing him. Beaver Country Day planned to install a new furnace, so the new janitor would have less to do. Over the ten or so years that were left of his life, he mourned for all that he had lost in that moment. The janitor work he found in a Post Office paid more, but it was never the same.

As the Second World War began, Tato's despair over the Ukrainians of Boston deepened. As he wrote, "The people argued tirelessly, mostly at church picnics when the flasks of whiskey were flying around the tables, about such useless things as to whether the Ukrainian flag should be yellow and blue, or blue and yellow, or maybe Soviet red. We were arguing over how the painting was proceeding, before we had even begun to build."

At about the same time, Tato began to feel a need to return to his Catholic roots. In 1941, he and eight other families, with the help of a priest from nearby Woonsocket, Rhode Island, petitioned Archbishop Bohachevsky for the ministry of a Catholic priest. The mass in Boston took place in the basement of the German Church where Anna had gone to Parochial School. Tato's brother, Streychu, together with his wife, Streyna, stayed at the Orthodox church. His sister, Chocha, and her husband, Vuychu, joined our family in the Catholic Church.

Undaunted by the vicious reaction of some of his former friends, he put his renewed energies into the nascent Catholic parish. He took part in the building of a temporary church out in the countryside, and became very active with a branch of a national, Ukrainian, fraternal insurance organization.

The extent of the devastating effects of the Nazi-Soviet conflict in Ukraine became known to him only after the war: Stalin's scorched earth policy for Ukraine, enacted so that the Nazis would find nothing of value if they won, resulted in the destruction of 28,000 Ukrainian villages; Hitler's declaration that Ukrainians were Untermenschen, sub-humans, was implemented by the establishment of the Nazi Annihilation Institute in Kiev. This Institute received a mandate from Hilter to direct the wholesale execution of Ukrainians with the goal of transforming Ukraine into a 100% German occupied Lebensraum or 'living space.'

Further evidence of Hitler's determination to obliterate the Ukrainian sub-humans came with the revelation at the Nuremberg Trials that 2.4 million Ukrainians had been forced into slave labor with the directive that they be worked to death. The actual number of Ukrainian war-dead was finally assessed to be between eight and ten million men, women and children, possibly the highest in Europe.

And the final blow of betrayal: the announcement from the Yalta Conference that Roosevelt, Churchill and Stalin had agreed that all of Ukraine would be given over to Communist Russia and would be henceforth known as the Ukrainian Soviet Socialist Republic.

Tato was proud when the governor of Massachusetts appointed Anna to the Displaced Persons Commission after the war. In that capacity, she greeted incoming ships with Ukrainian refugees with a welcoming speech, along with a record or two of some Ukrainian music. The parish priest, Father Tom, with Tato as his right-hand man, helped the newcomers to settle in to Boston. Years later, when Anna would be at some Ukrainian event in another part of the country, someone inevitably sought her out with thanks for her unexpected welcome at the dock, and for the material help provided by Father Tom, Tato and other Ukrainian groups.

I felt very fortunate that Tato lived long enough to see all six of my children born. He and Mama came often to New Haven, where my husband and I were in graduate school at Yale, to see the first two. When we moved to Los Alamos, N.M. where the last four were born, he and Mama came by car, bus or train every other year. We made the trip to Boston by car, in the odd years. One of the children's most cherished memories of their 'Diadia' was when he took them up into the cavernous attic in Mattapan to search for the toys he had made and hidden for them to find. They also loved the treats that their 'Babcha' made for them in her kitchen.

After one of his visits to New Mexico, Tato gathered Anna's 35-millimeter slides and movies and announced that he would give a travelogue at the church. A large crowd assembled, intrigued by this totally unknown part of America. Apparently all enjoyed his talk and Anna's pictures.

Not long before he died, he and Mama and Anna held a little mortgage burning ceremony in the back yard. Anna did not tell him how much it had all added up to. Tato died at the age of seventy-four, in 1961, of a massive stroke.

Mama

Mama was promoted to chief chef at the Chestnut Hill School within a few months of starting as assistant. She proudly reported the compliments she received, always adding, "It is not easy to be a tasty cook." She knew how frightened Americans were of carrying garlic on their breath, so in order to forestall any problems with Madame; she never put garlic on her shopping lists. Instead, she brought the heads of garlic cloves from her garden in her purse, sharing her secret only with her assistant cook. Mama maintained an untroubled relationship with the principal, and worried, like Tato, about the poor, little, rich children who didn't have breakfast. During the time she worked at the school, she was calmer and seemed to enjoy herself more. The tension between Mama and I slowly melted away at that time, as well.

When both she and Tato were told their services would no longer be required at Chestnut Hill School, she was devastated. She reluctantly went back to working full time at the needle factory, and when she turned sixty-five, stopped working and took Social Security which had accrued from the time she worked in the insurance building, the restaurant, and the needle factory.

Mama's sister, Katerina came for a visit in the early seventies during a thaw in Soviet-American relations. Mama was sure her sister's inability to understand her Ukrainian was due to her sister's extreme suffering in the two wars and the time between. Mama had no difficulty whatever understanding Katerina, so why was Katerina having so much trouble understanding Mama? What Mama did not understand was that she had added a great number of English words into her speech, which she then treated according to Ukrainian grammar. It sounded like Ukrainian to her!

When Tato died, Mama and Anna remained in the house. A crime wave had hit Boston, and Mama had twice become a victim in her own neighborhood. Anna decided to retire from her practice and move to New Mexico. I worried that Mama, now eighty-nine would miss her house. Also, there were almost no Ukrainians in Los Alamos. But, to my surprise, she was contented with her senior center lunches and coffee and doughnuts after mass at the Catholic Church. She responded happily to the friendly people that sat to chat with her and was happy to repeat her finely honed life stories to them. When her hundredth birthday approached, Anna and I invited all the eastern relatives, who were scattered from Canada to Florida, to help her celebrate. They were all from Tato's side, except for her sister's daughter from Philadelphia.

Mama at her hundredth birthday with Anna, right and me, left.

On the day of the celebration, Mama's face was wreathed in smiles all day. At the end of the day she said, "So then, I am really one hundred years old! And imagine, all these people came to celebrate with me! And not just Ukrainians and my family, but American people! When I was on that ocean, and then in the slums of Boston, and even in Mattapan, I never would have believed that such a thing would ever happen to me."

Three months after her party, she died in her sleep with Anna and me beside her.

Anna

By 1944, Anna was desperate to get out of the anti-women attitude at the insurance company. Walking through the Post Office Building, she passed a Civil Service Office. She signed up as an investigator and moved to New York. To her joy, the salary was the same for both men and women investigators and would be triple her salary of $55 a week. She was angered that the male attorney who took over her job at the insurance company started at $150 a week, however.

Within a year she was transferred to Washington, D.C. to work as an Attorney for the Opinions and Regulations Unit of the Civil Service Commission, a War Service appointment, then briefly, after the war as a Claims Adjuster, settling claims in connection with the mustering out of servicemen. She enjoyed the excellent salary and the challenging work, but once the servicemen began to return, women lawyers were bumped out of their positions. She found herself at loose ends again.

She returned home and established her own practice, after encountering the same prejudice as earlier in her career. The first year, after paying office expenses, she netted only $1200, or $23/week. Fortunately, living at home was inexpensive. Tato enclosed the front porch for an office. The tiny reception room at the head of the front stairs became the waiting room.

A few years later, she qualified for the right to plead cases in the United States Supreme Court. State Senator Leverett Saltonstall, who had spoken so often with Tato, introduced them to the justices before they took their oath of office.

Anna found it hard to build her practice as a woman. She had many prejudices to overcome. In the late fifties, she was appointed an Assistant District Attorney and later, an Assistant Attorney General.

She was rather shocked when she had announced her retirement and her move to New Mexico, the judge of the session, the court officers, and the assistant district attorneys, twelve men in all, took her out to lunch at a fine restaurant and presented her with speeches, a corsage and a gift. As they were leaving, a lady sitting nearby, said, "You must have done something very special to have those twelve men honor you." Anna smiled and said, "Yes." She didn't explain further, because how could this lady understand how she felt to be accepted as an equal by these men only as she was leaving the profession.

Anna is in a little in from the right, peering out behind a tall lady.

Once in Los Alamos, she became a director of a local Credit Union. She ran for the position of County Probate Judge and was elected three times. She continued traveling back to the east coast in various capacities for the largest Ukrainian Fraternal Association in the United States, later becoming president of their Senior Citizen group.

At the age of ninety-two, she was presented with an honorary Doctor of Law degree from the New England School of Law for her pioneering work as a woman lawyer in Boston. This school was technically her alma mater because it had taken over Portia law when the New England School of Law became co-ed. She alone of the honorees received a standing ovation from the graduates, all 4'7" of her. Perhaps it was because fully half the graduating class was women. She died in 2010 at the age of 97.

Stephanie

As my third grade teacher, Miss Frazier, had predicted, school went well for me once I calmed down. Though I enjoyed almost all of my subjects, I discovered a distinct affinity for math and science, with languages not far behind. When I read Madame Curie's biography in eighth grade, I sensed some connection between my beloved math and as yet unencountered physics and decided to follow in her footsteps.

In my senior high school year, my physics teacher independently determined that I should major in some science or mathematics in college. He heard that Northeastern University, formerly an all male school, would be admitting women for the first time in early May 1942. The tuition was low, and I could live at home. He filled out as much as he could on both an admittance and scholarship application and told me that my father should check it all over and then sign.

The two questions from my parents and Anna were, 'What in the world was physics, and what did a physicist do for a living?' I was glad I could use Steve Sydoriak, a tenor in our little church choir, who was in the wartime MIT Radar research laboratory as an example of how one earned a living in physics. Tato signed the papers, though he hadn't really understood.

I received a full scholarship as a freshman, then each year afterwards. I said goodbye to my high school friends on a Friday afternoon, and started college on the following Monday.

Steve had become interested in me during the time we sang in the choir together. He observed both my nebulous yearning to be a physicist and to enjoy out-of-door activities. At the beginning of my senior year, when I was sixteen, and he, twenty-five, asked me to go sailing. In turn, I found myself attracted by this scientist who sang so beautifully and who danced Ukrainian solos at our concerts in a bright costume his mother had embroidered for him. There was no objection from my parents. He was a priest's son, and a fine professional man. He introduced me to sailing, bicycling, hiking, skiing and square dancing, which we continued to enjoy our whole lives.

Northeastern was on a wartime accelerated program that offered two school years in the space of one calendar year. No vacations, however, only a week between semesters. We married between my junior and senior years. I was eighteen.

On our honeymoon backpack up Mount Katahdin in Maine, we heard that the war was over as was Steve's job. After only six weeks of marriage, he enrolled in the PhD program in physics at Yale. I returned home to finish the six months of my senior year.

My application to the Yale Graduate School of Physics was accepted. After my last final at Northeastern I took a train to New Haven for a joyous reunion, and began classes at Yale the next week.

In June of 1948, Steve received his doctorate. At the beginning of August, we left for Los Alamos where he was joining the Low Temperature group, each holding one of our two small children. Needless to say, I had not finished my Master's degree. On our first daylight view of the mountains on either side of us, we knew we wanted to stay forever. Besides the wonders of New Mexico, we traveled over every state in the west with the family that grew to six children

I was unable to pursue a career at the lab because of scarcity of full-time babysitters or day care facilities in the early years of the lab. I was able to contract with the lab for Russian, German and French scientific papers, later working for a company in New York that specialized in translating Russian physics journals. I was able to work at home, and in my free time, in spite of my dismal grades in grade school Home Economics, I sewed and knitted most of the clothes my six children and I wore and learned to cook large dinners.

When the need for such translations disappeared, and the last of the children were in their teens, I realized that physics had moved rapidly past what education I had. I turned to my piano. I studied and passed the rigorous Music Teacher's National Association tests and began my satisfying, thirty-three years of private piano teaching. I became active in the state Music Teacher's organization, eventually serving as president.

At the beginning of Lent, the dining room table became the center for egg decorating. I taught the children beginning when they were six or so. The door was always open to their friends, and there was never enough room around the table. Later some of our children earned pin money by selling their eggs to the International Folk Art Museum in Santa Fe. I taught classes at the local schools and to various organizations.

1968: Top left: Christine, Stephen, Katherine, Mary, Gene. Center: Walter. Front:
Steph and Steve

Using our eggs, embroideries that my mother-in-law and I had made, along with carved and inlaid wooden objects from his family in Ukraine, I put together many interpretive exhibits in local libraries. Soon after arriving in Los Alamos, Steve was doing his solo dance at several local variety shows, and we performed as a pair now and then in the schools.

For these events, I purchased records from New York with the proper dance music, remembering my unfortunate dancing debut at Chestnut Hill School. Steve's final dance of his life was in the barroom scene of the Fiddler on the Roof, put on by the Light Opera group in town. Two of our daughters danced Ukrainian dances with Folk dance groups. One of them danced with a professional group in Colorado.

For thirteen years, I was Liturgy chairman and choir director at our Catholic Church. I put English words to many Ukrainian choir pieces, which my choir greatly enjoyed. When Anna and my mother came, Anna and I arranged for an annual Easter food basket blessing at the church. I wrote a ceremony and led the singing of the responses. Mama enjoyed it very much. It has grown over the years to include people from many of the various Slavic countries.

We kept the tradition of the twelve Christmas dishes, though by common assent, we eliminated one of the foods, namely, the jellied fish. We always made sure to have a small bundle of wheat nearby to honor our parents and ancestors.

In 1990, Steve and I, my sister and two of our daughters, took a trip to Ukraine. We visited Kozova where we were hosted lavishly by our cousins. We saw Mama's house, now without the thatched roof she had been so proud of. Because of fire danger, all the roofs were now tin. Anna saw the room where she was born. We were then taken to Tato's house, two doors down the street, and immediately recognized the beautiful well and pump handle Mama had described. Disconcertingly, all the relatives seemed to know more about us, than we knew of them. When we visited the village of Steve's father, the hearty reception was the same.

We were in Lviv, the beautiful city where Tato served in the Austrian army and where Steve's parents courted, when we heard that Ukraine was making a declaration of their intention to make a Declaration of Independence from the Soviet Union. Many blue and gold flags suddenly appeared, hung from windows, poles, and flying out of car windows.

We went to a celebratory rally in the city's huge, packed soccer stadium. The main speaker addressed the diaspora, thanking them and their descendants for holding Ukraine close to their hearts, keeping the language, customs, music, dancing and the arts alive at the time when, in Ukraine, the language, the customs and arts were forbidden by the Soviets. We suddenly realized they meant Ukrainians like us.

When a band began to play folksongs, we proud, 100% Americans-100% Ukrainians, sang the Ukrainian words we had learned as children, while the native Ukrainians around us were mute. Someone asked where we were from, because if we knew the words to the songs, we couldn't be from Ukraine. The Russians had forbade almost from the beginning, all singing of Ukrainian songs. At the end of the event, the Ukrainian National Anthem began, and Anna, Steve and I, now feeling 100% Ukrainian, began with brave voices. Again, those around us did not sing. We didn't manage to sing long, because within two lines of the music, the three of us were sobbing with the joy that Ukraine might be free at last as well as with the sorrow of all that Ukraine had been made to suffer. And perhaps the greatest sorrow was that Steve's parents and Tato and Mama had not lived to see this unbelievable day.

Steve, around this time, had begun his long, fifteen-year journey into Alzheimer's disease. He died in 2003.

In 2011, I was honored as one of three Living Treasures of Los Alamos.